Dear Don,

I hope by reading this, it helps
you on your way to a healthier
life and happy living.
And, gives you a bit of insight as well to
help Eric and Sarah along the way.

Love your wife and
biggest supporter.
Jodi ☺ xoxo

"Of Farrell's many terrific books, *Father and Child Reunion* is his best. Wonderful advice, crystal clear writing, provocative discussion. Its insights are a gift to men and women."

—KYLE D. PRUETT, M.D. PROFESSOR OF CHILD PSYCHIATRY, YALE UNIVERSITY SCHOOL OF MEDICINE, AUTHOR OF *FATHERNEED*

"*Father and Child Reunion* introduces us to the nurturing side of fathers through a masterful blend of original ideas and hard data. It will inspire and persuade dads to become more involved with their children—a benefit not only to kids, but to moms as well."

—JOHN GRAY. AUTHOR, *MEN ARE FROM MARS; WOMEN ARE FROM VENUS*

"A book of incalculable importance and stunning originality. Written with lucidity and passion, backed by exhaustive and impeccable research. The best book I know of on the irreplaceable importance of fathers, plus a new way of thinking about the family."

—NATHANIEL BRANDEN, PH.D. AUTHOR, *SIX PILLARS OF SELF-ESTEEM* AND *MY YEARS WITH AYN RAND*

"Pure gold. . . . An astonishing book."

—SUSAN DEITZ. NATIONALLY SYNDICATED COLUMNIST, *LOS ANGELES TIMES SYNDICATE.* AUTHOR, *SINGLE FILE.*

"I come away from this book not only inspired to be a more involved dad, but with a much deeper understanding of exactly what I do that is helpful to my children, and why. It is brilliant, original, and inspiring."

—JACK CANFIELD. CO-AUTHOR, *CHICKEN SOUP FOR THE PARENT'S SOUL*

"Vital. An excellent and long overdue contribution to improving the lives of children, women, and men."

—KAREN DECROW. ATTORNEY; PAST PRESIDENT, NATIONAL ORGANIZATION FOR WOMEN

"*Father and Child Reunion* will change the lives of men, the women who love them, and the children they raise. He cuts to the heart of our conflicts and creates solutions we can use. Read this book!"

—MICHAEL GURIAN. AUTHOR, *THE WONDER OF BOYS*

"Stunning in its eloquence, thorough in its research, and passionate in its plea for valuing the soul that fathers bring to the heart of a child's well-being. This is simply an important work. A book of hope, comfort, and insight, but most of all, it offers solutions to restoring the spirit and healthy functioning of families."

—BETTIE B. YOUNGS, PH.D. AUTHOR, *A STRING OF PEARLS* AND *TASTE BERRIES FOR TEENS*

"A real eye-opener. An absolute essential for the man who wants to be more involved with his kids and for anyone who wants to help him do it."

—ARMIN BROTT. AUTHOR, *THE EXPECTANT FATHER,*
THE NEW FATHER, AND *THE SINGLE FATHER*

"A must-read. Farrell is a rudder of reason in a stormy sea of half-truths. He astounds and enlightens. Our children will reap the rewards!"

—DR. DENIS WAITLEY. AUTHOR, *SEEDS OF GREATNESS*

"When my daughter was four years old, I was depressed and almost suicidal at not being able to see her for two years. I heard Dr. Farrell share some of the findings that are now in *Father and Child Reunion.* I learned why giving up my daughter was not an option. Thank you, Warren, I now have custody of my daughter. This is the most important book a father could ever read."

—LARRY HELLMANN. PRESIDENT,
NATIONAL CONGRESS FOR FATHERS AND CHILDREN

"An amazing gift to men, women, and children. Unforgettable revelations that inspire us to change today's dysfunctional parenting."

—SUSAN JEFFERS, PH.D. AUTHOR, *I'M OKAY, YOU'RE A BRAT*
AND *FEEL THE FEAR AND DO IT ANYWAY*

"*Father and Child Reunion* shakes up my way of looking at the embattled world of fathers and families. Farrell's counsel is wise; his advice, sound and specific."

—HOWARD M. HALPERN, PH.D. PAST PRESIDENT,
AMERICAN ACADEMY OF PSYCHOTHERAPISTS; AUTHOR,
CUTTING LOOSE AND *HOW TO BREAK YOUR ADDICTION TO A PERSON*

"A great book! A unique blend of lively and humorous writing with rigorous documentation. A perfect gift for any father or mother—or anyone contemplating the adventure."

—HENRY BILLER. PROFESSOR OF PSYCHOLOGY, UNIVERSITY OF
RHODE ISLAND; AUTHOR, *FATHERS AND FAMILIES*

"Courageous . . . impeccable and responsible scholarship."

—LIONEL TIGER. PROFESSOR OF ANTHROPOLOGY, RUTGERS UNIVERSITY;
AUTHOR, *THE DECLINE OF MALES*

Father
and Child
Reunion

Also by Warren Farrell, Ph. D.

Women Can't Hear What Men Don't Say

The Myth of Male Power

Why Men Are the Way They Are

The Liberated Man

Father and Child Reunion

*How to Bring
the Dads We Need
to the Children
We Love*

Warren
Farrell,
Ph. D.

JEREMY P. TARCHER/PUTNAM
a member of
PENGUIN PUTNAM INC.
New York

Most Tarcher/Putnam books are available at special quantity discounts for bulk purchases for sales promotions, premiums, fund-raising, and educational needs. Special books or book excerpts also can be created to fit specific needs. For details, write Putnam Special Markets, 375 Hudson Street, New York, NY 10014.

Jeremy P. Tarcher/Putnam
a member of
Penguin Putnam Inc.
375 Hudson Street
New York, NY 10014
www.penguinputnam.com

Permissions can be found on page 303.

Library of Congress Cataloging-in-Publication Data

Farrell, Warren.
    Father and child reunion : how to bring the dads we need
to the children we love / Warren Farrell.
      p.   cm
    Includes bibliographical references and index.
    ISBN 1-58542-075-1
    1. Father and child.   2. Fatherhood.   I. Title.

HQ756.F3677   2001   00-061987
306.874'2—dc21

Printed in the United States of America

10   9   8   7   6   5   4   3   2   1

This book is printed on acid-free paper. ♾

Book design by Mauna Eichner

Contents

Acknowledgments

Father and Child Reunion has been thirteen years in the research and writing. I originally planned it as part of *The Myth of Male Power* or *Women Can't Hear What Men Don't Say,* but I slowly came to feel like a father watching the growth of a child whose voice was unique, and who could not be subordinated to any other. However, a father alone cannot nourish a child-as-child, or a book-as-child; over thirteen years, there are many contributors.

Perhaps foremost among these are the children whom my life has afforded me the opportunity to mentor, stepparent, and counsel—a process that has nurtured and matured me, even mentored and counseled me. My brother, Wayne, was born when I was twelve. It was as if his birth morphed within my twelve-year-old brain a parenting instinct. I felt his powerlessness, but also his power: When Wayne laughed, we laughed; when Wayne screamed, we became his servants.

When Wayne was eleven, my mother's sudden death afforded me the opportunity to witness the transformation in my dad's parenting with Wayne versus Gail (my sister) and me. With us, he was father-as-provider-and-firm-boundary-setter; with Wayne, he suddenly became father-as-provider-and-pal. In my father's time of vulnerability, he had a need for my brother's friendship, and this weakened his ability to set boundaries. The time pressures and guilt of single parenting compounded the problem, and my brother's shadow side soon haunted my dad. When I had relationships with women who were single moms, I saw these pressures overwhelm them as well. I came to have a deep compassion for the inner strength and selflessness the single parent must call upon within her- or himself. I hope that such compassion is reflected in this book.

My own experiences as a stepparent have made me aware of the walking-on-eggshells that Lee, my stepmom (aka "Mom"), silently endured as she juggled supporting my dad with confronting him. She adopted someone else's family and expected nothing but to give and receive love in return for her efforts. This she gave, and this she received. She has inspired me to do the same.

My years as a Boy Scout, as both a Scout and a Junior Assistant Scoutmaster, and as a camp counselor with both the Ridgewood, New Jersey, Y and the Newark, New Jersey, Boys Club, provided foundation experiences that are reflected in *Father and Child Reunion,* as are my relationships either as a stepparent or quasi-stepparent to Megan Hubbard, Erin and Alex Blanchard, and Kathy and Janet Brookins.

Perhaps as a result of these experiences, my interest in male-female issues found me especially aligned with fathers who wanted to be more involved with children. In the process, leaders of the National Congress of Fathers and Children, the Children's Rights Council, and the American Coalition for Fathers and Children provided much stimulation and support, as have the writings of Sanford Braver, David Blankenhorn, Jed Abraham, and Ken Canfield, and the activism of Wade Horn.

Father and Child Reunion benefited from the assistance of two editors, as well as the reading, friendship, and mentorship of Jeremy Tarcher. Its first editor was Marilyn Abraham; its second, Mitch Horowitz. Their contributions helped me rethink portions of the book. Mitch responded quickly, thoughtfully, and non-intrusively.

Joyce McHugh has brought her competence, caring, quick wit, and administrative skills not only to *Father and Child Reunion,* but to *Why Men Are the Way They Are, The Myth of Male Power,* and *Women Can't Hear What Men Don't Say.* She keeps the office running so I can keep the books coming (and do enough speaking to support my writing habit).

Research help has been provided by sociologist Lisa Broidy and economist Dan Johnston, who have both responded well to my insistence upon going to the primary source and often cross-examining the authors of government data (with some astonishing results). On numerous occasions, the resources of Larry Hellmann, Stu Miller, Elaine Mittleman, Augustine Kposowa, David Arnaudo, and Jimmy Boyd were given generously; and Richard Doyle's *The Liberator* served as an invaluable jumping-off point.

One of the most important "growth processes" each of my manuscripts enjoys (after some resistance) is its examination in whole or in part by at least twenty readers and experts of many persuasions. They are Art Barker, Jerry Boggs, Liz Brookins, Ellen Brown, Steve Collins, Alexa Deere, Greg Dennis, Liz Dowling, Mike Estes, Marty Fiebert, Suzanne Frayser, Larry Hellmann, Ron Henry, Steve Holzner, William Masterson, Sam Osherson, Sophia Ruiz, David Shackleton, Diane Sukiennik, Steven Svoboda, Hans-Günther Tappe, and Dianna Thompson. The book's shortcomings, though, are mine.

Being an author is the personification of postponed gratification: many days of isolation followed by the magnifying glass of publication. The deeper communications with my sister, Gail, have been nurturing and sustaining during these periods. I cherish also the continuing caring of Liz Dowling, as well as my special friendship and tennis partnership with Greg Dennis. Finally, I acknowledge the unique contributions to my life of Nathaniel and Devers Branden and Grainger Weston, as well as Eric Hornak, Fred Hayward, Steve DeLuca, David Dinn, David Shackleton, David Burroughs, and John Paoletto, the designer of www.warrenfarrell.com.

Ode to my Dad
on His 90th Birthday

You redefined the role of dad
Before it was in fashion
You taught me that a dad was more
Than the man who brought the cash in

That a dad was the guy who, when I cried,
Got up in the middle of the night
Changed my diapers and my formula
Until you got it right

That a dad was a guy who, when company came,
Was the one who made the dinner
Who baked the bread and raised the dough
But not just as breadwinner

You taught me to love tennis
When they called it a "sissy" sport
Now those mocking birds are flabby
(Or beggin' for a court!)

I can remember jogging behind you
Years before it was in style
(When meters were yards and kids traded cards
You were teaching me the mile)

Thanks for teaching me that eyesight
Was quite distinct from vision
From which I learned that all I saw
Was subject to revision

To see if the minister was boring
For knowing how God is hard to find
If there's too much snoring

Thank you, dad, for the investments you made—
In Gail, Wayne, Mom, and Lee;
And thank you for the 57 years
Of investment you made in me.

Love, Warren

Introduction

In almost thirty years of researching men's and women's issues, never has the research for a book I have written made me more emotional than the research for this book. I began the research feeling that dads were important, but I had no idea how important. It was not that I had never been exposed to children deprived of their dads. I have been fortunate enough to have been a stepdad—or quasi-stepdad—to children whose moms have each struggled to gently make it clear to their children that they and the children's dads would never be remarried, only to have their children yearn for the reunion. A womanfriend, Liz, received this picture from her then-ten-year-old daughter Alex—some seven years after Liz had separated from Alex's dad. . . .

When Alex later did a more-complete family picture (including sister Erin and the dog Champagne), she returned her biological dad to the picture as if her intact, harmonious family had never been disturbed. It was fine for a dog to be added and a hamster and sister subtracted, but not for Dad to be subtracted. It was as if there had been a starting lineup with a fixed number of positions, and if her dad were not in the starting lineup, he would be required to disappear from the playing field altogether. In reality, he lived 500 miles away. More accurately, in *one* reality he lived 500 miles away; in another reality, he was ever-present in her heart, and this reality was both too powerful and too vulnerable to allow Alex to be secure enough to acknowledge both realities. In the meantime, from my perspective as a potential stepdad, well, Alex was trying desperately to hold on tightly to the security of the old. Letting me into the picture would require juggling. Alex did not want juggling, she wanted Dad. That was Alex. . . .

Liz has another daughter, Erin. Erin occasionally interrupts a conversation with "I was adopted!" Liz and Jeff did the adoption immediately after Erin was born. Erin intellectually knows how much better her life is with Liz than it would have been with her biological mom (who had a history of drug problems, and had children with many men); nevertheless, for years, if Erin was tired, bored, or sad, she would have nightmares and crying spells of yearning for her biological mom. At other moments, she deeply missed her adoptive dad, Jeff.

It seems that when an early bond that signaled acceptance and security is broken, it is as if the boundaries of all the cells in our body are broken, allowing fears of rejection and abandonment to sneak in and contaminate our immune system. Whether we call it a psychic wound, a gaping hole, or an insatiable hunger, right now we live in a culture deeply wounded with enormous father hunger, not because fathers are more important, but because they are more often missing.

I sent an early draft of Alex and Erin's experience and the research on the importance of dads to Jeff. Coincidentally, his more recent marriage was coming to an end, and he was contemplating a career transition. Jeff began to make more and more frequent trips to visit Alex and Erin. Although he and Liz disagreed on many fundamentals and had markedly different styles of parenting, eventually they agreed she would build an addition to her home so he could move in and be with the children less as a visitor, more as a dad.

Within a year after their reunion with Dad, Alex and Erin made a transition from receiving extra help at school via a resource program as well as extra help at home via a tutor, to getting straight A's without either. Although Jeff's career and relationship transitions meant he was on the road about half the time, Alex and Erin knew he was coming back. They had father stability. Crying for a biological mom virtually disappeared. Alex's and Erin's academic achievement and emotional security both took a substantial leap.

This father hunger is not an American phenomenon. Almost all industrialized countries experience it. Why? **The more a country is secure economically, the more it permits divorce. The more divorce, the more the child lives with Mom alone, thus the more father hunger.**

As my books *Why Men Are the Way They Are* and *The Myth of Male Power* have been translated into other languages, the mail I receive from other industrialized countries reflects this hunger. As I was writing this, a college teacher sent me this picture from *Der Spiegel*[1] in Germany. . . .

My personal experiences with Alex and Erin touched my heart almost daily, but they did not allow me to know which experiences were idiosyncratic and which were normal for children who were missing their dad. It was only as I saw, for example, how children without dads suffer in school, and then watched Alex and Erin struggle in school, that I began to both deepen my sympathy for the myriad of minefields that Liz and the children faced, and the importance of encouraging Liz to keep their dad involved despite the self-interest that sometimes felt conflicting.

Fortunately, some shifts are being made. The twenty-first century began with two hopeful signs for fathers and children. First, the Harris poll tapped into father consciousness, finding that "young men in their twenties are seven percent *more* likely than young women to *give up pay* for more time with their families."[2] A full 70 percent of men vs. 63 percent of women. Give up *pay*. A generational shift without precedent.

This generational shift will require a new way of discussing careers and children. Recently, when children arrived, career-focused women who took time off to raise them spoke of "giving up my career," as in making a sacrifice. In the future, when children are planned, children-loving dads who are expected to work full-time will be speaking of the sacrifice as "giving up my *children.*"

In the process, the tension between couples will change. In the last quarter-century, couples often fought over who would "get to" focus on his or her career; in the next quarter-century, couples will fight over who will "get to" be with their children.

Just as the last third of the twentieth century was about creating equal opportunity for women as workers, so the first third of the twenty-first century will be about creating equal opportunity for men as parents. Neither goal will be achieved until both goals are achieved. The beneficiaries will be children, since dads in the family are even more important than women in the workplace: The workplace *benefits* from women, but the family *needs* dads.

The second hopeful sign for fathers and children was the father and child reunion of Elián González with his dad. It was a symbol of millions of dads' struggle to be reunited with their Eliáns.

Our response to the Elián González case tells us something about how far we have to go. The moment the news broke of the mother drowning and the U.S. relatives taking over, the first responses reflected suspicion of the dad: "Maybe Elián *should* be with the relatives; maybe the mom was bringing him to a better country, and helping him escape a dad who was perhaps abusive, incompetent and did not love the child." That is, we placed the father under suspicion until proven innocent.

The I.N.S. (Immigration and Naturalization Service) did investigate the dad, although he had already been investigated and awarded *legal custody* in Cuba (only to have it undermined by a lack of enforcement).[3] When all indicators pointed to a loving dad, the prevailing view was still one of the case being a struggle between a mother who sacrificed her life for her child, and a dad who merely wanted his child back. When the mother died, the American relatives fought to keep Elián as a way of fulfilling the mother's wishes, even honoring her sacrifice.

But if we substitute Dad for Mom, let's look at whether our view would be different. In real life, it was the mom *and her boyfriend* who took Elián. Had it been Dad and his girlfriend, would we be focusing on the dad sacrificing his life to create a better one for the child, or, suddenly, would our binoculars be on a man *and his girlfriend* unilaterally stealing a child from a mother who had won legal custody? As kidnappers, they would have been subjected to the Federal Parental Kidnapping Act of 1980. The focus would not be on the kidnappers' sacrifice, but on child endangerment.

Once the primary suspicion was on the relatives as co-conspirators rather than on the dad, it would not have taken more than two months to discover that four of Elián's Miami caretakers had recent histories of drunk driving, grand theft, and/or forgery: Lazaro and brother Delfin each had two convictions of driving under the influence; Jose Cid, another relative, stopped visiting when he started his thirteen-year jail sentence for grand theft, forgery, and violating probation, and his twin brother, Luis, visited Elián even as he was on trial for robbery.[4] All of these relatives had one thing in common: they supported Elián being kept from his dad. Lazaro's brother, who supported Elián's reunion with his dad, was barred from seeing Elián.

With this information, media pictures of a thief, a forger, and drivers with DUI convictions driving Elián around Miami and using Disneyland to distract him from Dad would be seen as child abuse, not child amusement.

In real life, the dad was in the headlines for five months, begging for the return of his son. But until he arrived in the U.S., almost no one knew his name. When the name of someone whose pleas surround us nevertheless remains invisible, it's a sign of a deep bias, a bias that prevents the dad from being heard as a person even when he does speak.[5] The image of a mom crying would be haunting our psyches, tweaking our hearts—we would know her pleas and her name. Distance would not make a difference.

I suspect that had it been the dad and girlfriend who had kidnapped Elián, our response to someone who said Elián might have a better life with his American relatives would be, "That's beside the point: the law cannot give permission for one parent to kidnap a child." Had it been a mom crying, feminists, Americans, and Cubans would have been of one mind: "Bring Elián home!" The immediacy of our response would have rendered moot the argument that Elián should not be disturbed from his stable Miami environment.

In brief, if a child were being deprived of Mom, our sympathetic minds would have opened the path to an immediate "mother and child reunion"; instead, when a child was being deprived of Dad, suspicious minds investigated the dad with custody even before investigating the relatives with prison sentences, inviting roadblocks to a father and child reunion.

The challenge of this book, then, is twofold: In Part I, it is to deepen our understanding of what's missing when Dad's missing and, therefore, deepen our commitment to bringing Dad home again. Part II challenges us to confront the gap between our conscious desire for father involvement and the unconscious ways in which we undermine that involvement.

In Part I, we'll see the psychological price that millions of Eliáns and their sisters are paying when either dads walk away or mothers keep them away; how dads contribute what they do, often without knowing it; at the psychology and biology of bringing Dad home again; at myths about fathers that keep dads away or at bay; at men's internal conflicts about being dads: fearing being swallowed up by the family; fearing being a wallet disconnected from family; fearing gentle touch; fearing disapproval for the way he touches; wanting to be a better dad than his dad; not knowing how . . .

Part I gives us an overview of how children fare with moms only, versus dads only, versus joint custody arrangements, versus stepparenting arrangements, versus the intact family. **Part I offers compelling new evidence as to why children raised by single fathers usually do better than children raised by single mothers.**

However, it does *not* say that men are better as fathers than women are as mothers. We will see that there are many reasons for this (differences in income, education, etc.), but most important among them the fact that the types of men who overcome the legal and cultural prejudices that this book discusses to become single dads tend to be exceptionally motivated. It might not be that kids do better with fathers per se, but that they do better with a highly motivated parent. Today's full-time dad is similar to the type of woman who overcame social roles to be a full-time career woman in the mid-twentieth century: Both are more motivated than their peers. Just as these women differed from their peers, so these single fathers differ from theirs.

Most dads still nurture their family by providing what I call a "financial womb." This process usually means a dad shows his love to his family by being away from the family he loves. This Father's Catch-22 adds to the discomfort men feel with the type of nurturing required by infants. So we are not at that point in history where findings about the man who is willing to be a single father can be applied to the average father—or, should I say, the average "working father."

Part I also looks at some counterintuitive ways about what makes the two-parent family tick. For example, it posits that the tensions built into the two-parent system operate similarly to the tensions built into the two-party system (or multi-party system) of government. That is, just as the tensions between political parties create a more balanced country, so the tensions between parents create more balanced children. Even the tensions among fathers, mothers, and children seem to work much like the tensions among the legislative, executive, and judicial branches of government: They create checks and balances that produce a better outcome than would any one working separately.

Ironically, children often benefit from exactly those differences between mothers and fathers that might have led to their divorce. The challenge is to see how the person we just divorced makes positive contributions to the children sometimes via the very characteristics that led us to divorce her or him!

Toward the end of Part I, I look at how, in the last quarter of the twentieth century, when it comes to the contributions of dads, the pendulum has swung from the Era of Father Knows Best to the Era of Daddy Molests; from Dad as family head to deadbeat dad.

This image—of daddy-as-nightmare—is not exactly an incentive for daddy involvement. And a family, like a finely tuned car, begins sputtering when fueled by influences that are out of balance. For example, lack of father involvement tends to lead to a mother overprotecting the children. Soon, theories of overprotection become the litany; then the litany becomes the law. One such theory is that everything should revolve around "the best interests of the child." Up to a point, yes. But when we don't raise a child to also consider the "best interests of the mother" and the "best interests of the father," we prepare a child for a world that revolves only around its own interests. Good luck.

In Part I, I look at the impact on our children of the transition from mother-headed homes to female-run elementary schools, often depriving our sons of positive male role models for the first decade of their life. Is it any wonder many turn to gangs for male approval and identity?

In Part II, I look at how this imbalance of overfeminization is reinforced by other imbalances, such as the government spending 340 million dollars on child support enforcement for each dollar on "visitation" enforcement, or focusing on a woman's right to choose with no comprehension of men's rights to choose. If we want fathers equally involved, we won't be talking about women's reproductive rights and men's reproductive responsibilities— we'll be speaking equally about what I call both sexes' ABC rights and responsibilities. (Speaking more about rights than responsibilities is the sign of being not an adult but an adolescent—someone who wants the right to the car while you pay for the gas, insurance, and repairs!)

I'll look at whether our current theories about the best interests of the child are in conflict with our laws about women's right to choose abortion, and whether, if they are in conflict, the conflict is a proper balance of powers. And if it is a proper balance between the fetus and mother, where in this picture is the dad?

On many of these questions, I do not have answers to which I am personally attached. But I am attached to reframing the dialogue so it is not stuck in one ideology or another; so that everyone is included, and theories that are in conflict are out in the open. At this moment in history, the father is the left-out parent. But **if the father was presumed to be the better parent, this book would be called *Mother and Child Reunion*.**

Part II looks at the chicken-and-egg interactions between our psychology and our social policy; it looks at how we can make the transition from what was functional in the past to what is functional in the future. The blueprint for change is specific: from men's ABC Rights and Responsibilities to the Octant of Equal Opportunity Parenting. It makes it clear why it will be a more complex challenge to make Dad an equal partner to Mom in the twenty-first century than it was to make women equal partners to men in the workplace during the twentieth century.

It will be more complex in part because we are still passing laws to replace the natural father by whomever the mother chooses. For example, in 2000, after a child's biological mother died, the Pennsylvania Supreme Court ruled that the child could stay with the *step*father, although the court deemed the *natural* father to be a good man and a good father who loved his child and wanted to raise his child.[7] When that son becomes a dad, he'll know his natural rights stop at his wife's whim.

The consequences? We will explore how neither animals nor humans become emotionally involved if they know they can lose what they love at someone else's whim. We would not expect mothers to emotionally invest in children if the dad could choose a different mother for the child should he someday fall more in love with another woman. We will see, then, how we are alienating the father from his parenting instinct in a way similar to the alienation of the domesticated dog from its parenting instinct when it discovered it wasn't needed to feed the puppies, and that the puppies could be taken away besides. More on that later.

If you think Part II is not for you because you're "not into politics," I'll ask you to challenge yourself: **if we are alive, we are into politics.** Politics comes from the Greek word *polis,* meaning people. Even when we are alone, we are considering people and considering people's considerations of us. The moment we see our dads more positively, we have a more positive view of our own worthiness of their love and attention, and we begin to alter our view as to how we want dads to fit into the family, and therefore the workplace, and therefore the laws that govern both.

Our attitude of dad-as-wallet is not fixed. It is a view that has been magnified since industrialization. However, it is now ubiquitous. For example, a womanfriend called me after reading the first draft of this book and said, "You won't believe this. When I finished your manuscript, I had to unwind, so I turned on *Jeopardy.* Their 'Answer' card read, 'The day of the year on which the most phone calls are made.' The correct response was, 'What is Mother's Day?' The next 'Answer' read, 'The day of the year on which the most collect phone calls are made.' The correct response was, 'What is *Father's* Day?' So here I am trying to escape from your book on the jeopardy of dad-as-wallet only to encounter dad-as-wallet on Jeopardy!"

The Quietest Revolution

One of the biggest demographic changes of the twentieth century's last two decades was the increase in the percentage of single-parent households headed by fathers from 10 percent to 19 percent; the percentage of single dads almost doubled![8] With neither sound nor fury.

Moms moving out of the home has been a headline-creating revolution; dads moving into the home has been the quietest revolution.

This trend will continue, to the point that father involvement will be to the twenty-first century family what Internet involvement will be to twenty-first century productivity. Dads are, if you will, in the infancy of their revolution to reenter the family, this time not only as money raisers, but as child raisers; not as killer-protectors, but as nurturer-connectors. Not to outdo Mom, but to do with Mom.

We can detect the psychological and political momentum by looking at the common denominator of perhaps the most diversified political (or quasi-political) movement (or quasi-movement) in recent history: the embryonic men's movement.

This men's movement harbors diversity: from New Warriors in the Woods to fathers in courts; from mostly white, Born-Again Christian Promise Keepers[9] to African-American Million-Man Marchers; from men who see feminism as constructive to those who see it as destructive. But all embrace one goal: preparing dads to reenter the family in the twenty-first century, just as women entered the workplace in the twentieth

The New Warriors, most often associated with Robert Bly and his book *Iron John,* prepares a man to be a warrior in a new world—that of his feelings; to understand his father wound—the void he feels because of a less-than-satisfying connection to his dad. It inspires him to alter that connection with his own children. If he retreats into the woods to learn how to listen, it's to retreat from a world that teaches him how to talk; if he experiments with drums to put him in touch with his feelings, it's to experiment with knowing he had feelings to be in touch with. Each step deepens the man, and the dad.

The feminist portion of the men's movement prepares men to participate in the family by telling men they cannot be egalitarian if they don't take equal childcare responsibilities. It sensitizes a man to women's needs and to men's role in female empowerment. It helps him support his daughter in pursuing options, and teach his son to be supportive of the woman he marries.

The Promise Keepers—the Christian men's movement—organizes men to keep the promise of commitment to their families. In weekly groups, men confront the barriers to accomplishing this, discussing their feelings and fears, and asking God for help. The Promise Keepers supports men to play the traditional family role of breadwinner, but in a nontraditional manner of creating permission to ask for human help and divine guidance. Similarly, African-American men in the Million-Man March made the same commitment to their families. As with the Promise Keepers, they turned to the church for human community and divine guidance—often to support them in turning their backs on drugs, drinking, and trouble with the law.

There is yet another portion of the men's movement—the fathers'- and children's-rights portion. It differentiates itself from the others by speaking not only of responsibilities, but also of rights. Not only the rights of the father, but also the right of the child to have a father—not as a wallet, but as a dad; not as a visitor, but as a parent.

Fathers'-rights groups, we will see, are not really fathers'-rights groups in the same way women's-rights groups are women's-rights groups. **The "right" for which fathers'-rights groups are fighting is the right to more responsibility for children. In contrast, the right for which women's-rights' groups fought was less responsibility for children, more for income.** (The right to abortion decreases family involvement and responsibility, as does the right to the three C's: childcare, careers, and contraception. Women's-rights groups focus on *increasing* women's responsibility in the *workplace*.)

How can we tell if these fathers'-rights organizations will amount to anything? Here's the litmus test. Most major movements and revolutions have three things in common: a *large number* of people experiencing *economic hurt* and *emotional rejection* at the same time. The catalyst of the women's movement was large numbers of women simultaneously experiencing the economic hurt of unequal pay and the emotional rejection of divorce. In the civil-rights movement, it was the economic hurt of unequal opportunity, and the emotional rejection of "sit in the back of the bus."

Fathers'-rights groups are also experiencing these two prerequisites to revolution: economic hurt and emotional rejection. Divorce leaves many fathers economically hurt (alimony, child support, mortgage payments on a home he doesn't live in . . .) and, as far as emotional rejection is concerned, they often feel a double dose: loss of both wife and children.

When the law requires large numbers of fathers to simultaneously pay more money than the mother for children they cannot see as often as the mother, **fathers experience a form of "taxation without representation"—the same basic injustice that drove the American Revolution.** In the case of fathers, economic hurt and emotional rejection are joined by a sense of legal injustice. The law has always been men's way of exercising their protector instinct—in this case, toward children. Thus, we have five powerful forces operating simultaneously to fuel the fathers'- and children's-rights portions of the men's movement: large numbers, economic hurt, emotional rejection, legal injustice, and a protector instinct.

Why, then, is the fathers' movement not stronger than it is? Because it confronts major countervailing influences that no other movement has had to face: the propensity of men—and especially married men with children—to protect women, and to not fight with them; the political power of the women's movement (created, in part, by men's propensity to protect rather than fight women!); the biology and socialization of men to fight to support a family economically, but not to be involved with a family emotionally; the biology and socialization of men to fight to protect others, but not themselves—lest they be called whiners or wimps, bitter or babies.

The influences that normally create a political movement, then, are in tension with influences that discourage a political movement. These influences are unique to women and men.

However, a countervailing influence unique to the male-female phenomenon strengthens the potential of the fathers' movement: When fathers lose, the family loses; and since the family includes women, many women are increasingly championing the father and child reunion. Organizations of Second Wives are emerging, and many parents, children, and siblings are deeply touched by the tragedy of their son, father, or brother losing the children they had all come to love.[10]

Many women, the apparent victors in the battle of the sexes, are realizing that when either sex wins, both sexes lose.

Men's fear of being dismissed as crazy, angry, or bitter should they speak up leads to our missing the life experience of millions of fathers. But ignoring them forces them to build strength and develop a major movement, with all the one-dimensional cardboard ideologies, counter-bureaucracies, and loss of soul that accompanies any group making the transition from emotionally repressed to visible and powerful. In the process of achieving equity, many of these men will be wasted, many of their children will be damaged, and generations will be provided with another distorted version of love. If we hear these men, we give their children dads.

Men's fear of confronting women has led to many men feeling paralyzed for fear of women's anger. So let me speak mostly to the dads first. . . .

A Message to Dads . . . Mostly

Anger. "Why Is She So Angry? She Seems Like Those 'Hell-Hath-No-Fury-Like-a-Woman-Scorned' Women of The First Wives Club."

Many dads are astonished that their former wives are so angry. They paraphrase Norman Mailer's "You never know your wife until you meet her in court." Not knowing what this anger is about, and feeling damned if they do communicate and damned if they don't, the dads feel their only alternative is the legal route. It can help a dad to know that although some of his ex's anger might be related to him personally, something deeper is often also going on.

Many dads feel frustrated that one moment they hear their former wife speak of independence, and the next moment she's asking for money. From his perspective this does not reflect a desire for independence, but entitlement and dependence. A dad can have more empathy for this contradiction when he recalls that for millions of years, women who didn't marry money didn't marry the best protectors for their children.

Sometimes he attributes this dream to his former wife's evilness. However, exactly because seeking protection via a man was so functional for motherhood, *most* women have been brought up with the dream of being swept away. It is as deeply woven into the female psyche as is your vulnerability to her pleas of being financially rescued. As is your dream about sex with a young, beautiful woman (à la *American Beauty*). Wasn't being "swept away" a pre-liberation dream? Hardly. Remember the Fox-TV special "Who Wants to Marry a Multimillionaire?" in 2000? Women called Fox-TV to marry an anonymous multimillionaire in such large numbers that Fox's computers crashed.

Both women's and men's dreams are as difficult to remove as syrup from a pancake. And both dreams affect and distort the mind like syrup affects and distorts a pancake.

Here is the point: The more embedded that dream is in your ex's psyche, the more **a divorce means her dream of being swept away has just been swept away.** And that has nothing to do with you personally.

Women and men have another parallel neurosis. You know how women accuse men of not being willing to ask for directions? Of denying we're lost? Well, women have a parallel area of denial. The five finalists in the show "Who Wants to Marry a Multimillionaire?" all swore that *money had nothing to do with their interest in marrying the man* (about whom they knew nothing, except that he had money). So if your former wife does desire to be swept away, don't look for the satisfaction of her acknowledging this.

"I'd never marry a man just because he had a million dollars. Not in today's market."

If divorce created her first nightmare (of her dream of being "swept away" being swept away), her second nightmare comes when she assesses her potential after divorce. That is, her potential for being swept away again. She looks in the mirror and sees what forty looks like, which wouldn't look that bad were she not observing men and seeing them swap one forty for two twenties. She feels disposable.

When her dream of being "swept away" is swept away, her fear of disposability makes her want to dispose of the husband she feels disposed of her. The anger emanating from that fear is best expressed by women's response to the movie *The First Wives Club*—a movie building its popularity on the creative ways women could combine their resources to ruin the lives of their former husbands—all of whom were portrayed as deserving it. In the first week of its release, half of all female moviegoers chose that movie, *above all others combined*. Your former wife's fear of disposability, and the anger emanating from it, then, has nothing to do with you personally.

She is angry at you in part because you were her hope, and her *hope* has been disappointed. That can easily be confused with *you* being her disappointment.

If you take her disappointment personally, you'll both be defensive. Defensiveness is the energy from which lawyers build swimming pools. Defensiveness is the enemy of flexibility, and lack of flexibility is the greatest road*block* to your children. The road *back* to your children starts with remaining in your ex's psychological family. Even though you are divorced, you can still be on her team.

Communicate What You Value About Her

Most dads who are in deadlock with their children's moms think they are good at acknowledging and valuing the moms, but when I ask the moms if they agree, they laugh. It makes no difference who is technically correct. From a communication perspective, if the mother isn't hearing it, it isn't happening. I'm not saying former wives are any better at this. For the reasons mentioned above, they're not. But right now I'm talking to the dads. And what I find is that it is hard for your former wife to refuse to value you when you are *consistently* valuing her.

Dads who do this best are especially good at looking for *small* and very specific acknowledgments: "The kids say they really liked the movie you took them to." Most dads don't acknowledge in part because they think in terms of grand and sweeping *superlative* statements ("You're the best mom . . .") or absolute statements ("You're a good mom"). Because they don't feel that way and abhor dishonesty, they say nothing. Other dads are afraid of saying something that can be used against them in court. But specifics like "The kids say they really liked the movie you took them to" create none of that downside and buy you plenty of upside goodwill. Besides, it tells your former wife she is actually being seen.

Focus also on something specific and small that you have *learned* from your children's mom ("Sara said you brush her hair in the morning. I felt she could do it herself, but I noticed that when I did it once, she seemed to feel more secure").

Search for even a small way she has grown and deepened ("I appreciated the way you mentioned to the kids that I didn't give them the answers to their schoolwork because they'd get more out of it if they worked it out on their own"). Look for contexts in which you actually experience her that way so the acknowledgment is not gratuitous.

One overlooked source of specific positive acknowledgments is examining the flip side of a criticism. You might have wanted to take the kids to the movie your wife took them to, but instead of saying, "Gee, that was a movie I was planning to take them to," you say, "The kids say they really liked the movie you took them to." Almost every criticism hides a compliment dying to be found.

Many dads, when they say something that they believe is a compliment about the way their ex has changed, compare it to the old, negative behavior. For example, if she is now giving him more notice about teachers' conferences than previously, he might say, "Thanks for not just notifying me the day before." He sees that as a compliment; she, as a criticism. Why? Because every word in the sentence except the "thank you for not" was about what she did wrong. Now try, "Thanks for giving me enough notice that I could rework my schedule to be there." Now every word is about what she did right, and why.

Many dads who do feel they focus on the positive still complain that their former wife doesn't see it that way. Sometimes that's their former wife's issue, but to be certain, check this out. How does, "Thanks for asking me to join in the teacher's conference this time" sound to you? What your former wife doubtless heard was the "this time." To her, that was a zinger. She would have preferred, "Thanks for asking me to join in the teacher's conference."

Too subtle, fussy and particular? If you've ever been in sales, or done comedy, you know how a word, a tone, or even just a well-timed hesitation can turn opposition into partnership. Many men are great at mastering those distinctions in sales, but when dealing with a woman by whom they have felt rejected, their mastery disappears.

Our former wives' minds are fully open only when they feel fully acknowledged. In this respect, former wives are exactly like their former husbands.

Children Aren't Just Children

When divorce occurs, men's biggest fear is emotional insecurity; women's is economic insecurity.

Although the divorce *settlement* might have transferred the fear of economic insecurity from her to you, the initial stages of divorce just magnify both sexes' insecurities, so some women might want the children *partly* because they're her *job security*. The degree to which your job was her income, and her contribution to create that income was caring for the children, is the degree to which your having the children is your having her job. **When you fight with your former wife for the children, it feels to her as it might feel to you to have someone fighting you for your job.** This is particularly true for a traditional woman. And particularly true if you're successful. (The more successful you are, the better her "job.")

Consider, then, helping her reduce her economic fears by helping her build her own economic muscle. I see this approach having the best chance of working when the woman sees the development of her own economic strength as a way of helping her daughters have a good role model. It often takes her viewing it this way to persuade her to pursue education that leads primarily to income rather than primarily to fulfillment. She needs to see her own economic muscle as part of what being a good *mother* is about. And it is part of being a good mother, because it frees you to be more involved as a dad, and getting you more involved is part of what being a good mother is about.

I guarantee, though, that this approach will not work unless she feels you feel you are still on her team.

A woman is most likely to be able to hear about your importance to the children only when her economic fears are reduced. Notice that I did not say your "right" to your children: Your ex is more likely to be interested in your children's needs than your rights. If you agree with me about that, then express it to her that way.

Articulate Dad's Contributions, but Be Sure to Include Mom's

Just as women took responsibility for bringing their values into the workplace (family leave, sexual harassment, gender sensitivity), men must take responsibility for bringing our values into the homeplace.

To introduce your ex to the value of *your* contributions to the children, include examples that incorporate *her* contributions. If you are perhaps introducing your value to the children by encouraging them to take risks, you might also discuss *her* value to the children in encouraging them to be safe. If your son or daughter is climbing a tree and your ex is more likely to say, "Don't do that—it's dangerous," first acknowledge that her attentiveness to the children's safety is her contribution. She will then be more open to hearing that your contribution, of risk taking, comes from your experience that a child who falls and breaks a bone is hurt less than a child who is overprotected—since that doesn't teach a child how to negotiate life. Once she is secure with your attentiveness to their safety, she will be able to hear that too much protection fosters mediocrity, creating mediocrity's offspring: insecurity.

Attentiveness to her contributions allows your ex to be open to the understanding that it is exactly that tension between the mother and the father that produces the best outcome for the child. (Input from both of you helps the child balance risk-taking with self-protection—either one without the other would produce a child who is out of balance.) If you let her know that you know her intent is to be the best mother she can be, she'll more easily be able to hear that **being a good mother also means doing everything possible to include the father.**

A Message to Moms . . . Mostly

If you are a mom reading this book, you might be suspicious about your ex's "sudden interest" in the children. If he were "so interested," why didn't he express that more when you were married? You might suspect his real interest is to reduce or eliminate his child support payments. Here is what is often going on that few men can articulate:

Just as you provided the children's physical womb, so your husband probably provided most of the children's financial womb. But, as we discussed, providing income also produces "The Father's Catch-22" (what it takes to love his family takes him away from the love of his family). To him, there is an unspoken deal: He provides financial security and receives emotional security. Divorce jeopardizes this.

Sometimes a divorce feels to a man like a requirement to work overtime for a wife he feels hates him and children he feels have been turned against him. This does not exactly inspire him to produce money.

A man often experiences divorce, then, not only as depriving him of his wife's love, but also as jeopardizing his children's love. He suddenly feels an enormous "love void." He, like you, had a dream, albeit less conscious. **The man's dream was that if he produced money, he would receive love.** He unconsciously believed that if he kept his promise of producing money, you would keep yours of giving love. (Thus the name of the nationwide Christian *men's* organization, the Promise Keepers, promising to produce money, hoping to give and receive love.)

Divorce makes him fear that his unconscious dream—to receive love for producing money—is being swept away. His bitterness comes partly from feeling he's still required to produce money for you; you're no longer required to give love to him. Or cook. Or clean. Or channel any money from your career to his bank. He might feel bitter that everything he produced is half yours under the theory that you created it together—as partners; but the children you also created together, as partners, aren't half his.

It is the void after divorce that catalyzes for many men the discovery (on a gut level) that the primary purpose of work is not work, but love. When he feels he no longer has yours, he discovers that the only people who both love him and need him are his children. Feeling loved and feeling needed are vital to the human psyche.

I mean the word "vital" literally. In the three decades I've worked with both sexes, I have consistently found four common denominators among people who commit suicide: feeling *unloved,* feeling *unneeded;* feeling *no hope of that changing,* and feeling a *lack of comfort expressing those feelings.* Think of whether any of these fit your former husband.

These common denominators are increasingly found in men. The risk of suicide has recently risen only for men—from four times higher than women's risk to almost five times higher.[12] And **divorce increases his risk of suicide even more, to ten times greater than a divorced woman's.**[13] Divorce does not increase your risk. Suppose a man divorces and lives in an environment that teaches him to repress feelings. Australia has such an environment. If he's a man who represses feelings, his probability of committing suicide goes up again. Thus, in Australia, separated and divorced men commit suicide at more than thirteen times the rate of separated and divorced women.[14]

This might be but the tip of your former husband's vulnerability. If he is fighting to be with his and your children, and he loses, I predict we will eventually discover that American men in that position are about fifteen times more likely to commit suicide than their wives; if he feels he has been falsely accused of abusing you, about twenty times greater; if he feels he has been falsely accused of child molestation, about thirty times greater. I say "I predict," because no one has cared enough to fund these studies. But you've got the point.

As a woman, it might be difficult to grasp this, since divorce and separation do not increase women's risk of suicide at all.[15] Why not? Women are more likely to have the children—someone to love them and need them. (Remember that people who feel loved and needed rarely commit suicide?) And women develop support systems. **Women's traditional support systems support women being vulnerable; men's traditional support systems support men being *in*vulnerable.**

This creates a paradox: The support men get to be invulnerable makes them more vulnerable; the support women get to be vulnerable makes them less vulnerable. It is just one example of how women's strength is their façade of weakness and men's weakness is their façade of strength.

Take, for example, the most archetypal of men's support systems—his football team, the cheerleaders, and his family. When a cheerleader says, "First and ten, do it again!" she isn't saying "first get in touch with your feelings again." Nor is his coach. Or his parents cheering in the stands. All of us are unwittingly supporting him to "risk a concussion again"—to get tough again. If, instead of getting a touchdown, he gets in touch with his feelings, and quits his position on the team to avoid the concussion, the cheerleader doesn't say, "Next week I'm going to cheer for you—I noticed how open and vulnerable you were when you were playing football." Yes, next week she does cheer. But she cheers for his *replacement*.

Expressing feelings of vulnerability brings women affection and men rejection. So men's support systems support men in being *in*vulnerable. The result?

Some men's inability to express the depth of their love to their wives—and therefore their hurt when that love disintegrates—leaves many women clueless about how the combined loss of his wife and children often leaves him flirting with suicide. Thus divorce often leaves Dad "suddenly discovering" his children—not a disingenuous response; rather, a *vital* response.

This "sudden discovery" is not just a theory: 87 percent of custodial fathers actually spend more time with their children after divorce than before (even though most are also working longer hours, and many have to drive for more than an hour to see them). Again, women's experience is different after divorce. Custodial moms spend less time with their children (since more moms are taking on additional work burdens).[16]

Many moms ask me a different question, this one with a lot more feeling: "If my ex cares so much about the children, why does he seem more preoccupied with this new, younger woman? If *I* didn't go seeking out a new, younger, admiring male, why did he seek out a new, younger, admiring female?" Why? In part, because of sexual attraction, to be sure, and in part because men get from the admiring female what women get from their womenfriends: emotional support.

Many women sever ties with their exes by sharing their version of the marriage with their womenfriends until they've honed a story line that creates maximum emotional support. Men are much more likely to lick their wounds by finding a new woman to love. But they often pay a price for this: The women most willing to do that are often dependent, which usually means young, and usually means they need, in return, his potential for financial security. Both sexes are healing by seeking support, but each does it in a different way.

The upside of the female method is that she does not take on new dependents; the shadow side is the anger she creates toward her ex (the "First Wives Club Syndrome"). The upside of the male method is that he does not build a support system based on a view of his ex-wife as a jerk; the shadow side is that he might continue to love his ex even as he loves someone new. He often remains in love with her exactly because he hasn't demonized her. He is most likely to prematurely take on someone new to love if he feels his wife is badmouthing him to the children and he has no one to confide in— that is, if he feels devoid of emotional support.

This male shadow side (of continuing to love his ex while loving someone new) was captured humorously in the "Cheers" episode in which Nick brings his new bride to Cheers, only to confess to his ex, Carla, that he still loves her, and wants her back. When a man is portrayed as doing this, he is usually portrayed as Nick is: a two-timing loser who knows nothing of love or commitment. However, if *The Cosby Show*'s Dr. and Mrs. Huxtable had broken up, and Mrs. Huxtable had remarried but never gotten over her love for Dr. Huxtable and one day confessed to him that, in her heart, she wanted him back, might we not see that as a sign of the depth of women's love?

The best ways to prevent a man from falling in love with a dependent woman? First, assist his connection to the love of his dependent children. Fathers who have an opportunity to fully share in their children's love are less likely to fall in love with an overly dependent woman just to fill the void. Second, offer emotional support. When a man feels caught between pleasing a new woman and receiving love versus trying to please his ex-wife but receiving anger, he chooses the new woman. Remember, even though you are divorced, you are still on the same team.

Many times the woman's negative feelings toward her ex—now reinforced by her womenfriends' agreement—spill over to badmouthing of her ex within the children's earshot. But children eventually look in the mirror and see how their body language—or nose, or rear—is like their dad's, realize that they are 50 percent their dad's genes and, well, if their dad is an irresponsible jerk, maybe they are, too.

Many moms have told me they hadn't thought about it this way. When they realize that badmouthing their ex is the same as badmouthing the child, they work on restraining themselves. **They can see how badmouthing the *dad* becomes a form of *child abuse.***

To children, badmouthing translates into a fear of loving Dad, the fear that "loving Dad is betraying Mom." Since it is love that inspires most men's responsibility, badmouthing deflates a dad's inspiration to take responsibility (his unconscious translation is "no love, no responsibility"). Put another way, men invest money in the bank of love.

A mother who has a true motherhood instinct will be fighting for the father to be involved as if her children's lives depended on it.

If you are reading this book as a single mother who has tried to get your ex involved but has not been able to, rather than condemn yourself for the hazards to which your children have been exposed, congratulate yourself for

Your father was a jackass.

navigating your children the best you could around those hazards, and in uncharted waters.

Similarly, although you will read below of the problems that children without fathers are more likely to suffer, remember that a certain percentage of children *with* fathers also suffer from these problems. So don't *assume* that these problems emanate from father deprivation. How can you tell? Get a hint by reading carefully the section on what fathers do that's different. And, most important, **as you look at the long list of hazards and see the ones from which your children do *not* suffer, think of them as being the long list of hazards that your mothering has helped them avoid.**

If your children have not turned out okay, remember, you grew up with one map and, halfway through your journey, it was exchanged for another. Divorce and children-without-marriage are our generation's equivalent of our parents' World Wars and the Great Depression. Each generation has a different burden, and both sexes a different challenge in meeting it.

Meantime, let me know the challenges of your sex and generation that I have right and have gotten wrong. (I have a one-sex, one-generation limitation.)

I invite you to write me directly:

Dr. Warren Farrell

PMB 222

315 S. Coast Hwy 101, Suite U

Encinitas, CA 92024-3555

And visit me virtually:

www.warrenfarrell.com

What's Missing When Dad's Missing?

What's missing?
One-quarter of
American children
are living without
their dads.[1] That's
17 million children
missing their dads, or
never knowing what
they're missing. . . .

Why Dad Is Crucial

First, Some Basics

I'm one of those men who is sometimes in the mood to skip the instructions and "just get into it." There are, though, two teensy-weensy paragraphs that will save you enough teeth-gnashing to make their reading worth it.

I'll often use the phrase "shared parent time" to replace joint custody. There are two types of joint custody: physical and legal. Physical implies about equal time with the children; legal doesn't. Unless I state otherwise, references to "shared parent time"or joint custody will be to joint physical custody.

Since I'll be mentioning what percentage of dropouts, successes, and failures grow up in mother-only homes, it will be helpful to know the percentage of all children growing up in mother-only homes. In 1970, it was 11 percent; currently it is 22 percent.[1] (The studies I cite will cover from 1970 to 2000.) But it is, of course, crucial to never confuse correlation with causality—the fact that single-mother homes are correlated with certain problems does not necessarily mean the problem is created by the single mother's or the father's absence. The problem might be caused by other factors, such as less education or more poverty. We'll explore all of that.

Now, for the possible impact of Dad. . . .

The Impact of Dad

The benefits to the baby begin at birth.

The Benefits Start Early

An Israeli study found that the more frequently a father visited the hospital of an infant who is prematurely born, the more rapidly the infant gained weight and the more quickly the infant was able to leave the hospital.[2] More important, the more the father visited, the better was the infant's social-personal development and its ability to adapt.[3] I wondered whether this might have been because the mothers of these infants also had more contact with the children; but the children with more paternal contact did better even when they had not had more maternal contact.

In a study of black infants, the more interaction the boy had with the father, the higher his mental competence and psychomotor functioning *by the age of six months.*[4] By the age of three years, psychomotor functioning is associated with the development of a higher I.Q.[5]

Psychologists at the National Institutes of Mental Health have found that boys who have contact with fathers display a greater trust level even by the time they are five to six months old.[6] For example, they are friendlier with strangers and more willing to be picked up. They also enjoy playing more, and are more verbally open.

Empathy

If there is one quality that I find is more essential to a successful and happy life than any other, it is empathy. It is at the core of family stability and love. I've never had a couple come to me and say, "I want a divorce; my partner understands me."

Similarly, children who don't feel understood rebel, join gangs or cults, disappear into a bottle, or seek another world at the point of a needle. Even in the work arena and the legal arena, it is rare for us to sue someone from whom we feel empathy.

We usually think of empathy as something transmitted via the mother. Thus one of the more surprising findings about father involvement is that "the amount of time a father spends with a child is one of the strongest predictors of *empathy* in adulthood."[7]

Although this finding emerged from a study that was done over a twenty-six-year period and was published in 1990, everyone still seems to be at a loss for a good explanation as to why Dad involvement leads to empathy. From my observation of moms and dads, I believe it has to do with men's style of discipline.

Dads and moms are both prone to set boundaries with their children—

moms even more so than dads, especially when safety is involved. But the big difference is in the enforcement. When the child violates the boundaries, Mom tends to repeat her request, escalate the volume of it, feel guilty about getting angry, and find reasons to be flexible with the promised consequences (or not have promised any consequences to begin with). Dad is more likely to mention a consequence up front, and when the boundary is violated, exact the consequence as if it were a deal made between the dad and child. The usual outcome is the child taking the father's boundary-setting more seriously.

How does treating boundaries seriously create empathy? **Teaching the child to treat boundaries seriously teaches the child to respect the rights and needs of others.** Thinking of another's needs creates empathy.

A child who learns that consequences are always negotiable focuses on how to manipulate the best negotiation, or on its desires, not the desires and needs of the person setting the boundary—or the person who is being intruded upon when the boundary was violated. I remember hearing when I was a kid, "good fences make good neighbors," without understanding the deeper reasons why.

Although dads bring these values, they perpetuate their own devaluation by just doing what they do, rather than thinking about why they do it clearly enough to articulate it. Conversely, no one has valued dads enough to ask them.

When a dad does not articulate his contribution, he also hurts his children. Studies are now finding that children thrive by their parents helping them interpret the world—for example, not just by setting boundaries, but by helping the children understand why . . . via kids' values. For example, a dad might explain, "Kids who think of others are often popular; if you want popularity, think of others." It's called the Child Incentive Plan. Or he might just take the children to a fence between two neighbors and ask them why they think the fence is there.

I. Q. and Achievement

ITEM. Students coming from father-present families score higher in math and science *even when they come from weaker schools.*[8]

ITEM. First-grade black and white children of both sexes raised in father-absent families recorded significantly lower I.Q. scores than those with fathers present.[9]

This last item is the second study I have cited showing the relationship between father absence and I.Q. This suggests that I.Q. might be a social problem with a potential social solution, rather than inherent in racial differences. This is significant because when we hear that blacks score lower than Caucasians on I.Q. tests, and that Caucasians score lower than Asians, we are sometimes tempted to assume that we are talking about a hierarchy of intelligence. If we refrain from mentioning this because we know it serves no constructive purpose, or for fear of being called "racist," it can nevertheless rest in our unconscious. Perhaps, though, it is not a hierarchy of intelligence and race, but a hierarchy of father involvement and race. Yes, Asians have the highest I.Q. scores among the three races, but they also have by far the highest father presence; blacks have the lowest I.Q. scores, but by far the least father presence. This suggests a social problem with a potential social solution.

But is the real issue the single mother's greater poverty or lesser education? Well, two Harvard researchers asked the same question. They reviewed four of the major national surveys with that in mind. They found the impact of father absence to still be profound. For example, *even when race, education, poverty, and similar socioeconomic factors are equal,* and regardless of which survey was looked at, living without Dad doubled a child's chance of dropping out of high school.[10]

Similarly, a study of boys from *similar backgrounds* revealed that *by the third grade, the boys with fathers present scored higher on every achievement test and received higher grades.*[11]

Elementary-school children living without their dads did worse on twenty-one of twenty-seven social-competence measures and eight out of nine academic measures.[12] They were also more likely to repeat grades, were absent more frequently, and were less popular with their peers. Overall, the boys suffered more than the girls.

The chances that a child living with both biological parents will have to repeat a grade in school are one in nine; the chances that a child living with a single mother will have to repeat a grade in school are one in four.[13]

Why? Children living without dads were more likely to be absent from school,[14] and to have more suspensions, more expulsions, and a higher rate of truancy.[15] In the end, "The more years children spend with single mothers, the fewer years of school they complete."[16]

Single mothers are not, though, the only issue. Dads who see their children frequently help their children considerably. The children who saw their fathers only once or twice a year (or less) did by far the worst. Dads who don't come around, or moms who don't encourage dads to come around, keep their children from "coming around."

The area of achievement most negatively impacted by father absence was math and science aptitude.[17] An article in the *Harvard Educational Review* suggests that fathers seem to help children develop the thinking skills that lead to success in math.[18] Could the poor educational performance in the United States in the past twenty years, especially in math and science, have more to do with the absence of fathers than with the quality of schools? Yes. As we saw in the "Item" above, students coming from father-present families score higher in math and science, even when they come from weaker schools.[19]

Is the impact short-term? No. Even six years after living with mothers, boys scored lower on ten social and an additional ten academic measures.[20] And students from father-absent homes score "dramatically" lower on college entrance examinations,[21] and are 1.5 times more likely to be unemployed, not only in their teens, but well into their mid-twenties.[22]

Furthermore, if this unemployed man has children, he is less likely to be present, because the mom can get economic support only if he is absent— that is, Temporary Assistance to Needy Families (TANF, which replaced the government program Aid to Families with Dependent Children [AFDC]) is available if Dad is *absent*. Thus, if we have an unemployed dad who has plenty of time for the children and an employed mom who doesn't, we turn his potential father presence into father absence.

Note that this unemployed dad could not only be present, but involved. And in a two-parent family. The significance? A recent U.S. Department of Education study finds that, "In two-parent families, fathers' involvement, but not mothers' involvement, is associated with an increased likelihood that children in the 1st through 5th grades get mostly "A"s. Among children in the 6th through 12th grades, after controlling for a variety of resources that parents offer at home, fathers' involvement, but not mothers' involvement, remains a significant influence on the likelihood that their children get mostly "A's."[23]

Our preoccupation with dad-as-wallet leaves us with a disposable dad when Dad doesn't have disposable income, underdeveloped children because we don't see Dad's value in developing them, and a fatherless family because we're paying Mom to make it that way. The result? Fatherlessness begets fatherlessness.

The Suicide Factor

The *American Journal of Orthopsychiatry* reports that women who commit suicide have one thing in common: a "strong influence exerted by mothers coupled with lack of involvement of fathers in the subjects' lives."[24] Similarly, **living in mother-only homes contributes more than anything else to suicide—for both sexes.**[25] (This is true even among groups matched for income, age, race, and religion.)

As I discuss at length in *The Myth of Male Power*, teenage male suicide is increasing rapidly. Even boys in their early twenties are six times as likely as girls to commit suicide.[26] Overall, the suicide rate among white American men between the ages of fifteen and twenty-four has *increased by 50 percent* since 1970.[27]

Why is this happening?

The Psychological Factor

ITEM. The more the father is involved, the more easily the child makes open, receptive, and trusting contact with new people in his/her life.[28]

ITEM. Eighty percent of pre-school children admitted as psychiatric patients in two New Orleans hospitals came from homes without fathers.[29] Similar percentages emerge from countries as diverse as Canada,[30] South Africa, and Finland, at ages from pre-school through teenage.[31]

ITEM. Sixty-five percent of juveniles and young adults in state-operated institutions come from homes without fathers.[32]

The National Center for Health Statistics reports that a child living with his/her divorced mother, compared to a child living with both parents, is 375 percent more likely to need professional treatment for emotional or behavioral problems.[33] They are also more likely to suffer from frequent headaches[34] and/or bed-wetting,[35] develop a stammer or speech defect,[36] suffer from anxiety or depression,[37] and be diagnosed as hyperactive.[38]

In the extensive Guidubaldi study of elementary-school children mentioned above, elementary school children without fathers were likely to have more nightmares, have greater anxiety, be less popular with peers, and be more hostile to adults. They were more likely to be dependent, inattentive, and either aggressive, withdrawn, or both. They were poorer at social skills in general and communication in particular.[39]

When fathers do not visit after a divorce, *girl* children show signs of being hyperactive, headstrong, and antisocial. Both boys and girls showed signs of over-dependency on the mother.[40]

The psychological problems reveal themselves in many ways. Take drug use: An adolescent who experiences her or his father as being distant is much more likely to use drugs heavily.[41] This is especially true of female adolescents. Obviously, older children use drugs more than do younger children, but aside from this age factor, **the most important factor by far in preventing drug use is a close relationship with Dad.**[42]

Similarly, 90 percent of homeless or runaway children are from fatherless homes.[43] Most gang members come from mother-only households.[44] Former neo-Nazi T. J. Leyden, who joined the skinheads after his parents divorced, reported that the neo-Nazis look for "young, angry kids who need a family"—which, in practical terms, usually means that they need a dad.[45]

If a child has been alienated from his dad, lives with his mom, and goes to a school with mostly female teachers, from where does he receive his male identity? It is exactly those circumstances that make young men turn to gangs for male approval and love.

Physical Health

Psychological problems cause stress, weaken the immune system, and make us more vulnerable to whatever physical problems our inheritance makes us prone to. For example, the National Center for Health Statistics reports that a child living with a divorced mother, compared to a child living with both parents, is more likely to suffer chronic asthma.[46]

Daughters Without Dads Become Mothers Without Husbands

ITEM. Daughters who live with only their mothers are 92 percent more likely to divorce than daughters of two-parent families."[47]

ITEM. In a study of inner-city Baltimore women who were teenage mothers, one-third of their daughters also became teenage mothers. But not one daughter or son who had a good relationship with his/her biological father had a baby before the age of nineteen.[48]

Connection with Dad leads not only to preventing daughters from becoming pregnant prematurely, but also to preventing sons from creating pregnancies prematurely.

Exactly what do good dads bring to children that leads to not a single child with a good dad having a child when she or he is a teenager? Best to ask teenage girls. In a 1997 national survey of teenage girls who were asked what would prevent pregnancy, here were some key answers:

- 97% said, "Having parents they can talk to;"

- 93% said, "Having loving parents;"

- 93% said knowing how condoms were used;

- 93% said being satisfied with life;

- 91% said carefully choosing boyfriends.[49]

Do fathers, then, allow teenage girls to feel they have someone they can talk to (which usually means listening more and lecturing less)? Are dads in some way helpful to girls in knowing what type of boys to choose—or avoid? Certainly mothers love their daughters as much as fathers do, but we will see below that the greater stress single mothers experience—even compared to single fathers who are also working—leads to mothers hitting and punishing their children more than do single fathers, and perhaps this leads to the daughters feeling less loved and less satisfied with life.

Notice that the girls' dominant concerns were about emotional issues more than technical issues. Yet when we think of education for pregnancy prevention, we think of contraception. Similarly, although professionals stress that young girls should resist peer pressure from boys, the girls themselves are slightly more likely to feel pressure from their female peers than from their male peers.[50]

The relationship between fatherlessness and teenage pregnancy is not a problem just in Baltimore or the inner cities. Researchers McLanahan and Sandefur, in a book published by Harvard, examined four major surveys of youth and discovered that daughters who live with only their mothers are 2.5 times as likely to have a teen birth, and twice as likely to have that teenage birth out of wedlock. The samples with and without dads had similar socioeconomic backgrounds.[51]

Is it possible that girls living with dads are less likely to become pregnant because their sexuality is more repressed? Apparently not. Girls who lived in father-absent homes tended to go to extremes in their relationships with males—being either very withdrawn, or overly aggressive and flirtatious.[52] Both extremes seem to come from a lack of comfort with men. And there are other indicators. Females from homes with dads experience more orgasms when they become sexual in their adult relationships.[53] Most women who have overcome difficulties reaching orgasm know that they have done so either by becoming more relaxed in general or with their partner and their sexuality.

When Father Goes, Crime Comes

ITEM. Seventy-three percent of adolescent murderers come from mother-only homes.[54]

ITEM. Eighty percent of rapists who were evaluated as raping out of anger and rage came from father-absent homes.[55]

ITEM. Ninety percent of adolescent repeat arsonists lived with only their mothers.[56]

Overall, 65 percent of juvenile prisoners were brought up without dads.[57] *The Journal of Research in Crime and Delinquency* reports that the more absent the father, the higher the rates of violent crime.[58]

Were these associations with crime due to poverty? No. When the children in homes *with* fathers with *more* income were compared to the children in homes *with* fathers with *less* income, there was no difference in the rates of violent crime. **The difference in crime rate could be predicted only by comparing the children *without* fathers at home to the children *with* fathers at home.** This study is especially significant not only because it controlled for the poverty factor in this way, but because it analyzed data from 11,000 individuals in different urban areas.

Why is our image of fathers at such odds with reality? In part, because of the media. Although three-quarters of adolescent murderers are brought up by mothers, we don't see front covers of major news magazines saying their mother gave them "a Motive for Murder." Yet look at this front cover of the *Los Angeles Times Magazine* and how it portrays the Menendez brothers as brought up by Dad—the only parent holding them, the only parent mentioned on the cover, and the only parent accused of maybe giving his sons a "Motive for Murder."

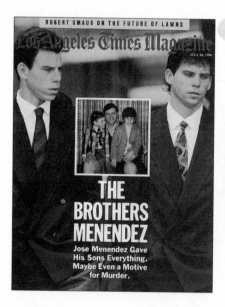

I was therefore surprised to discover that, in fact, it was the mother who had brought up the sons while the father was the chief of a worldwide record division at RCA. The father might also have been abusive, as the sons later claimed, but this article was written and published before that claim was made public and, whether true or not, *the mother had the primary role of bringing up the children, yet only the father is shown holding the future murderers.*

If a dad had brought up the children while a mother had been a corporate executive, we would have blamed the children's murder on their being raised by a dad and neglected by a mom—"who cared more about her company than her kids." We use our stereotypes to keep moms as mothers and dad$ as dough.

If Divorce Is the Only Way, Then What's Best for the Children?

The intact family definitely gives children a jump-start in life; but, as we saw with the Menendez brothers, it is no panacea. A jump-start can lead to disaster if no one is maintaining the tires. And divorce can be better than the message to children that marriage is a trap with no way out—no matter how miserable you are.

How a child adjusts after divorce is only partially dependent upon the parenting arrangement. A child is much more likely to adjust well if . . .

- there is a smaller amount of conflict between the parents;

- the parenting is not authoritarian, but authoritative (the children's input preceding the decision, then the parents making decisions they stick with);

- there is access to both parents; and

- the child has good support systems available (*e.g.,* friends, other family members who listen well).[61]

However, other things being equal, here is the impact of shared parent time (joint custody), primary father time, primary mother time, stepparenting, and moving the child away from the non-resident parent.

The Impact of Shared Parent Time (or Joint Physical Custody)

I am introducing the expression "shared parent time" to replace joint *physical* custody (as explained above, in "First, Some Basics"). Similarly, I will be using "sole parent time" instead of sole custody. "Custody" has the feel of prison time. I'd prefer parent time.

Divorce's biggest disaster, from the child's perspective, is loss of contact with a parent.[62] The visiting pattern that incurred the most intense dissatisfaction was the traditional one of every other weekend.[63] Both boys and girls found it a loser, but the greatest feelings of deprivation and depressive behavior were observed in the boys.[64]

Children in a shared parent time arrangement were found to have higher self-esteem (especially girls[65]), be less excitable, and be less impatient than children in arrangements with one parent having sole parent time.[66] One study finds that boys' overall adjustment in shared-parent-time arrangements was similar to that in happy, intact families.[67] Children of all ages benefited, but children under ten express the greatest interest.[68]

Children with shared parent time were also much more likely to be happy with the length of time they were with each parent—not feeling as if one parent was really more like an aunt or uncle.[69]

Shared parent time resulted in less sibling rivalry and fewer negative attitudes toward the parents even within the first few months after separation.[70] Both parents are perceived to be less rejecting[71] (especially fathers[72]), and less controlling and manipulative,[73] which doubtless contributes to the almost unanimous findings that children in shared-parent-time arrangements are better-adjusted.

Shared parent time also leads to better relationships with stepparents and greater overall family cohesion than do sole parenting arrangements.[74] The opportunity to share parent time brings the opportunity to build a cohesive family.

From the parents' perspective, shared parent time leaves each parent feeling less stressed out,[75] and leaves mothers more time for social support.[76]

The evidence in favor of shared parent time would seem to make it the presumed jumping-off point. It has met, though, with three forms of political opposition: traditional couples, traditional legal assumptions, and feminists. Traditional couples feel it is natural for the woman to raise children and the man to raise money—or, even, that God intended it that way. Traditional judges and the law developed the "tender years doctrine," that children are better off with their moms during their young and "tender years," a doctrine most popular when songs with titles like that were popular. And feminists, initially pioneering advocates of full father involvement, reversed themselves when many women objected, saying they wanted to have the first option of having the children if they wanted them. By the mid-seventies, most N.O.W. chapters supported female choice over shared parent time. They still do.

Although shared parent time seems to be best for the children, it cannot, nevertheless, always be worked out. So, if we must stop at the Inn of Last Resort called sole parent time, which works better—Mother Time or Father Time (ahem)?

If Shared Parent Time Isn't in the Cards, Are Children Better Off with Their Mom, or with Their Dad?

If for some reason divorce is necessary and shared parent time cannot be worked out, are the children better off with the dad or the mom?

We prepared society for women entering the world of work by challenging ourselves to acknowledge that *sometimes* "the best man for the job is a woman"; as we prepare men to enter the world of children, we need to be open to the possibility that *sometimes* "the best mother for a child is the father."

Despite the fact that there are now almost two million single dads who have full parent time,[77] neither government nor private funding sources have generated much data on the impact of full-time father versus mother time, almost as if they were afraid of what might be found.

The research that has been done surprises virtually everyone with the degree to which it shows how well children do with dads. Yet, at the outset, I said this book will not show that dads are inherently better than mothers.

Am I contradicting myself? No. The men who have chosen to be fathers with sole or primary parent time are still a small percentage of all fathers— self-selected almost always by their interest in parenting, if not by their gifts for it. They are unlikely, therefore, to be representative of the average father—only of the average father who currently cares enough to overcome male socialization, the social stigma of being a full-time father, and the isolation from support systems that so many full-time fathers report that they encounter.

So the following section should be distinguished from the first part of the chapter, which dealt largely with a comparison of the family with the single mom to the two-parent family. In the two-parent family, it is not possible to say that children do better with fathers or mothers—only that they do better with two parents.

When I first looked at this research, I was also critical of it for two other reasons that, fortunately, have recently begun to be addressed. First, I felt it was biased against mothers because dads who fought for primary parent time had to have enough income to engage lawyers and were, therefore, usually better off financially than the average father. So the first question was, were the children better off with the dad because of the income or because of the dad? (Then I'll get to the second concern.)

Do Children Do Better with Dads Because Dads Have More Income?

Few people know that children do better with dads. Those who do assumed until recently that it was because of dads' greater income, thus allowing children to have advantages like their own computers. What is true is that, yes, dads who have sole father time *are* more likely to have higher income— not only higher than single mothers, but also higher than the average father.[78] And yes, their children living with them are more likely to have computers. It is also true that children from poor environments experience higher levels of conduct disorders,[79] behavior problems,[80] and depression,[81] and lower levels of education and socioeconomic achievement as adults.[82]

Recent research finds, though, that **even when the father and mother had *equal* income, the children who were with their dad full-time did better than those with their moms full-time.**[83] This is true for both girl children and boy children.

This is so crucial because it tells us that the dads' greater income is not *the* benefit to the children, but an *additional* benefit. More important, his income is much less likely to come from the government. This allows the children to have a role model of how to juggle the world of work and children, without having to be dependent on financial assistance. (To say nothing of what it does for taxpayers to have more money to send their own children to college rather than someone else's.)

Do Dads Get the Problem Children?

In brief, yes. Nearly half the children now with their dads full-time initially lived with their moms. Why did the moms give them to the dads? Usually it was "because the mother felt incompetent to care for them,"[84] most often because of one or more of the five Ds: drugs, drinking, delinquency, disobedience (including swearing viciously at the mom), and depression.

Do dads get children who are challenged when they are younger as well? It appears so. The National Health Interview Survey, drawn from Census data,[85] reveals that dads are more than 15 times as likely as moms to be in charge of children with developmental delay who were under one year of age.

Whether infants or teenagers, developmentally delayed or delinquent, dads are more likely to get the problem children.

Psychological Health

A study reported in the *Journal of Social Issues* found that boys who live with their fathers after divorce to be warmer, have a higher degree of self-esteem, be more mature, and be more independent than boys who live with their mothers after divorce.[86]

Boys who lived only with their moms grew up to be more demanding[87] and tended to develop a coercive relationship with their mothers.[88]

The impact of dads begins when life begins. Kyle Pruett of Yale studied infants living with just their dads and found that in the areas of personal and social skills, they were two to six months ahead of schedule. The older babies followed suit.[89]

A new Danish study of 1,200 children aged three to five, half with single moms and half with single dads, found that children living with their dads were much less likely to experience problems of feeling like victims.[90] For example, they were less sensitive to criticism and had fewer temper

"During the next stage of my development, Dad, I'll be drawing closer
to my mother—I'll get back to you in my teens."

tantrums. In many of the "victim" categories, the size of the reduction was enormous. Children living with dads were only:

- half as likely to have frequent nightmares, feelings of low self-worth, and lonesomeness;

- one-third as likely to feel victimized by other children; and

- one-quarter as likely to experience frequent seizures of fear.

Quite relevant to American boys with Attention Deficit Disorder, the Danish children living with their dads were only half as likely to experience problems with concentration.[92] And, perhaps as a result of all the above, they also had more playmates.[93]

We often hear of the stress single mothers experience from the juggling of work and family. The Danish study verified this and compared this to the single dads' stress. Did single dads experience as much stress? No.[94] The single moms had a harder time combining working outside the home with childraising, even though they are more likely to receive financial assistance. However, the Danish author notes, as have I, that the type of man who becomes a single dad today is exceptionally motivated.

Educational Achievement and I.Q.

ITEM. When dads had the primary responsibility for infants, the infants often performed problem-solving tasks at the level of those four to eight months their senior.[95]

Girls' difficulty with math and boys' difficulty with verbal skills are legendary. The solution to both might have less to do with scholarship money than with father involvement. In the area of math and quantitative abilities, the more involved the dad is, the better both daughters and sons do.[96] Ditto for boys' increase in verbal intelligence.[97] And the amount of time a father spends reading to his daughter is a strong predictor of his daughter's future verbal ability.[98] So both sexes improve in both sets of skills when fathers are more involved.

Among children living with only Dad, the children in grades 1 through 12 who enjoy school more and get mostly A's are the ones whose dads are not only present, but involved—not only at home, but at school, a recent U.S. Department of Education study found.[99]

Young teenagers do as well grade-wise living with Mom, but do better on all standardized tests if living with Dad.[100] What are the implications of grades versus standardized tests?

Grades are more likely to reflect study skills related to short-term memory, knowing what a teacher wants, attentiveness to getting homework in on time, help from parents on home projects, being able to look up answers at home, and willingness to ask parents for answers. Standardized tests are more likely to reflect what the child knows without those aids—to reflect whether there's real learning of the subject.

Both have their value. In real life, knowing what a boss wants leads to promotions, meeting deadlines is crucial to teamwork and production, asking others for help makes others feel important, and, with computers, more answers are available for the asking than ever before.

Innovation, though, requires understanding the underlying reasons why things tick. When we don't understand the reasons, the right questions evade us. The questions that separate what is the common wisdom from the un-common wisdom. That separate the politically correct from the politically courageous. Both prepare our children differently: one for leadership and innovation, the other for supporting leaders and innovators. Pictures and frames need each other.

When it comes to the differences in education between the average woman and man, a woman today is *more* likely than a man to graduate from college—it is just that the type of man who selects to be a single father tends to be more educated than the average dad; conversely, the type of woman who selects to be a single mother tends to be less educated than the average mom.

How big is this education gap? Census data shows that *heads of households* who are single fathers are 25 percent more likely to have graduated from college than single-mother household heads.[101] I predict, though, that the real education gap between single dads and moms is much greater than 25 percent. Why? Think about single moms. Especially in poor communities, single moms are often not heads of households—they are often teenage mothers living with their parents, with less than a high school education—doubtless making the education gap between these single moms and single dads (an average of eight years older) significantly larger than that revealed by the Census Bureau data.

This education gap creates three important advantages for the children with single dads. As a rule, the more educated the father, the better his child-rearing.[102] And the more educated the father, the more positive the impact on both the children's educational and occupational achievement.[103] When variables such as a parent's education, income, and race are the same, the children attain similar quantitative and verbal skills with moms as with dads.[104]

Effectiveness of Discipline

Overall, children living with dads are less likely to have discipline prob-lems.[105] However, the data is mixed as to whether children living with moms or dads have more difficulty getting along with others in school.[106]

Are dads more likely to use physical punishment to prevent discipline problems? No. Moms are. And moms used physical discipline more frequently.[107] Nevertheless, the children living with moms were more likely to exhibit frequent temper tantrums.

Health and Safety

ITEM. The U.S. Department of Health and Human Services finds that of the approximately 275 children killed each year by single moms or dads, that **single moms are 24 times more likely to be the killers.**[108] (There are about five times as many single moms.)

ITEM. Frequent headaches and stomachaches are two to three times more common among younger children living with only their moms (than with only their dads).[109] And five- to eleven-year-old children with moms are 259 percent more likely to go to the hospital.[110]

Why these differences? I will explore the reasons for the differences in abuse of children in Chapter 3—when I deal with all fathers and mothers, not just single parents—but let's explore here why children with single dads are so much less likely to be sick.

One possibility is immune-system breakdown. Single moms are more than three times as likely to let younger kids get away with late or irregular bedtimes.[111]

Why *that* difference? The literature has no answer. In my personal experience with single moms and dads, the single mom is as likely as the single dad to set an early bedtime, perhaps an even earlier bedtime, but the children are more likely to succeed in manipulating her by calling upon her protective and nurturing instincts ("I have a tummy ache" . . . "I need water" . . . "I have to get my homework done").

Of course, they initially try the same thing with Dad. The difference is in the response. Mom says, "Okay, but next time I want you to get your homework done before you play." Emphasis on "next time." Dad says, "Sorry, you had the opportunity to do that before—to bed, to bed, or off with your head," and playfully chases the child to bed. Emphasis on the invisible "*this time.*"

The child picks up the difference: "With Mom, I got away with it. With dad I didn't." Once the boundary is weak, it's a matter of who has more energy. Guess who "wins"? And guess who becomes stressed and over-whelmed? And guess whose immune systems suffer (hint: systems is plural)? Once the mom sees the child go to the hospital, she becomes even more protective and guilty, setting her up to be more easily manipulated, and thus the cycle continues. It all started with the weaker boundary.

Attitude Toward the Non-Resident Parent

ITEM. When children live with only their moms, the parents are *nine* times as likely to have conflict as when children live with their dads.[112]

Children living with their dads felt positively about moms; children living with moms were more likely to think negatively of dads.[113] Similar findings were reported in the large Danish study. When mothers had the children, the children were more than twice as likely to have no contact with the other parent.[114] Why?

One possibility? Badmouthing. Moms are almost five times as likely to badmouth dads as dads are moms.[115]

Another possibility? Traditional roles. Women's entrance into the workplace did not knock men out—work is too entrenched in men's tradi-tion. Similarly, men's entrance into parenting does not knock women out—mothering is too entrenched in women's tradition.

Whatever the reason, the result is that children living with their fathers are not sacrificing their positive feelings toward their mothers.

Do Boys Do Better with Dads and Girls with Moms?

The belief in the special connection between children and same-sex parents is so strong that approximately half the people to whom I mention that I'm writing a book called *Father and Child Reunion* say to me, perhaps when they say "good-bye," something like, "Good luck on that *Father and Son Reunion* book you're writing."

The prevailing wisdom has been that, if boys and girls must be with one parent or the other, boys should be with dads and girls with moms. As we've seen, this isn't true—both boys and girls do better with their dads. At all ages. Even when the dad has no advantage in income.[116]

What is true is that the advantage of father time is greater for boys than for girls. For example, boys do *much* better psychologically with their dads than with their moms; girls just do better psychologically (not much better) with their dads than they do with their moms.[117] (Psychological well-being was determined by tests of self-esteem, adjustment, mood, and lack of depression.)

Other researchers, who focused more on how well the children did in school, found that while both sexes do better with Dad, the performance level was not any greater for the son than for the daughter.[118]

The Impact of a Stepparent[119]

More than *half* of Americans will spend some of their life as a stepchild or stepparent.[120] Eighty-six percent of stepparent couples are a biological mom and a stepdad.[121] This stepdad is likely to have originally been better off than the biological mom since the more money a divorced man has, the more likely he is to remarry; conversely, the more money a divorced woman has, the less likely she is to remarry.[122] Thus their family income is only slightly less than that of the intact family.[123] *Economically,* the stepfamily resembles the intact family.

That's the stepparents' profile—what about their impact on the kids? There's good news and bad news.

Some good news first. Children whose *close* ties with stepdads were *both long-standing and stable* did as well as those who grew up with their biological fathers.[124] Although stepchildren have many more problems than if they are in an intact family, between two-thirds and three-fourths of the time their problems are not serious, and they eventually adjust. If the stepfamily is long-standing and stable, the chances of adjustment are greater.[125] If a stepdad comes into a boy's life when he is young, the outcome is very likely to be positive.[126]

The bad news begins with the difficulty of making a stepfamily long-standing and stable. Unfortunately, 60 percent of second marriages fail.[127] The bad news continues with the difficulty of getting stepfather and children close. Why? Lots of reasons. The children have usually become the parent's confidant prior to remarriage. The daughter especially doesn't like being replaced with the stepparent as new confidant.[128] Second, daughters in particular show more anger toward Mom and more difficulty relating to stepdads,[129] resulting in younger girls displaying more antagonistic, disruptive behavior toward both parents, and adolescent girls becoming increasingly noncommunicative, sullen, and avoidant.[130]

The result? After two years of marriage, most stepfathers are minimally involved and have low levels of rapport, control, and discipline.[131] Remember, the stepdad has been chosen from among the best breadwinners, which tends to leave him neither the time nor the propensity for lots of interpersonal intimacy or the skills to unravel the bond between the mother and daughter. In essence, he usually feels he has little real say, and returns to the arena in which his contribution is appreciated, or at least non-conflictual: breadwinning.

In comparison to an *intact* family, the children in stepparent families have lower GPAs and more discipline problems, and are less likely to stay in school, attend college, or graduate from college.[132]

In comparison to single-mother families, most studies show the outcome for children is about the same.[133] Better if it's stepfather and son, better if the barriers to closeness can be overcome and the relationship endures, but it is, in brief, a minefield.

Let's end with some good news. William Beer looked at the children of stepparents years later to discover whether they considered themselves happy.[134] Ironically, the happiest adult women grew up with the mother-stepfather combination; and daughters growing up with biological father and stepmothers were also happy. Both combinations resulted in between 80 percent and 90 percent being either "pretty happy" or "very happy."[135]

Stepparenting is an extraordinarily important area for the therapeutic community to work on—especially therapists with the courage to help Mom, daughter, and stepfather untangle that most complex of webs.

One area in which the evidence is very clear, and which can perhaps be effected logistically—as opposed to psychologically—is the impact of moving on both stepchildren and children in single-parent homes.

The Impact of Moving the Child Away from the Non-Resident Parent

When I was a kid, my parents moved a lot;
but I always found them.

RODNEY DANGERFIELD

ITEM. Within four years after separation or divorce, three of four custodial mothers move at least once.[136]

ITEM. Residential mobility is the single most important factor determining a stepchild's likelihood to succeed . . . accounting for as much as 60 percent of the overall negative difference between children in stepfamilies and children in two-parent families.[137]

There are many good reasons for a parent and child to move—A better job or school system, a new spouse, or just a fresh start. Some new research, though, signals a need for careful deliberation prior to moving children away from the parent who lives where they don't.

This research discovers that children—especially daughters—benefit considerably when the parent they are not living with nevertheless does everyday things with the child, from "shopping, reading, visiting, doing homework, watching TV together," to "spending holidays together."[138] The authors conclude that, **for a school-age daughter, this "doing everyday-type things together" with the parent she is not living with is the *only* predictor of psychological well-being.**

This finding takes on additional urgency in light of the recent California Supreme Court decision that rules that the parent with the children can move out of state at will, no longer needing to justify the move.[139] And frequently, California decisions become national decisions, for better or worse.

This decision usually switches the burden of proof to the dad, who must now demonstrate that the relocation would severely injure the child. Economically, a dad who doesn't have the money to hire a lawyer each time such a decision might be made should be especially aware of how vulnerable he might be should his children not live with him. This is a good example of how a dad can be an even better dad by being aware both of how and why he is important, and of the laws that might prevent him from acting on his knowledge. (More on those laws in Part II.)

What is a viable solution? Obviously, the law should not prevent either parent from moving if both agree. If one parent does not agree, the law could require the parent who moves to pay the expenses of the parent not living with the child seeing the child (*e.g.,* about twice per month, totaling five or more days).

This solution does not *require* the non-resident parent to see the children, but also does not *prevent* or discourage him or her from seeing the children as a result of the burden of additional expenses created by a unilateral decision of the resident parent.

In Conclusion

The policy implications emanating from the larger picture of the value of Dad begin with educating our children to dad-as-nurturer-connector rather than dad-as-provider-protector; they include education to prevent divorce—both legal divorce and psychological divorce; and, if divorce is the only way, to make shared parent time the starting way. Just as the pen can be mightier than the sword, so a little education about fathering can be mightier than lawyers, judges, police, and social workers.

But many specific findings also have policy implications. For example, the Danish study's finding that children living with dads are only half as likely to have difficulties concentrating is especially relevant to American children—especially boys—who are often put on Ritalin to control Attention Deficit Disorder. Should we perhaps take them off Ritalin and put them on dads?

In industrialized countries, there is perhaps no area of greater underlying tension between men and women than women's feelings of being victims (especially of men) and men's less-often-articulated feelings that the very women who are the most educated and privileged are the most likely to yell "victim." The Danish study finding that children living with their dads are less likely to manifest the seven "victim characteristics" (*e.g.,* feeling victimized by other children, seizures of fear, frequent nightmares, low self-worth, sensitivity to criticism, temper tantrums, feelings of lonesomeness)[140]

has enormous implications for reconciling that underlying tension between the sexes. It is difficult for a victim to trust. And it is difficult to trust someone who cannot trust—who needs to create a perpetrator when not everything goes her or his way.

Perhaps the group of women who feel most victimized are single moms. On top of the stress is fear—fear of poverty, and fear that her situation will scare men away. As I mentioned above, her fear of economic deprivation is matched by his fear of emotional deprivation.

What the success of today's single fathers points to is that for millions of single moms and dads, there is a win-win-win solution: Have the children be with the dads for the first couple of years after divorce until, for example, the children make a natural transition (*e.g.*, beginning or graduating from grade school). Here's why this is a win-win-win alternative:

During this period, Mom has the time to build up her economic muscle, thus reducing her economic dependency and fear; Dad feels emotionally needed by his children, not by a younger woman substitute for child; the children benefit, both for themselves and for their future view of alternatives to dead-end dads and stressed-out moms in the event that their own marriage ends in divorce; as for feminists, well, feminists get role models to die for. Okay, so it's not win-win-win. It's win-win-win-win.

The full-time-fathering option should not replace the shared-parenting option as the first choice. But if full-time fathering leads to more trust and fewer victims, it will also lead to our children having better marriages and fewer divorces, thus reversing the children-of-divorce pattern. Less victimhood, more trust, and more fathers bringing up daughters will translate into fewer workplace sex-harassment and sex-discrimination lawsuits. Most important, it leads to a deepening of the love between the sexes that is everyone's common goal.

If all this data was to reach one conclusion in one sentence, it might be: **Mommy is no substitute for Daddy and money is no substitute for Daddy.**

Knowing that Dad is important does not, though, overcome that nagging feeling underneath it all that there's a mothering instinct but not a fathering instinct. Nor does it leave us with a clear understanding of exactly what dads do with children that's different from what moms do. Here's what that is. . . .

2

Is There a Mothering Instinct?
A Fathering Instinct? And What
Does It All Mean for Our Kids?

Exactly What Do Fathers Do with Children That's Different from What Mothers Do?

No one can say with 100 percent certainty why Dad's involvement seems to affect children so positively. Perhaps the most important reason is a bit ironic: Children who live with their dads are likely to have more contact with their moms and feel better about their moms than vice-versa. Put another way, children who live with their dads are more likely to have, in effect, two parents.

Fathers' contribution is not better, just different. For example, when mothers play, they are more likely to let the child direct the play and to proceed at the child's pace.[1] Mom's play is much more likely to emphasize emotional security and personal safety—warning the child not to swing too high on the swing. Dad is more likely to teach him how to swing higher, and jump off at its highest point, always providing a safety net, but not making the safety net the focus.

Dads are prone to using play as a teaching tool. He doesn't compartmentalize play and teaching. He uses a different style of play—encouraging risk-taking and competition, pushing the child's boundaries of physical and mental skills, leading the child to win more and lose more (and, therefore, laugh and cry more); and, through the play, he is teaching the child to im-

"Pass 'em, Pop."

prove her or his skills and focus, and to deal with losing without cheating or becoming vindictive or violent.

Some dads consciously help their children make these connections; others leave the children to make the connection unconsciously; other dads are unconscious that there is a connection, but the connection is nonetheless made (unconsciously!).

Even with young children, studies consistently find men's style of play to involve more roughhousing, more tossing of the children in the air,[3] less talk, less containment, and less limb-holding.[4] As Armin Brott, a dad who writes wonderful books on dads, writes: "Both my daughters, for example, spent most of their first year on an extended roller-coaster ride on my back and could stand up on my shoulders—without using their hands—before they were eighteen months old."[5]

These forms of play seem to improve child development in three major areas: the management of emotions, the development of intelligence, and academic achievement.[6] Let's look at the management of emotions.

A child not used to roughhousing will usually bite, kick, and be physically violent when something doesn't go her way. That becomes an opportunity for the father to stop the playing and explain what is unacceptable and why. The child has an incentive to learn because each time she does not, the playing stops. The child also learns when "enough is enough" and when to "shut it down." The child is learning, then, self-control and "socially acceptable forms of behavior that do not include violence and aggression."[7] This might seem counterintuitive to the mom who notices that when Dad plays, the kids seem more aggressive. In fact, the kids *are* more aggressive. But it is exactly the flirting with the boundaries between acceptable assertiveness and unacceptable aggression which helps the child have real-life experience in knowing where to draw the line. The roughhousing seems to assist both girl and boy children to discover what they can achieve, which methods of assertion work, and how to deal with success and defeat—all of which are important components of identity, and prerequisites for success.

We often hear that mothers do the caring; fathers just do the playing. This is a false dichotomy—even a dangerous one—because fathers' particular style of play involves a conscious focus on teaching and, as the research is now showing, is also instructive to children even when it is not consciously designed to be so. It is therefore more accurate to view dads' playing as his form of childcare, his contribution to child development.

In my own experience of play-wrestling with children or playing games of tag or soccer with them, I often notice that this dichotomy is reinforced when the mother is sought out for comfort by a child who falls or loses. The solution? Well, I notice that if there is no mother around, the child will come to me for comfort. One of the values a child receives from playing with a male teacher or parent is knowing that the ability of a man to roughhouse does not exclude his ability to be a comforter.

In my personal observations during my twenty-nine years of working on gender issues, I notice that dads' style of play serves many other vital functions. Because kids love to play dad's way, it creates an incentive for the child to obey if it wants more play. Playing bonds. This allows dads to set boundaries without creating rebellion, because the child's incentives to stay connected discourage rebellion. In contrast, **boundaries without bonding can create rebellion.** Dad's style—"Play hard 'til eight o'clock, then see who can get ready for bed first"—models how a parent can be both fun and responsible.

When I have observed women establish boundaries and still fail, what seems to be missing most often is a sense of humor, playfulness, shared physical activity, and fun that bond parent and child as allies.

I am sometimes asked, "Which is more important for child development, playing or obeying?" which is like asking, "Which is more important for a salad dressing, the oil or the vinegar?" I remember after my first week of student teaching, I had done a lot of playing and role-playing with my classes; I encouraged them to call me by my first name, to disagree; I had never raised my voice. But then . . .

I gave my first exam. A lot of students failed. Their response, to my dismay was, "We had so much fun that we never expected you to give a tough exam." I had failed to prepare my students for the possibility that fun and discipline, like oil and vinegar, are better together than separate. I acknowledged my failure, told them I would give them another tough test next week and they could choose the better grade. That was the last time they didn't study; and somehow, word got to the next class even before I got there!

I want to make it clear that the solution is not just in exerting more discipline. Seventy percent of poor pupils in the Soviet Union, for example, came from families with autocratic mothers.[8] When a child expresses her or his feelings and the parent argues rather than discusses, or when the child volunteers that she or he has done something wrong and the parent disciplines or restricts without reward for the volunteering, it's a setup for a child who either pretends to be good, or withdraws and rebels, or some combination of the above. In any case, the child unbecomes itself around the parent, which is a frequent precursor to depression.

One of the most powerful contributions many fathers make to their families is getting their children involved in team sports. Not sports, but team sports. I will discuss the value of team sports in greater depth in the Solutions portion of Part I, but for now, suffice it to say that team sports teach children a balance between cooperation and competition, between "letting go" and "rules of the game," between fun and discipline, between winning and being a good loser, and between inspiration and perspiration— all while not thinking you're learning anything. Obviously, a mother's support of this process and attendance at events creates added value.

It goes too far to say that a family that plays together stays together; it is more accurate to say that a family that knows how to play together has the tools to stay together.

Male socialization to take risks—whether it is the high-risk job or the approximately 150 risks of rejection between first eye-contact and inter-course—teaches dads that risks involve failure and that rejection isn't the end of one's life, and seems to prepare fathers to help their children take risks and handle loss and rejection. It also helps dads discipline their children and risk the possibility of the child's rejection-after-discipline.

In my own contact with single moms, many seem to exhibit what I call "Single Parent Syndrome": being needy of their children—both as a friend and as someone who makes them feel needed. They fear their child rejecting them. The possibility of conflict with her child makes a single mother fear she is a failure as a parent on top of being a failure as a spouse, so "maybe no one can get along with me and the divorce is my fault." Fearing additional rejection, she is unwilling to enforce consequences for disobedience. How-ever, the degree to which she fears her child's rejection is the degree to which her children sense her fears, test her boundaries, and drive her to ex-haustion.

Many a dad's natural way is to teach and mentor. Researchers find that women who grow up successful in their professions tend to have two things in common: fathers who respect and encourage them;[9] and male mentors.[10] Think about this in relation to the profession or sport you know best.

Aren't men threatened by successful women? Particularly fathers by successful daughters? In general, no. They encourage it. Fathers, husbands, and men were the coaches of almost all the female medal winners at the 2000 Olympics (*e.g.*, Venus and Serena Williams; Marion Jones). Why do we think otherwise? Because Stage I fathers (fathers who lived when women spent their lives raising children) encouraged their daughters' success in a different way—by encouraging them to marry men who could raise enough money to help them raise six or eight children. Stage I fathers did not see this as discrimination against their daughters any more than they saw the preparation of their sons to possibly die in war as being discrimination against their sons. The fathers were just doing the same as the mothers were doing—preparing their children to marry and be the best possible protec-tors of another generation of children.

Fathers often adapt to the mother's values without a real dialogue. For example, prior to marriage, fathers are much less likely than mothers to be churchgoers. Many dads tell me they would like to discuss openly with their kids such issues as whether or not there is a God, but they feel pressure from their wives to "not confuse the child." Mom might feel that church is a good moral education and source of stability; Dad might feel that the exploration process is the moral education and source of stability. Children can benefit from the parents having an open dialogue about their perspectives—but the parents can't have a dialogue if the dad treats parenting as "her job."

Is mothering, though, "her job" because it is her instinct, not his? Not quite.

Is There a Fathering Instinct?

Many wild animal species boast dedicated fathers. Yet the dedication disappears with domestication. Thus no domesticated male animal assists the female in raising young.[11] Why not?

Let's look at what happens to the paternal instinct of the wolf—or even the wild dog—versus the domesticated dog to see if there is a parallel among humans. Genetically, wolves and dogs are virtually the same—only a 1 percent difference.[12]

In *The Emperor's Embrace,* Jeffrey Masson describes the typical fathering behavior of a wolf. Daddy wolf returns from hunting. His six cubs "leap up to his face and kiss him wildly about the mouth, pawing, nuzzling, nipping his mouth and head."[13] The dad has taken the food from the hunt, and stored it in his stomach, as if his tummy were a shopping bag. Now he opens his mouth wide—very wide—and disgorges the food to the puppies. He doesn't want to trigger a competing frenzy among the cubs, *so he has already chewed it up and organized the food in his tummy into several little piles!*[14]

The daddy wolf often licks and cleans his cubs, guards the den from predators, and then, when he feels they are ready, leads them out of the den and teaches them how to hunt. He does this by teaching them the rules of the game, so to speak. He and the mom socialize the cubs together. Similarly, coyotes and foxes are active and loving dads.[15] As are dogs *that live in the wild.*

What happens to a domesticated dog, which is usually a neglectful, nonparticipatory dad? With domesticated dogs, Masson explains, the human family replaces the wolf pack. The human family takes care of the puppies, feeds the puppies, pets the puppies, holds and loves the puppies, and often gives them away. Daddy is not needed—he has no incentive to do the caring. He does, though, care—he cares for what can give him love. Thus he cares for his owner, and the owner's children. His protective instinct is transferred to protecting the human children, from whom he also receives love.[16] He will often guard the human children, protect them from danger, and protectively play with them.

The implication for humans? **Domestication is to dads who are animals what mother custody is to dads who are human: Dad's daily love is not needed, so Dad's daily bread is not provided.** Thus 85 percent of fathers with shared parent time (joint custody) pay child support in full and on time; when mothers have custody but do not discourage or deny fathers the opportunity to see the children, 79 percent of these fathers paid child support in full and on time; when seeing children is undermined or denied, only 56 percent of fathers paid child support.[17]

Howard Halpern, past president of the American Academy of Psychotherapists, explains that among humans, the job of the father is two-fold: to help the mother and child separate; and to nurture "the little child within the mother" who may be threatened by this separation.

What would happen if a dog owner required the daddy dog to "make a killing" for its puppies, only to have the owners take the food out of the daddy dog's mouth, give it to the mother puppy, and have the mother puppy feed the puppies with the food the father has just killed? The daddy dog would go off and never return.

Suppose the owners could always track down the daddy dog, and then punished him until he "made a killing"? The daddy dog might produce a little food, but as little as possible—just enough to avoid punishment. Meantime, during his outings, the daddy dog would search for someone who wanted his love, someone for whom he would be willing to hunt.

The human father thus acts similarly toward the government's mandate to pay child support. He begins hiding money and tucking it away, hoping to find a new family for whom he may use his money and love to receive love. In brief, as any animal psychologist would immediately intuit, the papa dog will have no incentive to risk being killed (in order to make a killing) without the puppies leaping up to his face, and kissing him, as Masson puts it, "wildly about the mouth, pawing, nuzzling, nipping his mouth and head."[18] (I am not, of course, opposed to a mother or the government playing substitute father when the father is a genuine deadbeat—only to the mother believing she can be a substitute father and the government paying her to believe that.)

The United States has one other experience trying to get people to work by force, without the fruits of their labor adding to their ability to give and receive their family's love. It was called slavery. Smart slaves—slaves who survived—began acting toward plantation owners like some fathers act toward the government or the mother with sole parent time: doing as little as possible to not be beaten, making it *appear* like they're doing as much as they can.

How powerful and universal is a father's "instinct" to father? Until early in this century, hundreds of thousands of mothers died in childbirth each generation. The government didn't step in. Fathers did. The father may have chosen to protect the children by working harder at the work he knew best to provide the children with a governess, or bring a family member into the home, but, in one way or the other he stepped up to the plate. We didn't read articles about the plight of the single father. There were no child-support payments from the dead mother. No government-as-substitute-mother programs to rescue the father. The fathers were not domesticated by rescuers. They were needed. And, like wolves in the wild, they responded.

Maybe the "instinct" isn't a fathering instinct per se, but an instinct to protect, provide, and take responsibility in whatever form it takes—with the reward being to receive and give love. This male instinct seems to be triggered when needed by someone who loves him, and when trusted by someone who loves him.

This male instinct to protect and provide can be called upon on behalf of a beloved country or a beloved child. For war, or for love. It is adaptable and transferable. As long as it's for what he loves and he's loved for what he's doing. Let's look at its transferability.

We all know of families in which the father has died, and on his dying bed, passes on the baton of responsibility to his oldest son, saying, "You're the man of the house now. Take good care of your mom, and your sisters and brother." And we've all heard of boys who were transformed into mini-men when their dads left to war, returned to being children if their dad came home, but became men prematurely if their dad was killed.

The Promise Keepers and Million Man March used the church to "pass on the baton" of responsibility from God the Father to the sons of their ministry. If it was only an instinct, it wouldn't need to be taught. But if it wasn't deep within, it wouldn't stir so many men's souls so quickly when called upon.

This transferability difference between the mothering and fathering "instincts," if you will, can also be seen in male versus female patterns of step-parenting. It is common for a man to marry or live with a woman whose children are living with her, have no new biological children with her, continue to work full-time earning more money than she does, and contribute both money and time to his wife's or womanfriend's children, receiving nothing but his wife's or womanfriend's love and the hope of her children's love in return.

Now reverse that situation. Think of how many women you know who married or lived with a man whose children were living with him, who had no new biological children with him, and who continued to work full-time earning more money than he, contributing both time and money to him and his children, receiving nothing but her husband's or boyfriend's love and the hope of his children's love in return. Almost always, a stepmom also has biological children of her own, or plans to have one with her new husband, or receives some financial advantage in being a stepmom, including the ability to cut back on her hours at work.

A difference between male and female parenting, then, seems to be that a woman's is both more specific to her biological child and more dependent on being coupled with financial support, either from a husband or the government. The man's is more transferable, less conditional upon receiving money, but quite conditional upon his ability to give and receive love, to feel needed and wanted.

I say that the instinct may be as much an instinct to give and receive love as a fathering instinct per se, because although many men want children, many are perfectly happy to live out their lives with only their wife or womanfriend, giving love to and receiving love from them alone.

In *Why Men Are the Way They Are,* I labeled men's need to give and receive love as men's primary need. The power of this is perhaps best illustrated by an experience Liz, the mom of Alex and Erin, whom you met in the introduction, tells me about how she and her former husband, Jeff, couldn't, for a long time, have a biological child. Liz suggested adoption. Jeff was lukewarm, but eventually agreed. They adopted Erin. No sooner did the adoption come through than Liz became pregnant with Alex. About six months later, Jeff had fallen so deeply in love with Erin that he momentarily expressed the fear "I can't imagine loving a biological child as much as I love Erin." No sooner was Alex born, though, than he found more love than he had been able to imagine.

None of this is to say that women's parenting propensities are only biological, or not transferable. Women also adopt, stepparent, and make their own lives secondary to the lives of children who are not theirs biologically. For both dads and moms, the power of love can exceed their instinct to personally survive, and, functionally at least, be as strong as the motherhood instinct to protect her own biological children at all costs.

Whether we call it a need, or call it an instinct, loving and being loved appears to be, for some people, as primary as the need to live. As I discuss in the introduction, when people feel they are unloved and unneeded, they become candidates for suicide. Men, especially, are vulnerable to this deprivation of love—which is why men commit suicide ten times as often as women after *either* the death of *or* divorce from a spouse.[19]

The father's movement is fighting to keep men's protector instinct focused on the father's biological children. The only upside of its minimal success is the millions of stepdads we have bred—often men hoping to receive love they felt they could not get enough of from their own children.

Is There a Mothering Instinct?

For hundreds of thousands of years, countless mothers have left the world to bring their children into the world. They have died in childbirth. Many moms still do, and millions make their own lives secondary to their children's. Does this suggest a mothering instinct? On one level, yes.

On another level, mothers are much more likely than fathers to neglect their children, physically abuse them, and kill them. There are many reasons for this, as the next chapter makes clear, but it's not quite what we think of when we think of a mothering instinct.

A mothering *instinct* would imply something so automatic and reflexive that the mother would not question it. It cannot be said, though, that virtually every mother is unquestioningly willing to forfeit everything for her child, or is devoted, or even happy about her time as a mother. For example . . .

ITEM. Ten thousand women responded when Ann Landers asked her readers, "If you had to do it all over again, would you have children?" *Seventy percent said, "No."*[20]

In a nationwide survey of children, 39 percent said they felt closer to their father; 46 percent said they felt closer to their mother.[21] Given the amount of time mothers versus fathers spend with their children, if a mothering instinct were added and a fathering instinct were nonexistent, we would expect virtually all children to feel closer to the mother.

Most of us have read that infants protest separation from their mothers more than from their fathers. And that seems to suggest a maternal instinct. But we didn't read that the data was collected from the *reports of only the mothers.*[22] The studies were done in the early sixties. Since then, more than a dozen researchers have participated in eight separate studies using a variety of methodologies that included *both* parents. They agreed on one thing: There was *no* significant preference for either parent staying or leaving.[23]

Think of how often, when we reach out to a child, he cries and grabs for his mom, and our belief in the maternal instinct is unconsciously reinforced. But remember that we saw above that the more father involvement there is, the more trusting the child?[24] What we are really seeing is how too much mother and not enough father makes a child distrustful.[25] We are witnessing mother dependency leading to distrust. If it leads to distrust, it is really overdependency. By calling mother overdependency an instinct, we blind ourselves to the need to balance dependence with independence. And the need to examine maternal co-dependency (something to which single dads are not immune).

The more the father is involved with the child, the less the child protests separation from its mother. Some fathers have even reported breathing over their newborn baby as animals do to solidify the bonding process.[26] These fathers report an "inexplicably deep bond" with these children as they grow older.

Ironically, we solve the problem by giving the child back to the mother, thus reinforcing the child's overdependency. Of course, the child stops crying when we give it more mother, just as it would stop crying if we gave it more candy. It is not responding to an instinct but to its demands being ful-filled.

Just as some dads' propensity to encourage risk-taking can go overboard without the checks and balances of an involved mother, so some moms' propensity to protect children can go overboard without the checks and bal-ances of an involved father. With mothering, the result can be smothering.

Mothering Versus Smothering

ITEM. Smothering mothering is characteristic of men who join the military at an early age.[27]

Smothering is to mothering what workaholism is to masculinity: a ten-dency to fulfill our traditional role too well. What was intended as the means (raising money or children) becomes the end (addiction to money or children). Workaholism and smothering are the traditional divisions of labor as neuroses.

Divorce magnifies this division of neurotic labor. Why? Most of us have childhood wounds. A good marriage offers childhood wounds a protective coating. Divorce not only exposes those wounds, but slices them open. Edna St. Vincent Millay put her finger on the postpartum void after love's loss: "Where you used to be, there is a hole in the world, which I find myself walking around in the daytime and falling into at night."

To avoid the void, both sexes run for a new protective coating. Men run to work; women run to children. Men attend to their calling; women hear their children calling. Both sexes convince themselves that someone else has the need that is really theirs.

Many men who date single mothers share with me stories of mothers being so dependent on their children's approval that they cannot break ties or set boundaries. They're afraid of their child crying, throwing a temper tantrum, or speaking to them with an attitude. When their teenager calls for Mom to come, Mom leaves what she's doing rather than expect the teenager to leave what he is doing, thus leaving the child unprepared to enter a world far less willing to wait on him. The mom fears that if she puts her foot down, the child will only get angrier, which indeed is true . . . until he knows the attitude or tantrum will make things worse for him.

Ironically, many of these men who are critical of these mothers are themselves fearful of women's disapproval, and for exactly the same reasons: They have their emotional eggs invested in the basket of women's approval and love in the same way a single mom has her emotional eggs invested in the basket of her children's approval and love.

The result of a mother who smothers? A child who's entitled. And is usually an underachiever. When fathers smother, the result is the same. And when Mom and Dad are competing for the child's love, the result is a child who has a choice of entitlements.

For many single moms, guilt magnifies the problem. She already feels guilty for not spending enough time with the child, so she doesn't want to deprive the child of anything else; in her marriage she's seen arguments and anger lead to the failure of love—she's not going to fail again with her children, so she tries to settle arguments and eliminate anger by giving in. Besides, giving in makes her feel giving; giving up her needs makes her feel altruistic and mature. Those are reassuring characteristics—they are not qualities her ex often attributed to her, either just before or since the divorce.

The smothering problem is magnified by our gender biases. I know of mothers who occasionally sleep with their thirteen-year-old daughters. But if a father slept with his thirteen-year-old daughter—*or* his thirteen-year-old son—he would soon be in a separate bed. In prison.

When the traditional female role of mothering becomes overbearing, we tend to call its upside "devotion" and its downside "domination." The child might eventually complain about the mother, as in *Mommie Dearest,* but that's a different response than our response to the traditional male role taken to its extreme, as in sexual harassment or date rape. Then we use the law to exact a price: imprisonment, financial punishment, and public humiliation. Yet when a parent smothers a child, we rarely go farther than to complain about it. Despite the fact that the smothering occurs prior to the age of consent.

The loss of parent-child boundaries that result from, usually, a father being sexually dependent on a daughter, is part of what makes incest so damaging; the loss of parent-child boundaries that result, usually, from a mother being emotionally dependent on a daughter can be thought of as emotional incest, and can be, as we will see in a minute, equally damaging.

Before we explore the potential damage of emotional smothering in its extreme form, though, let's look at a form of smothering by which fathers can be equally tempted—I'll call it "vicarious achievement smothering." It can come in the form of a mother who needs her daughter to be a beauty queen more for her own glory than the child's. Or in the form of a father who needs his son to be a famous athlete.

In my sport, tennis, many fathers—and some mothers—are mentors who sacrifice much of their lives to their daughters' careers, and create extraordinary benefit for the daughter. But this can easily drift into smothering. This boundary is pushed by Chris Evert's dad, Jimmy; Jennifer Capriati's dad, Stefano; Steffi Graf's dad, Peter; Andrea Jaeger's dad, Roland; Mary Pierce's dad, Jim; and Venus and Serena Williams's dad, Richard.[28] As these daughters began to be their fathers' achievement and to supply their fathers' income and the families' income, then the parents started needing the children—and the ability to effectively discipline was often eroded. More than half of these daughters came to have major conflicts with their dads.

Back to smothering mothering. As we saw from the Item above, smothering mothering is characteristic of the background of men who join the military at an early age.[29] In the military, they receive the boundaries they did not receive from the smothering mother, the opportunity to have men as role models, and an understanding of how to survive when they are not being protected. In the process, many of these boys are lost not only to the mother, but to themselves. The mother who smothers the child often literally loses the child.

Smothering can create much more severe problems. A singular degree of closeness and attachment to the mother is a characteristic of 83 percent of child molesters.[30] Similarly, assassins of presidents almost always have domineering mothers, coupled with fathers who are either weak and ineffectual or absent and/or unresponsive to the child. (Even twenty-seven inmates who had indicated an *intention* to assassinate the President had this type of background.[31])

Sirhan Sirhan and Lee Harvey Oswald were also dutiful sons "reared under the maternal shadow"[32] and deprived of fathers and normal male associations. As Patricia Sexton explains, "Such assassins often pick as their targets the most virile males, symbols of their own manly deprivations."[33]

Smothering mothering is not associated only with men who pick men as the targets of abuse. It was, for example, a defining characteristic of "Vasseur the Terror" . . .

Once upon a time in France there lived a little boy named Jacques Vasseur whose overly indulgent mother "catered to his every whim" and isolated him from other children, neighbors, and especially men. During World War II, "Vasseur the Terror," a French collaborator with the Nazis, was responsible for the horrible deaths of 230 Frenchmen. His reputation for enjoying cruelty was widespread. He evaded arrest for seventeen years after the war. When he was finally brought to trial, one man testified that Vasseur had bullwhipped him for ten hours, and a woman testified that Vasseur had burned her breasts with cigarettes. Vasseur was not caught for nearly two decades. His "Mummy" had kept him hidden in the garret above her second-story apartment. His greatest suffering after being imprisoned was that he was not able to see "Mummy" more than once a week.[34]

It is sad for a mother to devote so much energy and love to a child who betrays every value she tried to instill.

The key litmus test revolves around the parents' introspection as to whether they are giving love or money to "buy" the children's love because they are in need of the children's love. When the parents start needing the children, the ability to discipline effectively erodes.

Do Children Want to Be with Their Fathers?
Do Fathers Really Want to Be with Their Children?

Eighty-six percent of children surveyed nationwide said they had no preference *at all* regarding which parent they would prefer to live with after divorce.[35]

Although approximately 90 percent of children spend more *time* with mom, only 46 percent said they felt *closer* to Mom. (39 percent felt closer to Dad.)[36]

That's the kids. What about the dads?

In workshops, I ask men whether they would want to be with their children full-time, part-time, or just on evenings or weekends for two or more years after each child was born *if* the following three conditions prevailed: The society felt that emotionally balanced babies needed Dad's energy for a year or so since they had been exposed for nine months to Mom's; there would be no financial hardship were they to be full-time with the children; and their wife approved of their full-time involvement with the children. The men range from college age with no children to grandfathers. (Some workshops are in corporations or government agencies; others are sponsored by churches, universities, or professional associations.)

When I ask the men for their preference should those three conditions prevail, about 80 percent prefer full-time involvement for two or more years per child; 10 to 15 percent part-time; 5 to 10 percent evenings and weekends. The women are usually stunned. The three conditions are provided to isolate men's emotions from the prevailing beliefs (wives should parent), their fear of their wife's disapproval, and their assigned role of showing love by providing money. Most fathers who work full-time nurture the family by providing an opportunity for their wives to nurture the family. This is, if you will, a fathers' financial womb.

What about polls more scientific than the Farrell polls?

ITEM. Roper polls of both sexes in western Europe, Japan, and the United States found one thing in common: *Both* sexes considered the family role more satisfying than the job role.[37]

ITEM. In a nationwide poll, when fathers were asked what part of their lives they would "most like to change," almost three-quarters said, "I'd like to spend more time with my children." This response, in 1993, was almost 20 percent greater than it was in 1984.[38]

As I discussed above, by the year 2000, Radcliffe's national survey found 7 percent more men than women in their 20s willing to put their money where their mouth is—to give up pay for family time.

That's men's attitudes. What about men's behavior?

First, men's fathering behavior is also a-changin'. In the last twenty years, single-father families increased at almost five times the rate of single-mother families.[39] And many married dads are now the primary caregivers.

Men's fathering behavior increasingly defies many myths. The first is the myth of the deadbeat dad, which I will take apart piece by piece throughout this book. But a part of that myth that has one of the strongest fixes on the public consciousness is that of the economically poor man who provides neither money nor love—the hit-and-run lover. According to the U.S. Census Bureau, 37 percent of fathers of working wives living in poverty were the primary childcare providers for their preschoolers.[40] When a father cannot provide a good financial womb, he is much more willing to provide a womb of love than we give him credit for—but often the mother in poverty is told by the government that she'll get pay only if the man is away. This makes her feel caught between money and love.

Second is the myth that men are motivated by money, not by a nurturing instinct. A study of stay-at-home dads found that their average annual loss of income from their "Daddy Track" decision is $27,000.[41] About two-thirds of these dads report that they stayed at home "because they did not want to put their child in day-care—not because of economic necessity."[42] During the time of the study (1996), the times were economically booming, so the dads at home full-time are rarely doing it for want of being able to find jobs.

A third myth about men's behavior is our belief that men don't spend much more time caring for the children when a woman works than when she doesn't—that her children's primary caregiver will most likely be some form of day-care or preschool facility. Not true. A dad is 170 percent more likely to be the child's primary caregiver than all day-care, group care, nursery school, kindergarten, and preschool facilities *combined*.[43]

A fourth myth about men's behavior is that "Even when paternity leave is made available, men don't take advantage of it." Only half true. Men do not take advantage of formal paternity leave that offers them significant amounts of unpaid time off, but 74 percent of men take an average of five days off when each child is born and sacrifice their vacation days or personal leave days.[44] These men are doing their best to nurture their wives and children without sacrificing the financial womb that nurtures their wives and children in a different way. What gets sacrificed is their vacation days.

Why don't we hear about this? Because surveys ask company personnel managers how many men take advantage of their formal paternity-leave program. The question assumes the formal female model of parent leave, and thus misses the more informal male mode of participation.[45]

When fathers are *not* with their children, is it because they don't care? Rarely. As we discussed above, "The Father's Catch-22" is that the earning of money it takes to love his family takes him away from the love of his family.

When we hear about a dad not seeing his children after divorce, we think of the "typical deadbeat dad." This was believable until a nationwide study by Glynnis Walker of the children of divorce found that 42 percent of all children who lived with only their mother reported that their mother tried to prevent them from seeing their fathers after the divorce. (Only 16 percent of the children who lived with only their father reported that their dad tried to prevent their mother from seeing them.[46])

The deadbeat-dad myth is reinforced by the polling of only women. Whether it be a quarter-century's worth of Virginia Slims polls focused on women, a Roper poll, or even the Census Bureau, information about men (e.g., why they don't pay child support) was obtained only from women—like asking only Republicans about the motivations of Democrats. Which is why Glynnis Walker's survey of the *children*—and the children's *actual experience* with their fathers—is so important. The children paint a different picture of the frequency with which their fathers were able to overcome barriers to see them:[47]

Frequency of Dad Seeing Children After Divorce

Weekly	54%
Monthly	23%
Yearly	10%
Never again after divorce	13%

When we consider that 42 percent of mothers present barriers and 54 percent of fathers see their children weekly, despite the fact that three-quarters of custodial mothers move at least once within four years of divorce, we get a different image than that of the "deadbeat dad" portrayed by the media and based on surveys of only women.

Exactly what are some men, besides Robin Williams as Mrs. Doubtfire, willing to do to be with their children? Kenny Rogers was averaging 150 nights a year on the road. One day he went for a walk with his six-year-old son, Christopher.

> We sat down on the grass and I started talking about all the travel-ing I have to do in my job. I told him I really miss him when I'm on a road tour. Christopher looked up at me and had the biggest smile on his face. He said, "Dad, I want us to be together."
>
> I knew what I had to do. I was brimming with tears of joy as I reached over and hugged my little boy with everything in me.[48]

49

What Kenny Rogers had to do—and did do—was give up 100 nights per year on the road. And ten million dollars a year in revenue.

Similarly, Yo Yo Ma, arguably the best cellist in the world, refuses to play on weekends (with some of the best symphonies in the world) because he wants to spend his weekends with his wife and children.

"Powerful" men in government and business are increasingly beginning to express their father love differently than as "dad-as-dough." In business, the president of American Express, Jeffrey Stiefler, resigned so he could work near his family in Connecticut, and is now an involved and playful-with-his-family dad who lives near me in California. As I've had the oppor-tunity to spend time and play with him, his wife, and their children, I am struck by the centeredness and security of their children—a quality often missing among the children of high-achieving absentee dads.

In government, some fathers and I had but a brief opportunity to meet at the White House with William Galston, who was the Domestic Policy Adviser to President Clinton prior to resigning to join the faculty of the University of Maryland so he could spend more time with his ten-year-old

son Ezra. Frankly, I would have suspected "family reasons" as a coverup ra-
tionale for resigning had I not heard both President Clinton (on C-SPAN)
spontaneously praise Galston on separate occasions, and repeatedly heard
Galston himself express awe for Clinton's breadth and depth of knowledge
and his boundless energy.

In Conclusion . . .

Is there, then, a fathering or mothering instinct? I think it is fair to say that
the instinct of women to mother is more *directly* connected to her biological
child than is men's instinct to father. Men's instincts are more *indirect*. The
instinct of men to protect is able to be channeled toward women and children in the form of father love. And the instinct of men to take risks creates
in men one of the most powerful of parenting skills: transmitting to children
the paradox that taking risks is the best protection.

The fact that the male instincts do not require a biological child to be
triggered seems to make them more transferable than women's, as evi-
denced in men's greater willingness to stepparent without pay.

Margaret Mead pointed out that fathering is more of a social role. True.
But it is more than that: The ability of fathering to be a social role comes
from the flexibility of the male protector instincts, designed to be adaptable
to society's varying needs—from war to love. By using tools such as appreciation, society gets men to express their love by either sacrificing their lives
to fight enemies or spending their lives loving children.

However, the variation within each sex and the adaptability of both
sexes means it doesn't make much difference what is an instinct and what is
socialization, or which sex has more of what. What's important is that each
sex brings to the table its own head-start program.

So what's preventing that from happening? More than any other thing it
is our belief that men have been programmed to protect by killing, not loving; by being aggressive, not nurturing—and this is more likely to result in
children who are harshly abused, not gently raised. This belief allows children to quickly be removed from dads after a hint of abuse, thus making
dads afraid to fight for their children lest they become accused of abusing. Is
the belief true? False? Or both? Let's look.

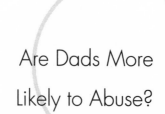

Are Dads More Likely to Abuse?

Are Children More Likely to be Abused by Their Mothers, or by Their Fathers?

QUESTION 1: The most common child batterer is:

    a. a suburban, middle-class father

    b. an uneducated father

    c. a divorced father

    d. none of the above

QUESTION 2: The most common family characteristic predicting a battered baby is:

    a. poverty

    b. mother as head of household

    c. illegitimacy

    d. father as head of household

    e. none of the above

ANSWER TO QUESTION 1: None of the above.

ANSWER TO QUESTION 2: Mother as head of household. The mother as head of household is one of the most important single predictors of a battered baby—a more important predictor than poverty, illegitimacy, and almost all of twenty-nine family characteristics.[2]

The 1999 release by the U.S. Department of Health and Human Services of their report on child maltreatment reinforces this counterintuitive picture.[3] Four starter facts:

FACT. Each year about 350 parents in the U.S. kill one or more of their children. Almost two-thirds of the parents who *kill* their children are mothers.[4] Almost two-thirds of the children between eight and fifteen who are *killed* by their parents are boys.[5] Overall, when it comes to children being killed, it is most likely the mother killing the son.

FACT. Children are 88 percent more likely to be seriously injured from child abuse or neglect by their mothers than by their fathers.[6]

FACT. Children are more than twice as likely to be victims of *neglect* by their mothers than by their fathers.[7]

FACT. Boys who are abused are 24 percent more likely to suffer serious injuries than girls who are abused.[8]

Why? Domestic violence, as I document in *Women Can't Hear What Men Don't Say,* is a momentary act of power designed to compensate for a continuing experience of power*less*ness. This is why adult women abuse adult men as often as the other way around, and why **single-mother households account for 43 percent of all abused children.**[9]

Single parenthood does not, by itself, create the powerlessness. As we saw in the Danish study, single moms were more likely than single dads to use physical punishment.[10] But the mothers in female-headed households are younger than the fathers in male-headed households. And single dads aren't your run-of-the-mill men—they have more resources, such as education and income, and exceptional motivation.

The fact that moms spend more time with the child is also not as important a contributor to abuse as is this experience of powerlessness. As we have seen, single moms are twenty-four times as likely to kill children as are single dads.[11] In these families, the time spent by mother versus father is about equal—and the mom and dad have equal responsibility.

All of this surprises us only if we think of women as inherently better mothers than men are fathers.

Social expectation is a double-edged sword. In intact families, fathers are often assigned the role of physical abuser ("Wait 'til your father gets home!")—and then are blamed for being abusers. However, in the school system, if a male teacher hits a girl, he's hit with a lawsuit. It is not coincidence, then, that corporal punishment in schools is almost always a female teacher hitting a boy. And certainly anyone who attended a Catholic school taught by nuns when I was growing up knew of physical abuse by someone in a maternal role who had permission to inflict it.

All this said, the degree of female-perpetrated abuse of children did surprise me. Perhaps the two biggest of these surprises is, first, that **two-thirds of mothers acknowledge hitting children who are under six** *three* **or more times per** *week*.[12] The second of the biggest surprises was learning that the interviewers for the National Longitudinal Study of Youth reported that **7 percent of mothers with children under six hit their child right in front of the interviewer!**[13]

Despite this reality, perhaps nothing symbolizes the ingrained nature of the image of dad-as-abuser more than a "science" invention that won the grand prize for a nationally syndicated children's TV show.[14] A child puts the invention on his or her back and, when the child does something wrong, he or she pulls a string and gets punched in the face and kicked in the rear. The eight-year-old boy who invented it calls it "The Portable Dad." Ironically, the eight-year-old boy is of the sex more likely to be abused or killed—and he is blaming the sex *less* likely to abuse or kill him. Had the invention been called "The Portable Mom," would it have won the grand prize at a science convention or been demonized at a NOW convention?

What's the solution? A father who has bonded with a child during the first year—especially in early infancy—almost never abuses that child, or even passively allows others to do so.[15]

Is Sexual Abuse Basically a Father-Daughter Phenomenon?

We often think of sexual abuse as basically a father-daughter phenomenon. However, sexual abuse of daughters is most often a result of an *absentee* father,[16] a cool and distant mother,[17] and/or a stepfather or live-in boyfriend of a single mom.[18] Even by the current broad definitions of abuse, only 2.3 percent of daughters growing up with their biological fathers have been abused by them.[19] Sole parent time by the mother was much more likely to lead to a girl being sexually abused than sole parent time by the father, because the mother was often living with a stepfather and 17 percent of daughters growing up with stepfathers have been abused by them.[20]

The safest environment for a girl or boy child is living with the two biological parents. Preschoolers living with only one natural parent plus one stepparent were forty times more likely to become child abuse victims than if they were living with the two birth parents.[21]

There might be significant consequences of boys being sexually abused by mothers or other women. Nearly 60 percent of convicted rapists were sexually abused as children by women.[22] I say there "*might be*" significant consequences, because we don't really know whether the consequence is, for example, the result of sexual touching or whether the sexual touching is just a manifestation of too much mother involvement and dependency, or "smothering." My guess, based on what happens to a boy when a mom smothers him, is that the smothering is the underlying problem.

Are Fathers Often Being Falsely Accused of Sexual Abuse?

Sexual abuse can wreak havoc on a child's life. It leaves many children—especially girls—never able to regain trust. When it happens with a father, it often leaves the daughter unable to love men or feel sexually secure. It leaves her feeling torn between sharing and not sharing her trauma with her mom. If she doesn't share, it can eat her up. If she does, she is eaten up by the guilt over the conflict and frequent separation that ensues. If there is no separation, she can feel betrayed. Sexual abuse from stepfather to stepdaughter is a common problem. To create such a minefield in a child's life is not parenting, but poisoning. Because of the potential devastation, it becomes easy to overlook the damage done when the hint or accusation of abuse is acted upon without checking out its reliability.

MYTH. *False and unsubstantiated accusations of sexual abuse are a minor problem compared to sexual abuse itself.*

FACT. *Un*founded or *un*substantiated sexual-abuse allegations increased from more than half to more than three-quarters of cases in the short period from 1989 to 1993 in New York City.[23] (Almost 40,000 families are investigated *every year* in New York City alone. Most investigations involve officials cross-examining the children, their friends and relatives, their neighbors, teachers, and virtually everyone who knows the family well. An unsubstantiated accusation still turns family love into family suspicion. The next Kodak moment becomes a Maalox moment.)

MYTH. *Both sexes make false accusations about equally.*

FACT. When Hollida Wakefield and Ralph Underwager reviewed their files of court-referred cases of false accusations occurring during divorce and parent-time battles, they discovered that 94 percent of those who made false accusations were women and 96 percent of those who were falsely accused were men.[24] The men usually had passive personalities; the children were usually females under eight;[25] the mothers who made false accusations were characterized by their anger when an expert did not find evidence of abuse, and by their resolve to find an expert who would prove the child abused.[26]

MYTH. *You can count on children to tell the truth about being sexually abused.*

FACT. When asked specific questions about both sexual and non-sexual touching, children were accurate only 9 percent of the time in initial interviews, with 0 percent accuracy after repeated interviews.[27] Nearly one-quarter of children described sexual-type touching, when *none* had occurred.[28] (The sexual touching would be classified by adults as sexual abuse.)

How do we *know* there was not a single instance of inappropriate touching? Dr. Jane Rawls, a New Zealand child and clinical psychologist, video-taped 100 percent of four sessions in which a male adult played a dressing-up game with each child, putting on special hats, jewelry, etc. She then conducted interviews with the children about what had happened. Although there had been no inappropriate adult-child touching, nearly one-quarter of the children, when asked questions, reported that there had been. Ten per-cent of the children reported genital touching. Two others also said they were touched under their upper clothes. Two more children reported that the man touched their bottoms or they touched the man's bottom. Finally, two others reported mutual touching under clothing.

What was most frightening was that the two techniques used most fre-quently by specialists in child abuse—repeated interviews and showing to the children diagrams of body parts while asking them if they were touched on that body part—were what resulted in the 0 percent accuracy rate. Only a quarter of these children inaccurately termed their reports as sexual abuse, but none answered all the specific questions accurately.

The implications of this research are enormous since, as we will see be-low, a child often complains about something when at his or her dad's, and the complaint understandably leads to questions by the mother. We will see that the initial complaint is not necessarily sexual, but the complaint under-standably leads to a mom asking, "Did dad touch you here?" and, if the "here" is in a "sexual" zone, she might be too shocked to discuss it with her ex (whom she might already be angry at). *If she knew that the rate of accuracy was only 9 percent, she would be more likely to discuss the situation with her ex-husband.* But when she believes "a child has no reason to lie," and she has rea-son to mistrust her ex in other areas, she feels she has no alternative but to call child services or the police. If this is magnified by anger or vindictive-ness . . .

Thus the child is subjected to repeated questioning by social workers, psychologists, medical doctors, and police—and, as Dr. Rawls found, it is the repeated questioning that resulted in 0 percent accuracy for these thirty children.

Had the thirty children in Dr. Rawls' study been questioned *without* the safety provided by the videotaping, the papers might have reported it to the public with a headline like this. . . .

Seven Children Accuse Male Child Psychologist of Sexual Abuse

Imagine how you would feel after hearing on CNN Headline News that a psychologist accused of sexual abuse by seven children was still in practice. (I know I wouldn't refer any children to him!) Yet it takes only *one* such description by a child to ruin a dad's ability to ever see his child again. And one child's description would lead to social workers questioning all the children a child psychiatrist had seen. If even just one child confirmed sexual touching, not only would the child psychiatrist's career be ruined, but so might his marriage, and any attempt he made to see his children would be futile. If he moved to a new community, instead of hanging up a psychologist's shingle, he would be wearing a scarlet "A."

The solution? Talk with both the parent and the child *before* the professionals are called. See if there is a commonsense explanation. Was there a misunderstanding? A desire for attention? A desire to avoid seeing the dad for different reasons? A discussion of child abuse at school that provoked fears? And problem-solving should be modeled for the child by family meetings at home rather than by outside meetings at family court.

Why Not Understanding the Nature of the Father's Contribution Leads to Accusations of Sexual Abuse

Some fathers and mothers do sexually abuse their children, and the interference of authorities is not only valuable, but crucial. *So* crucial that it creates the "Crucial Cause Syndrome": The more crucial the cause, the more willing we are to suspend the need for a balanced investigation, and the more we "rush to judgment."

Fathers' style of play makes fathers especially vulnerable to false accusations of sexual abuse. For example, a father lifting his daughter onto his shoulders might boost her to his shoulders with his hand on her rear, but done in a bathing suit at a public pool, that behavior is subject to interpretations by dozens of people. During the 2000 Olympics, the male coach of

Lisa Davidson, the U.S. gold medal winner in the women's diving competition, lifted Lisa in her bathing suit by her rear and held her closely for an extended time in a congratulatory, full-body embrace; child winners from Russia were kissed on their lips by their adult coaches—all acceptable in the dual context of emotions and culture, but all subject to misinterpretation when taken out of context.

Single fathers—more than single mothers—are likely to feel that nudity is natural, and that open discussions of sexuality are healthy. However, if a dad who used to hot-tub with his wife and children in the nude is now hot-tubbing without his wife, and his daughter mentions at school, "When my dad and I were hot-tubbing in the nude . . . ," and just one child with a strict religious background overhears this, the father's days as parent can quickly become numbered. Yet it is exactly such an environment that leads teenagers to feel they have a parent they can talk to. And remember that in our national survey of teenage girls asked what would prevent them from becoming pregnant, 97 percent said, "Having parents I can talk to."[29] This fathers' style apparently works: As we saw with positive father contact, 0 percent of the daughters of inner-city teenage mothers became pregnant when they were teenagers and 0 percent of the sons of these mothers fathered a child when they were teenagers.[30]

The most frequent parent-time arrangement after divorce—mothers having the children—leads to the fathers leaving home. Yet research shows us that from one to three months after the father leaves the home, young children typically suffer sleep disturbances.[31] They have trouble falling asleep, have nightmares, and awaken with a profound sense of anxiety or panic. The link of this panic to the father leaving the home has only recently been recognized.

Now think about these characteristics of sleep disturbance. Tens of thousands of social workers have been trained to associate these characteristics with child abuse—not separation anxiety, or what might more specifically be called "Absentee Father Anxiety." So here's what sometimes happens. The children return from visiting their father. The mother notices them awakening with nightmares. If the child is rash-prone, then pants-wetting, bed-wetting, or genital shame that leads to the child not drying properly, combined with a depleted immune system, can lead to a rash in the genital area.

The mother puts the nightmares together with the rash and with "just returned from Dad's." She asks the child if the dad touched her or him "down there." The child says yes. The answer is either inaccurate (as in Rawls' finding of the 91 percent rate of inaccuracy) or accurate (as in Rawls' finding of the 9% rate of accuracy). If accurate (*e.g.,* the father might have dried the child's genitals or put medicine on the rash), the mother panics: "Sexual abuse!"

She takes the child to a social worker and a medical doctor, and if the doctor confirms the rash, the social worker reports the linkage to a judge; the judge issues an injunction to prevent the children from seeing the father. And from that moment on, instead of the children's anxiety being reduced, it is reinforced. Just when a child is reacting to "father hunger," it is forced into "father starvation." **The mother's genuine love for the child— when not coupled with an awareness of "Absentee Father Anxiety"—*can* unwittingly beget child abuse.**

Wait . . . Exactly What Is Sexual Abuse?

ITEM. A study of male sex offenders found that 30 percent had themselves been sexually abused as children; 78 percent had been abused by women.[32]

The woman therapist conducting this study asked each man questions like, "Did a babysitter ever touch you on your genitals?" When a man said "Yes" to one or more of the questions, she called it sexual abuse. But the men, hearing her definition, objected. Some explained that, as boys, it had been sexual pleasure for them. Others, more neutral, just said they loved the attention—and, yes, the sex, too.

These men were now in a treatment program to "cure" them of passing on to other children what some men considered a pleasure they had received as children. They were being told they were victims and perpetrators, which might be true, but the defining was being done largely by women, with little consultation of them.

Isn't it obvious what is and is not sexual abuse? Let's look. In educated urban areas from the late 1960s to the early 1980s, showing children a book such as *Show Me!,* with its nude pictures, was considered progressive; massaging children who were nude was considered a healthy form of needed nurturing and touch; undressing in front of children was considered natural. *Glamour* magazine ran stories encouraging mothers to feel fine about having orgasms from breast feeding.[33] By the late 1980s, the very behaviors considered healthy just years before were increasingly used in court as evidence of child sexual abuse.

I do not have, as it were, the "Final Answer." The closest I can come is to caution that we are creating final answers in an arena where "final answers" are not final. Not only does the definition of sexual normality vary enormously from generation to generation within a culture, but even more enormously from culture to culture. Premarital sex, homosexuality, and how a parent should touch or kiss a child are all subject to adults imposing very varied judgments of morality and abuse on children.

With the crucial exceptions of adults forcing themselves on children, or pressuring children sexually, children experience as abuse largely what adults define as abuse. They are also often traumatized by being sexual in ways that adult society considers sinful or abusive ("What?! You had sex *before* marriage?!"); and almost never traumatized by being sexual in ways that adult society considers acceptable (*e.g.,* tribes in which a middle-aged woman is an adolescent boy's first lover, both to teach him and give him a good first experience; and tribes in which men do the same for girls).

When we make it politically incorrect to hear with respect the sexual experiences and desires of the men above—who had their victimization and perpetrator status defined for them—or to hear the perspectives of the "Show Me" generation, or of other cultures such as those of Scandanavia, or of African tribes—the overall impact is increasingly expanded definitions of abuse dictated by feminists, social workers, and a Victorian sexual heritage. Our children's new heritage will be one of "touch neglect," especially "male touch neglect" by single dads worried about bathing their children, taking them into the security of their bed after a nightmare, camping with them, or sharing a hotel room together so they can afford a vacation; and by the absence of men teaching in nursery and elementary schools—absent for fear that today's job could be tomorrow's labeling with a scarlet "A" for Abuser.

Is Our Belief in the Superiority of Mothers Related to Our Adopting the Female Definitions of Sexual Abuse?

Our belief in the superiority of mothers was only one prerequisite to our adopting the female definitions of child rearing and sexual abuse. When divorces in the seventies left mothers unprotected, our desire to protect women led us to give women the option of being paid to be with the children (child support; Temporary Assistance to Needy Families [TANF—almost exclusively aid to mothers]; Women, Infants, and Children [WIC]; and other government programs). Between 1970 and 1998, the combination of divorces and the government playing substitute husband led to an increase in the percentage of children who lived with only their mother—from 11 percent to 22 percent.[34]

This left only women in charge of the definitions of sexual abuse—of sometimes assuming that sexual abuse was occurring when "Absentee Father Anxiety" was occurring. Yet in the past when women had been in charge of children, sexual-abuse allegations were almost nonexistent. What else is going on?

As men began having sex without commitment, often with younger women, and as single moms with children felt that they were especially disposable in the eyes of men, issues that had always bothered women, but remained largely hidden, began to surface. Especially the "eight anger at-male-sexuality issues": sexual harassment, sexual abuse, incest, prostitution, pornography, acquaintance rape, spousal rape, and stranger rape.[35]

As women aired their feelings, they realized others felt the same. The validity of their perspectives, the intensity of their emotions, and the political power of feminism combined to allow these issues to quickly become politicized and ultimately become politically correct. Men who had families or wanted a future quickly learned to keep their mouths shut. By the last two decades of the twentieth century, these social issues became, in essence, female legislation against male sexuality with no male response.

Sexuality became dichotomized—female good/male bad. As Glamour magazine was singing the praises of women having orgasms while breast feeding,[36] feminists were explaining that fathers who sat their daughters on their laps were really seeking sexual pleasure—and were therefore sexual abusers. Women were encouraged to feel pleasure, men to feel shame. Men, by ignoring women's magazines and women's issues, missed the double standard. Sometimes they missed the entire issue until a sheriff explained it to them.

This made men afraid to touch children in the way that most men felt was healthy, and stopped in its tracks the movement to get men and children involved with each other in childcare centers and nursery schools. It scared men whose desire to be with their children after divorce threatened their ex-wives' desire to have income from childcare. These men knew that if they pushed the issue, they could be accused of sexual abuse with virtually no ability to prevent their reputations from being ruined and their lives from being destroyed. All of this created a new sexism: the "presumption of perversion"[37]—only for men. It created a dad who wasn't "at home" at home; it was more walking on eggshells on the path to the fatherless child.

4

What Prevents Dads from
Being Involved?

The Dads Themselves

On one level, father involvement is the quietest revolution. On another, its quietness has prevented a revolution.

Dads were quieted by thousands of years of being selected based on their willingness to die on behalf of others, but not cry on behalf of themselves. Spies are taught to self-destruct before they self-reveal. All this makes for a

pretty quiet revolution. A self-help book that reaches out to Dads often watches Dad commit suicide before he walks down the self-help aisle.

Only dads themselves can lead the charge to change this, but the process will be slow, because dads are usually selected by women who are choosing men who will earn enough income to create options for the woman, not for themselves. Men are reluctant to change what they think brings them love. Nevertheless, women also want men's love. So men's first confrontation is learning more about how to love, so women will value men's love more.

Men's second barrier is comprehending why the industrial revolution led to many steps backward for fatherhood but has, nevertheless, laid the foundation for many steps forward. If we can find the steps . . .

The "Catch-22s" of the Industrial Revolution

The Industrial Revolution meant that a dad who raised food on the farm could no longer raise his family as effectively as a dad who raised money in the city. On the farm, family and food were raised on the same soil. Industrialization meant that the family was raised in a house while the father raised money in a factory. For fathers, industrialization meant isolation from his family.

Industrialization created the "Father's Catch-22": a dad loving his children by being away from the love of his children. The better he "loved" them as a human doing, the worse he loved them as a human being. Fathers had always been human doings, but industrialization magnified the problem.

Marx identified the alienation from self and work that industrialization created. Practically speaking, though, it was much more an alienation of males from self and work than of women from self and work. And more of fathers than of mothers. In fact, it allowed women to become the nurturing specialists. And, because the larger the man's family, the greater the alienation, the more children, the more alienation. Industrialization created the alienation of dads proportionate to the degree that they were dads!

The Industrial Revolution, then, took men's occasional absence from home—previously needed only in wartime and for hunting—and made it the norm. This increasing division of labor magnified the division of men's and women's interests. It magnified the belief in the maternal instinct and the reality of the distant father. Prior to industrialization, divorces usually led to children living with dads. But not after.

"The Father's Catch-22" was compounded by "The Husband's Catch-22." Few women fell in love with aspiring househusbands. Even if the househusbands were reading Dr. Spock. So a man learned early in life that a good career was a prerequisite for a good woman's love. That had always been true, but industrialization now magnified the degree to which he needed to be away from a woman's love in order to receive the love of a woman. Or, as a husband, he needed to be away from his wife's love in order to be loved by a woman who would be his wife. Thus the "Husband's Catch-22."

Both Catch-22s delivered to men the same message: Receive love by being away from love. The Industrial Revolution accentuated both "Catch-22s" and thus deepened men's unconscious fear of spending too much time with the people they loved for fear of ultimately losing their love.

The Industrial Revolution not only deprived the son of his father as a *personal* role model, but deprived the son of his father as a *professional* role model—he was no longer his dad's apprentice. In contrast, daughters still had their moms as both personal and professional role models.

While the daughter experienced her mom's teaching and her mom's temperament, industrialization created two "Sons' Catch-22s": First, he experienced his *mom's* teaching ("be neat" and "don't play rough") and temperament, but to find love, he needed to be more like his dad. Second, the more successful his dad, the more he should emulate him, but the less he saw of him. These are what I call "The Son's Catch-22s."

Children and wives began to blame the father for his absence. No one understood that Dad's absence was his form of slavery, his commitment to providing the family's "financial womb." Had he been unwilling, his wife would never have selected him to begin with, and thus the children wouldn't exist to register their complaints!

That's the bad news. The good news is that industrialization began to sow the seeds to reduce the division of labor. Which would, in turn, begin to sow the seeds to bring the father back home. How? Industrialization produced enough appliances and conveniences to allow the woman to work outside the home, enough cost to *need* the woman to work outside the home. Thus industrialization initially reinforced the division of labor, and then created the conditions to reduce it.

However, before this created a father and child reunion, it led to our sons being deprived of yet a third role model: male elementary-school teachers. Prior to industrialization, the boy also had mostly male elementary-school teachers. But industrialization increasingly produced female elementary-school teachers. Why? Dad was still the primary breadwinner, so Mom needed a work schedule to be compatible with the children's school schedule.

Industrialization's good news for fatherhood is that it laid the foundation for technology, and technology is increasingly allowing the father to once again raise money and family "on the same soil." Technology is creating the conditions for a father and child reunion. It allows for home offices on cheaper, more rural land, freeing him from paying the price of a home in the suburbs; freeing him from commuting in rush-hour traffic; freeing him from suits and, nowadays, from sexual-harassment lawsuits. Most of all, though, he has had decades to discover what happens to children when Dad is absent. Men, like women, respond to being needed. And now technology is allowing him to have the need for his love be under the same roof as the need for his productivity. Welcome to the Era of the Fatherhood Juggling Act!

The biggest barrier to helping men love will be expecting men's money. . . .

The Banker Barrier (or the "Daddy Track")

A father is a banker provided by nature.

FRENCH PROVERB

Nothing threatens a father's involvement in the family more than his obligation to be the family's "financial womb," creating "The Father's Catch-22": loving the family by being away from the family. It is the irony of traditional fatherhood: being a father by not being a father.

Creating fatherhood means creating a major psychological shift. Both sexes find it's difficult to fully share the psychological responsibility for the other sex's traditional role—especially when the other sex is around. Just as mothers take on twenty-four-hours-a-day psychological responsibility for the childcare—even in homes in which the father is spending more hours with the children—fathers similarly still retain a twenty-four-hours-a-day psychological responsibility for the family's "financial womb"—even if the mother happens to be making more money at some given moment in time.

Even in Sweden, where men are offered paid paternity leaves of six months and media campaigns show sports heroes tending their young, only 22 percent of Swedish fathers take the leave, and their average leave is not six months, but forty-seven days.[2] Why? Because even in Sweden, men know they will jeopardize their career advancement and therefore jeopardize their wife's and children's welfare (and therefore, possibly their wife's love) if they go on the "Daddy Track." It has become easier for Swedish men to take longer leaves because the government plays substitute husband so well for women in Sweden that women can afford to live with, and marry, men who earn less. Which is why the amount of leave time Swedish men have taken to be with their children doubled between the seventies and eighties.[3]

In the United States, the Family and Medical Leave Act of 1993, providing for up to twelve unpaid weeks off to care for a new baby or seriously ill family member, has been used by a half-million men and 1.4 million women.[4] But for the most part, dads use accumulated sick days instead of leave days. And overall, women are still 135 times more likely than men to leave the workplace for family reasons.[5]

I hope this social backdrop allows fathers and mothers to see that we've all been caught in a system dictated initially not by the needs of men, or of women, but by both sexes' needs to survive, and that more recently we've been caught in the transitions that have resulted from that system succeeding. Our desire to do more than survive included the desire for freedom to exercise options—from divorce to raising children without Dad. To give ourselves permission for that, we changed our image of father from "father knows best" to "father molests." The same German colleague who sent me the cartoon above also sent me another from *Der Spiegel* (roughly the German equivalent of *Time* magazine) in which the child says, "Mummy, please tell me something about Daddy," and the mom replies, "No, no, dear! No horror stories before sleeping."[6]

This daddy-as-nightmare image is ubiquitous in industrialized countries, to such a degree that the only way we can now envision Dad with our children is if Mom is unable to be available. Let's go to the movies and see . . .

Next Time You See a Full-Time Dad in a Movie, Notice This Formula

In the mythology of the fairy tales we learned as children, the stepmother was the horror story (*e.g.,* Cinderella). Today's children have more frequent exposures to the Homer-Simpson-as-horror-story.

During the 1990s, Hollywood turned into a formula what began as an experiment in the 1980s. Any time Dad was seen as the primary caregiver for his children in a positive way, something would be required. See if you can guess what was required. A hint: What do the following movies have in common (aside from this positive image of a father who is the primary caregiver)?: *Sleepless in Seattle, Friends and Lovers, The American President, Clueless, Casper, Fly Away Home, Sabrina, Milk Money, Contact, She's All That,* and *Arlington Road.*[7]

The answer: The requirement is that the mother be dead. Or, more occasionally, inexplicably out of the picture. The formula "If Dad is the primary caregiver, Mom must be dead" was the theme of only one movie in the 1970s, of four movies in the 1980s, and of at least twenty movies in the 1990s.[8] I might be off by a movie or two, but you've got the picture.

What's happening? On the one hand, Hollywood was adjusting to a new reality: the doubling of single-parent fathers during the 1980s and 1990s (from less than 10 percent of single parents to 19 percent of single parents). On the other hand, in this era of the deadbeat-dad image, Hollywood was rejecting a second reality: the possibility of an abusive mother, or a drunk or drug-using mother; the possibility of an immature, teenage mother; the possibility of a mom in prison; the possibility of an uninterested mother, a career-focused mother, or a mother who was in any other way inadequate.

In those last five categories of mothers, there are thousands of yet-to-be-made movies based on fathers who have, in reality, either come to the rescue or become fathers by mutual decision—or even by greater competence!

Hollywood is in denial out of fear that we are in denial. That is, as the image of Father Knows Best has disappeared, our collective unconscious prevents us from feeling comfortable with a father as the primary caregiver for his children—*unless* the "real parent" is dead. Let's look. . . .

In *Sleepless in Seattle,* Tom Hanks' character, while standing next to his wife's casket, explains to his son, "Mommy got sick, and it happened just like that. Nothing anybody could do." In *The American President,* Michael Douglas as President is described merely as having "lost his wife." In *Clueless,* the mom died in a freak accident. In *Casper,* the mom's death is described only as "sudden." In *Fly Away Home,* the mother dies in a car crash. In *Contact,* Jodie Foster's character's mom died before she was born. In *Arlington Road,* the mother was killed while serving as a federal agent, and vindicating her death was the focus of the movie. In *Sabrina*, we are told of the mother's death, but given no explanation; and the same is true in *Milk Money* and *She's All That*.

Even if the father is merely *living with* his *adult* children, as in *Sabrina*, there is a good chance the mother will be dead. In *Friends and Lovers*, a 1999 movie, the mother is dead so that a dad can be portrayed as merely trying to improve his relationship with his adult children. And the mother is sometimes dead in the movies depicting warm, loving relationships between a father and an adult child, as in *Meet Joe Black* (1998) and *Absolute Power* (1997) with Clint Eastwood. As a rule, the younger the children, the more likely the mother is dead; and the more the child is being raised by the father—as opposed to just having a loving relationship with the father—the more likely the mother is dead.

In contrast, in movies about *mothers* raising their young children on their own, the *father* is almost always *alive*.

So why do we need the mother to be dead for the dad to be desired? Because any scenario other than death or an *inexplicable* absence would risk making Mom look like she might have *chosen* to forfeit her maternal responsibilities. Or, heaven forbid, that she was on drugs, or in prison, or unable to handle the child. **Implicit in the Hollywood formula of Mom-by-option and Dad-by-default is Mom never at fault . . . to a fault.**

More subtly, the death of Mom makes no one have to look at the possibility that Dad is a dad-by-option, a dad-by-desire, or a dad-by-greater-competence.

Ironically, we have rejected a world in which Rosie can be a riveter only if Johnny is in a war, but replaced it with a world in which Johnny can be a dad only when Rosie is in a grave.

Now Rosie can be more than a riveter. For example, even in the latest macho James Bond movie, *The World is Not Enough*, Hollywood assesses its audience as secure enough to handle James Bond's boss being a woman. (Fortunately for James Bond fans, James Bond did not have to be dead!) In essence, even the macho man has become more secure with a woman as his boss than the average female moviegoer is with a dad as her equal.

Notice that I am not blaming Hollywood for "foisting this image on us." Let me suggest that *both American and non-American sales foist this image on Hollywood*. A film that Americans call foreign—like *Kolya*—presents a poignant story of a man's journey from self-centeredness to substitute fatherhood that nevertheless allows the mother a shadow side: The mother manipulates a fraudulent marriage and deserts the child. Hollywood supports the film by giving it the Academy Award for best foreign film. Yet Hollywood does not foist on us what we do not buy. The worldwide publicity of winning the Academy Award still leads to fewer sales than almost all its American counterparts in both American *and non-American* markets.

When viewers speak, Hollywood listens. Hollywood is entertainment's politician; our ticket purchases are our votes. When the payment is high enough, the prostitute will appear.

Even in *Kolya*, the mom-by-option and dad-by-default formula always lurks behind the scenes. Mom returns, and "Dad," who had turned his life and heart around to adapt to the child, has the child taken away when the

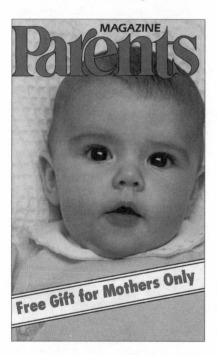

mom decides she wants the child back. The seizure is without regard for the adjustments "Dad" made to either his life or his heart. The mother's change of desire counted even as the child's needs were not considered. When the love that enters a dad's heart can be stolen, his heart will be sealed. We create not a deadbeat dad, but a deadened dad.

The presumption of "mothers only" prevails, even when we pretend to be including fathers. Images like this one from a *Parents* magazine[9] advertisement insert soliciting subscribers are ubiquitous . . .

Imagine the *Readers' Digest* offering a "Free Gift for Caucasians Only." Or a publication called *Managers'* magazine offering a "Free Gift for Male Managers Only." If such an ad did appear for a *Managers'* magazine, a lawsuit would also appear. But our collective unconscious is so aware of this discrimination against women executives that a "men only" banner could no longer be run on a managers' magazine; and our collective unconscious is so unaware of this discrimination against fathers that it doesn't even generate an organized protest.

How Our Discrimination Against Men's Style of Nurturing Keeps Men from Children

The "Presumption of Perversion"

ITEM. The success of Big Brothers of America has rested on the emotional trust between a boy who has never had a man as a friend and a man who is volunteering his time to love the boy. Oftentimes, this connection is built while the two spend extended time together, such as during *overnight* visits. Now Big Brothers has advised its 488 local agencies against overnight visits and substituted instead sexual abuse information.[10]

The presumption of perversion drives men away from children at exactly that point in history when men are rediscovering children. When women entered the male-dominated workplace and their attitudes toward sexuality were not understood by men, they said, "Men just don't get it," and they sued men for sexual harassment. But when men entered the female-dominated homeplace and elementary-school system with more hands-on touching and playing, and a freer attitude toward sexuality, they didn't even think of suing women for depriving children of this type of touch and play, but once again found themselves the target of lawsuits as **the legal definitions of sexual abuse began to overlap with men's style of playing and touching children.** While the actual number of lawsuits was small, the headlines petrified men.

Men soon feared taking jobs in childcare centers, nursery schools, and elementary schools; tens of thousands of men feared giving their love to children as a Big Brother, or even as a leader in Boy Scout groups and Boys Clubs of America.

Here's how this fear operates in practice: A mother tells me her son wants to go on an outing with the Boy Scouts. However, the Boy Scouts of America's national policy bans any scout leader from being alone with a boy (the presumption of perversion)![11] The mom tells me that as a result no one can find enough men to go with the boys. Here's the deeper dilemma. . . .

One man who recently quit being a scoutmaster explained it to me this way. "If I have to bring another man with me to drop all the boys off, I have to drive that man back to headquarters (to get his car) from the home of the boy who lives farthest from headquarters. It's a pain. But what's worse is when a kid asks me, 'Why don't you just drop Bill and me off on your way home, and Mr. Martinez can drop off Sammy and Frank?' Of course it makes sense, so then I'm left in the position of having to either bullshit my way out of it or explain to the boy the presumption of perversion. Boy Scouts is supposed to give boys a positive image of men. What does that do? If I take a weekend away from my family and then I'm made to feel like a criminal, it's just not worth it."

On a personal level, few moments in my own years as a Boy Scout were more important than the long walks I had with two different scout leaders—one in which I was told how my behavior was alienating some of the boys, and what I could do differently; another in which I was told why I would grow up to be a very special man. It is only now that I look back and remember when one leader and I got lost together, how we found our way back after dark, how he had put his arm around me during the walk, how he had held my hand for awhile as he was leading me back through the trees after it was dark. Today, any man who got lost with a child in the woods after dark could be accused by anyone of sexual abuse; and, no matter how popular he was, the institution he was with would be forced to let him go—especially, as Dr. Rawls' study helps us see, if the boy was questioned repeatedly to "be sure" everything was fine.

There were only two of those walks, but I remember both of them. I wouldn't trade those moments for any others I had during my years of scouting. I often think of being a scout leader today. Although I love children, and the best of me surfaces when I am around them, I, like many other men, am afraid to volunteer. I believe the best moments with children are quiet moments, alone moments, one-on-one moments, and yet in today's atmosphere it takes just one misinterpretation of those moments to ruin a career and, in my case, the credibility it takes to alter that atmosphere. So I feel caught between a rock and a hard place.

My sister, Gail, shares my love for children. She demonstrates that by extending invitations to her third-grade students to go hiking during weekends. She knows that mentoring comes naturally in nature. But unlike Boy Scout leaders, she does not worry about being accused of sexual abuse. She is not subjected to "the presumption of perversion."

Unfortunately, the children most vulnerable to sexual abuse are those who are starving for affection. **By starving our children of men, we have made them more vulnerable to the very abuse we are trying to prevent.** We reinforce this every time we focus on men as molesters and neglect the contribution of men as caregivers. The presumption of perversion has led us to *guaranteeing* child abuse to prevent the *possibility* of sexual abuse: We have taken a generation of men who were ready to benefit from connection to children and forced them to back off out of fear.

How Does the Presumption of Perversion Begin?

Imagine a mother explaining to her children the *joys* of sex and the beauty of male sexual energy. Or a high-school teacher saying, "Today's lesson is called 'The joys of sex and the beauty of male sexual energy.'" *Not.* They are more likely to cover up the joy of sex with "safe sex" or *substitute* sex-positive discussions with discussions of AIDS, pornography, sexual harassment, sexual abuse, date rape, rape, or incest. Sex gets so caught up in the blender of dirt, death, disease, and disgust, and of obscenity, criminality, immorality, and deviation, that it completely disappears as something with a positive value.

The warnings are not only about sex, but about our sons. Even medical institutions turn *male* sexuality into the enemy. Imagine, in this ad from Summit Medical, the sperm running *away* from the egg, so that "How to Avoid a Hostile Takeover" referred to the egg gobbling up the sperm rather than the sperm penetrating the egg.

On an unconscious level, the demonization of sexuality usually implies the demonization of males and the victimization of females.

How does this affect our sons? At an age when he knows virtually nothing about sex or girls, he begins to feel his body filled with testosterone and desire for sex and girls. And his ears filled with female fears of sex and boys. He hears horror stories of boys "always wanting it," boys getting girls pregnant, boys skipping out on girls, "making passes," "coming on," not being able to be trusted . . . he hears, in essence, that sex is dirty, and that he should be ashamed.

Then we say to him, "Your job is to initiate the dirt." As he rehearses initiating scenarios that will bring him the least rejection, he begins not to trust

HOW TO AVOID A HOSTILE TAKEOVER.

At Summit Medical you can expect highly qualified professionals, state-of-the-art facilities and professional counseling – all under one roof. So, whether it's pregnancy termination or a tubal ligation, our doors are always open. Also providing HIV testing and free pregnancy testing.

TUBAL LIGATIONS
SUMMIT MEDICAL ASSOCIATES · 770-452-1919

himself. He feels manipulative and begins to think of himself as taking advantage of "innocent" women.

The less our sons are trusted, the less women are able to really love them, and the more women feel entitled to use them as wallets. On a deeper level, **if our sons are learning they are obscene, disgusting, and untrustworthy, is this the best preparation for fatherhood?** And is it the best preparation for becoming a mother—to feel this way about her son?

This fear of not being trustworthy triggers a boy's desire to prove himself. If he fears failure, he might just feel, "I'll give up, it's hopeless." If he chooses success, sensing that success is the best preventive medicine to avoid the cancer of female rejection, and he succeeds, he is nevertheless left feeling insecure under the shell of his mastery.

What can we do to decrease the demonizing of male sexuality and the distrust it creates for our sons? We can approach sexual desire more the way we approach our children's desire to drive. Driving, like sex, can lead to death or life-altering damage in exchange for a few seconds of carelessness. We can see how absurd it would be to tell our children that driving is dirty and then tell only teenage girls that they're responsible for driving and picking the boys up. If we did this, we would be suggesting that parents and schools tell boys it's fine to have a desire to drive, and we'd encourage boys to drive and pick up girls as often as girls do for them.

The presumption of perversion is best reduced by giving our daughters permission—even encouragement—to discover their sexual desire, and expecting both sexes to share responsibility for the risks of sexual rejection. Girls today initiate a lot more than they used to, but they initiate by option, not expectation; they initiate less if they are attractive; they initiate more in this freshman and sophomore years, and *much less during their junior and senior years in high school*. Sharing responsibility implies not just feeling okay about our daughter calling a boy, but letting her know she has that obligation if she wants a real partnership; it implies being vigilant that our daughter continue as she gets older, especially if she is attractive; it implies letting her know that when she is the one to do the selection she is more likely to control her sexual experience.

Instead of limiting her to the *veto power* of saying no to unwanted men or sex, we give her the added tool of *original choice power*. Veto power creates a watchdog mentality of fear of boys and fear of sex; original choice power in the area of sex teaches her to extend control over her life into the sexual arena. This reduces her need to use the veto power tools of breast enhancements, tight sweaters, or make-up. "Make-up" is basically what a woman uses to make up the gap between the selection power she has and the selection power she desires.

As we resocialize our daughters to share responsibility for sexual risk-taking, we create less need for our sons to have to neurotically "rev" themselves up to risk the rejection. This allows our sons to balance receiving love by performing and providing (the traditional form of "*male make-up*") with receiving love by giving love.

When the demonizing of male sexuality is combined with devaluing fathers' style of play and the headlines of fathers as sexual abusers that emanate mostly during parent-time disputes, and these are combined with the propensity of child-protective services to cross-examine children until they "acknowledge" that they have been inappropriately touched, the result is a multi-pronged approach that scares men away from nurturing roles in child-care, elementary-school teaching, Scouting, and all the preparation for fathering.

The Female Value System

It is not only the childraising process that is dominated by women as mothers and elementary-school teachers, but also the enforcement of values related to childraising, in the form of female social workers and child-protective-service workers. Even when we matriculate in a university, if we heed the Latin origins of the word matriculate, we are, in effect, enrolling in the mother's womb of the university. In recent years, as the university has increasingly played the role of *in loco parentis,* the parent it has most resembled is the protectiveness of Mom more than the risk-taking of Dad. We are increasingly matriculating, not patriculating.

In aggregate, this creates a value system based on female socialization. Female socialization toward sex should be 50 percent of the curriculum, but now it permeates every aspect of childraising in the same way that male values previously permeated every aspect of money-raising. And, just as women who entered Wall Street or the armed services usually absorbed male values in order to succeed, so men who enter nursery-school or elementary-school teaching, or who become social workers, absorb female values in order to succeed. In universities, where family is the topic, women also dominate.

We saw from the Danish study of children living with their dads versus their moms that children of both sexes who lived with their moms were more likely to feel like victims—they experienced a children's version of what the mom was experiencing. The children were more than three times as likely to feel victimized by other children, four times as likely to experience frequent seizures of fear, and more than twice as likely to have frequent nightmares.[12]

More importantly, when female values are so dominant in raising boys, I believe it leads to boys not feeling lovable for their core energy, thus tempting feelings that they must perform to be loved rather than love to be loved. Some examples:

The journey of an inner-city boy is often from mother to female teacher to all-male gang. Is it possible he is joining a gang to feel respect for his core male energy? Is it any wonder he turns to gangs for a sense of male identity? How does this work in practice?

A boy who deals drugs rarely hears his mother or a teacher say, "Drug dealing has helped you develop skills of risk-taking, experimenting, and breadwinning; now let's take the skills you learned as drug dealer and make them work for you as a car dealer."

Teachers who have adopted the female value system are more likely to value speaking in turn, raising hands, sitting still . . . also useful values, but they are not ones that offer him respect for the way he learns to take risks, to blend cooperation with competition. Athletic boys often hear "male competitiveness" criticized as if it were a disease (at the same time that the cheerleaders compete to cheer and compete to love the best male competitors).

Even skills he learns that are compatible with the female value system are rarely seen that way. The male athlete, who might be praised for the way he "reads" his opponent's every move in a basketball or football game, rarely finds his "intuitive" skills praised for this anticipation, or his relationship skills praised for his teamwork. Few teachers say to him, "You have a sensitivity and the intuitive skills to be a wonderful father and husband," and proceed to help him channel those skills that way, or even appreciate all the ways in which they can be channeled.

Boys often feel discounted as their Gary Larson–type far out, off-the-wall perspectives that are the training ground for creativity and entrepreneurial skills are given less credence than correct answers, turning in homework neat and on time, proper grammar and spelling, the correct historical date. Life gives high grades to the skills that lead to the successful entrepreneur, not for remembering the year the Treaty of 1812 was signed. (Don't look for a source note on that one.)

Feminist theory has taken the discrimination against men as fathers a step further. It takes the biological finding that a female brain has a thicker connection between the left and the right side than the male brain does, and translates it into an assumption that that is why women are better at juggling children, dishes, laundry, etc., thus making them better mothers. But this is contradicted by two things. First, we have seen that single dads do better than single moms. While this is a selective group of men, it is also a superior performance at juggling.

Second, the male role requires every bit as much juggling as the female role does. For example, major corporate CEOs, more likely to be men, must juggle not just two children's egos in competition, but a thousand employees' egos in competition—he juggles their desire for more promotions and for more free time with his need to keep costs low enough to sell enough products to keep them employed. He must juggle each employee's overvaluation of self and undervaluation of others; he must juggle OSHA regulations with IRS obligations; stockholders' needs with humanitarian deeds . . .

He must juggle developing perhaps a dozen products and, therefore, the egos behind each product line, each group feeling that their product should be test-marketed better, advertised better, marketed better, have more sales reps, be better distributed. . . . He must decide what can better be done in-house, and how to get his in-house employees to make an honest recommendation as to what can be done better by outsourcing to someone else. He must then juggle his employees with perhaps a hundred different subcontractors. And then comes the juggling of all this with government regulations concerning safety, affirmative action, taxes, sexual harassment. Today that means taking responsibility for any one of his thousand employees saying something to anyone else who might interpret that as sexual harassment.

That's only what the CEO who's a working father must juggle at work. When he comes home, he must juggle all this with a wife who feels he doesn't spend enough time with her and children who want him to be a soccer dad. But, once again, men have said nothing. This man juggles so much, he has no time to write academic articles complaining about it!

Men often prepare for this juggling act as boys, via team sports, preparing as much for blue-collar as white-collar jobs. The quarterback juggles the patterns twenty-one other men are running; he faces eleven men trained to destroy his plan and his body in the process. His toss must avoid all eleven of their routes, be as far as possible, yet not out of bounds. . . . If everything is not executed with virtually 100 percent precision, at the right second, in the right place, he is considered a failure. When he fails to juggle, he gets feedback! It's called a concussion or a spinal cord injury. Yet few teachers, trained in the female value system, tell him how valuable his juggling act on the football field will be for juggling his role as a working father. Instead, he faces a feminist ideology that tells him his brain connection is too narrow to juggle.

13

When we add the devaluation of male values to the demonizing of male sexuality, we produce many boys who feel like perverts before they know who they are. He feels even his basic energy is held in contempt. And as the girls learning this from female-value-system teachers become mothers themselves, these mothers are bringing up boys for whom they feel this contempt. In brief, in the past we believed both sexes were born with original sin. Today, we have come to unconsciously believe in the original sin of boys, but the original *innocence* of girls.

As technology has minimized the need for men's physical strength, boys who grow up poor, and especially black boys, have taken a particularly hard hit. The flight from fatherlessness in the black community is, I believe, related not only to boys growing up without fathers, but to boys growing up amid mothers, female teachers, and female social workers who create a value system that does not honor his energy and, therefore, does not know how to channel it constructively. Thus we have worried little that the black male is an endangered species—which is why we hear more about saving the gray whale than about saving the black male.

The Mom-as-Gatekeeper Barrier—Keeping Dad Out of "The First Wives Club"

The decision to keep the child with the mother is theoretically made in the best interests of the child; however, when children were surveyed later in life, fewer than half felt their mother's motives had anything to do with their best interests.[14] Only a quarter felt it was because their mother loved them.

ITEM. "Almost 40 percent of the custodial wives reported that they had refused at least once to let their ex-husbands see the children, and admitted that their reasons had nothing to do with the children's wishes or the children's safety but were somehow punitive in nature."[15]

ITEM. Research by Drs. Judith Wallerstein and Joan Berlin Kelly revealed that approximately 50 percent of mothers either saw no value in the father's contact with his children and actively tried to sabotage it, or resented the father's contact.[16] For example, "One gently bred matron smeared dog feces on the face of her husband when he arrived to see his children."[17]

The acknowledgments by mothers of their undermining of fathers are especially important because when dads don't see their children, we often call them deadbeat dads before we ask whether Mom is discouraging the contact. In addition to the dog-feces example in the Item above, some of the methods Wallerstein and Kelly described that mostly mothers (but not exclusively mothers) used to discourage contact are: "forgotten appointments, insistence on rigid schedules for the visits, refusal to permit the visit if the father brought along an adult friend—a thousand mischievous, mostly petty, devices designed to humiliate the visiting parent and to deprecate him in the eyes of his children."[18]

The real issue was the self-fulfilling prophecy the father and children experienced that emanated from this behavior. First, the children felt "in jeopardy between two warring giants" and reacted with anxiety and fear; and then the mothers used that anxiety and fear "as proof that the visits were detrimental to the child's welfare and should, therefore, be discontinued. Attorneys were called by aggrieved mothers who blamed their husbands for the child's lapses"[19] which, of course, just magnified the children's symptoms, thus "proving" that the problem is Dad.

From Berkeley to Boston, both female and male researchers have found mothers who said they wanted fathers to be more involved with their children but nevertheless acted as "Gatekeepers": controlling the "when" and criticizing his style if it wasn't like hers. This "Gatekeeper Barrier" is strongest among women who stay at home full-time.

A full-time mother is not only protecting her job, but also her love interest. Anyone who develops the style and the psychological investment of a full-time parent is likely to believe her or his method is the best. In fact, though, children benefit most from the synergy between men's and women's different styles.

Full-time mothers who had a background as homemakers were more likely to act as if they were protecting turf[21] and full-time mothers who were former executives were more likely to say, "It'll take you forty-five minutes to dress the baby. Let me do it, it only takes me ten minutes."[22] The men feel either criticized or unappreciated. They "pick up the hint" and, to keep peace, back off. Just as she feels the executive suite has a "glass ceiling," he feels the playpen has a "glass barrier"—and she's on patrol.

Both mother and father need to do some creative rethinking here. It is helpful for a woman to recall how devalued she felt when, as a dinner guest, she helped load the dishwasher only to notice the host reload it "the right way." It is helpful for a man to think of his wife's gatekeeping as some combination of mentoring and hazing. Any man who has succeeded in a competitive profession has also succeeded at handling hazing—and also understood its function as a rite of passage. Nevertheless, it is important for a father who feels pushed away to say, in effect, "When you do that, I feel unwanted as a father," or "I feel my roughhousing is not bad parenting; it's my contribution to helping our child take risks." Women can't hear what men don't say. Or something like that.

Men's assertiveness is especially important with daughters. Census data shows us that parents with two daughters are the most likely to divorce, followed by parents with a son and a daughter; the most stable family with children is one with two sons.[23]

Why? A father often doesn't feel he has a right to interfere with the bond he believes his wife has established with his daughters. Mom becomes a gatekeeper of her daughter's morality, dresses and undresses her, nurtures and protects her—and if he plays too rough or criticizes too much or brings her to tears or disciplines her too strongly, he feels he receives both their disapproval. He feels as if he has been told by the mother, "This is *my* kingdom, *my* gate, *my* lock, and only I know the right combination." Thus, he distances and, feeling disposable, is more likely to become disposable. Men who fight to integrate their value systems into their daughters' lives are fighting, even if unwittingly, to keep their marriage together.

When our binoculars are focused on the dad as "deadbeat," it often even leads us to missing concrete cues a dad gives to show his desire to be involved. Rent a video of *The First Wives Club,* a film which attracted almost half of all the female moviegoers during the first week or two of its release. Note how Diane Keaton's character and her daughter plot to "vaporize" the dad-as-enemy. As you focus on this, do you somehow miss appreciating how delighted the dad felt to be making contact with his daughter—so delighted that he allowed her access to his private life and files, hired her, and was her mentor? Did you miss how his love for her blinded him to the conspiracy that his daughter and ex-wife were perpetrating against him?

The deeper issue, of course, is how your missing this (if you did) is symbolic of how a society which focuses its attention on the "deadbeat" part of Dad misses the loving part of Dad. Similarly, even the daughter's need for the approval of the mom was so great that she also could not see her own dad's desire to love her.

The Badmouthing Barrier

We saw above that when mothers have primary or sole parent time with the children, the relationship between the father and child deteriorates,[24] and one reason for that is perhaps the badmouthing of the dad. When Glynnis Walker conducted a nationwide study of children interviewed an average of eight years after their parents' divorce, she found the following:

- 54 percent of the children said that only their mothers spoke badly of their fathers in front of them;

- 12 percent said that only their fathers spoke badly of their mothers.[25]

The damage from badmouthing the other parent is done mostly to the child. A friend of mine who wrote me about a childhood memory put it this way:[26]

When I was at my best friend's home, I often witnessed my friend's mother verbally rip his dad to shreds [they were divorced], blaming him for almost everything that was a problem in her life. I saw my friend's anger at his dad when he believed her, his protectiveness when he didn't, his embarrassment that I was there, and his isolation because I could not identify with his feelings.

Only as an adult have I thought how his dad must have felt paying alimony and child support to support his own son's hatred of him, and, therefore, his son's hatred of himself. My friend's mother seemed to assume that along with sole custody came a right to transform her son into a captive audience for her bitterness against his dad. I watched my best friend's anger toward men and himself grow and grow.

Some children seem to internalize the badmouthing: "I always felt that no one is all bad, but maybe if he was, then so was I."[27] Mothers who badmouthed fathers eventually produced children who resented their mother more than their father. Walker quotes a daughter:

I began to lose respect for my mother. She made the entire process of divorce and what came after into pure hell for me and my father. This put a wall between us that still exists today. She was constantly trying to persuade me of my father's awfulness and force me to leave him and come and live with her. I think she felt that if she could not have him, then neither could I. When that did not work, she succeeded in driving my family away from me with cruel lies about how I was responsible for the divorce. To date, I have relatives who won't acknowledge my existence. The worst thing about the divorce was that I saw my mother for the person she really was.

Therapists, of course, can help. They can facilitate both parents helping the children understand what is going on. My personal preference is for

VS.

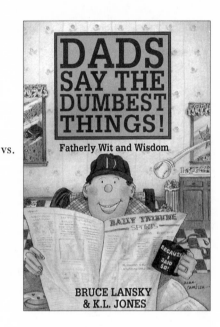

parents to discuss this both with the children and separately in the company of a counselor. Like anyone else, children will distort things based on their own fears. And when the parent hears a child's distorted version and cannot check it out, animosity is built toward the other parent.

However, the helping profession is not always helpful. . . .

The Helping Professions as Barrier

In a study of therapists, two separate groups watched a videotape of a simulated counseling session. Each group saw the same "client" with the same problems. However, in one video, the client claimed to be an engineer whose wife stayed home to care for the children. In the other, the identical client said his wife was an engineer and he stayed home to care for the children.[28] Not a single therapist questioned the domestic arrangement of the client who pretended to have a traditional arrangement. Almost all the therapists did question the "client" who pretended to be a househusband, with questions like, "What messages do you have from your childhood about what a man is?" Typical solutions were, "You probably need to renegotiate the contract that you've got at home." The therapists rated the man who pretended to be a househusband as much more severely depressed, even though in both tapes the client insisted he was very happy with his work arrangement, his wife, and his family.

It is this type of bias that leads therapists to make observations critical of the mother yet still draw conclusions favoring the children being with their mother.

Helping professionals at hospitals have made it easier for men to be with their wives during labor and delivery. That's real progress, given the father-infant bonding we now know occurs immediately after delivery. Ads that

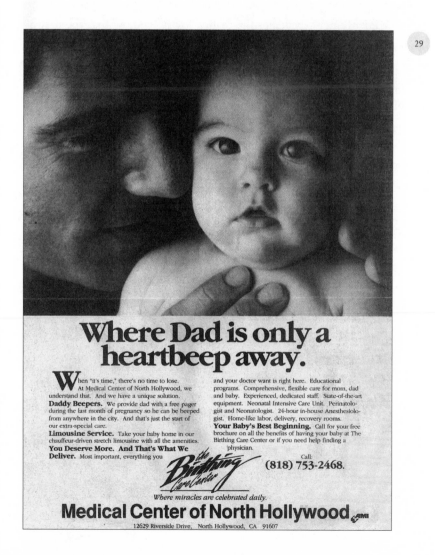

29

Where Dad is only a heartbeep away.

When "it's time," there's no time to lose. At Medical Center of North Hollywood, we understand that. And we have a unique solution. **Daddy Beepers.** We provide dad with a free pager during the last month of pregnancy so he can be beeped from anywhere in the city. And that's just the start of our extra-special care.
Limousine Service. Take your baby home in our chauffeur-driven stretch limousine with all the amenities.
You Deserve More. And That's What We Deliver. Most important, everything you

and your doctor want is right here. Educational programs. Comprehensive, flexible care for mom, dad and baby. Experienced, dedicated staff. State-of-the-art equipment. Neonatal Intensive Care Unit. Perinatologist and Neonatologist. 24-hour in-house Anesthesiologist. Home-like labor, delivery, recovery rooms.
Your Baby's Best Beginning. Call for your free brochure on all the benefits of having your baby at The Birthing Care Center or if you need help finding a physician.

the **Birthing** *Care Center*

Call:
(818) 753-2468.

Where miracles are celebrated daily.

Medical Center of North Hollywood
12629 Riverside Drive, North Hollywood, CA 91607

picture the dad with the child and that feature "daddy beepers" are beginning to tell dads that we value their loving.

On the other hand, as I mentioned above, we are still calling it "progress" when hospitals create "women's units" even as we call it "Neanderthal" for companies to create "men's clubs." Yet "women's units" relegate dads to the role of visitor after birth, while divorce laws relegate dads to the role of visitor after divorce. The message to men is clear: "You are your children's visitor." And then we wonder why men don't participate equally in childcare.

Calling birthing centers "women's units" not only discourages the vision of father involvement, it denies the reality. We now know that about two-thirds of expectant fathers experience many of the same symptoms their pregnant mates experience—loss of sleep, weight gain, nausea, backaches, abdominal and leg pain, *and even postpartum blues.*[30] It turns out that men *are* part of the process. So "birthing units" acknowledges the reality of Dad's experience.

But do men really need to be invited? In West Virginia, the nursing staff in "maternity" rooms were trained merely to have a different expectation of the newborns' fathers, inviting them in to be with their babies rather than treating them as peripheral or chasing them away. The results of making fathers feel included? The rate of paternity establishment went from 18 percent to 60 percent.[31] Which suggests that even small changes in awareness and behavior can have impact. Let's try some bigger changes. . . .

5

Toward the Best Interests

of Everyone . . .

Some Solutions

There are few solutions to replace a caring and boundary-setting, but non-authoritarian, intact family—although the best combination of shared parent time and stepparenting arrangements can come close. Family structure definitely is not everything; but, other things being equal, and at a time when dads must be motivated enough to buck the system to be full-time dads, research seems to justify the following ranking:

1. the intact family

2. shared parent-time (joint physical custody)

3. primary father time

4. primary mother time

Is the "Best Interests of the Child" Theory in the Best Interests of the Child?

Divorce makes everyone feel guilty about the "best interests of the child." The point is so valid that we take it to the extreme. Am I questioning the current approach to the "best interests of the child"? Yes. More precisely, I am introducing **"the paradox of the best interests of the child"**—that the real best interests of a child do not come from focusing only on *its* interests, but that **a child's best interests are served only when everyone's**

interests are considered. To raise a child with only its own best interests in mind creates an adult who keeps only its own interests in mind. It is healthier to raise a child who understands that its own interests are best served when everyone else's interests are carefully and consistently considered.

When it is assumed that the best interests of the child are best decided by Mom, this often leads to treating the father with benign neglect, and this tempts the desertion by Dad, if not physically, then psychologically. This destabilizes the family and damages the child in the name of its best interests. Why?

No one commits to a bad deal. If a mom was being badmouthed by her ex even as she was expected to be on call as a babysitter, she might consider that a bad deal. Moreover, if a dad or mom does commit to a bad deal, it can be *harmful* to the child—it teaches the child that he or she can form relationships by treating a loved one as a wallet (or a housecleaner) while disregarding him or her as a person. Talk about divorce training!

Paying Men to Stay, Not to Go Away

How do we get dads to stay: Instead of paying moms when dads disappear, we reverse the incentives. . . .

Fathers' Corps

The Fathers' Corps would train men to be nursery- and elementary-school teachers, and teach men how to communicate with their children.

When we train men for war, we lose some part of every man we train—even if we win the war. When we train men to be better nurturers, even men who fail the course will have won. And so will every child they ever meet. **Training men to love is a nation's best investment.**

The Man-in-the-Family Plan

The Man-in-the-Family Plan proposes to give men equal opportunity to enter the homeplace, just as women have equal opportunity to enter the workplace.

When I conducted an all-day workshop for the Community Baptist Church in Brooklyn, New York, most of the mothers were working outside the home. They all wanted dads more involved in the family—but the underlying assumption was that the dads' primary role would be to earn income, even though most of these women were already earning income.

I asked the audience if any of them had grown up in single-mother families with fathers who contributed neither income nor love. Many had. So I asked what they missed most in their childhood—their dad's income or his attention and love. I asked for a show of hands. But the hands were not raised, they were waving.

I was to hear an outpouring of testimonies about wounds they still felt from looking into the audience when they were doing a recital, hoping their dad would magically appear; or making it to their Little League playoffs, hoping their dad would see their name in the paper and show up; a woman wishing she knew what it was like to be hugged by a man without his wanting sex; a man wishing his dad would have taught him how to throw a ball . . . tie a tie . . . ask a girl out . . . take the lead in dances. Another man confessed he told himself his dad must be great, created a fictional figure, and joined the army to emulate the dad he hoped was his. To this day, memories of those stories are with me. And I expected a show of hands.

Each person in the church audience—and therefore each person who spoke—was black. Almost all had grown up poor. Most mentioned the poverty, but it was not the poverty that created the tears or the wounds. Yes, they missed money. But they missed Dad more.

This was not just a black issue. My dad grew up down the street from this church. He was one of ten children. My sister, Gail, and I heard most about his childhood at Christmas. When we would hint about what we hoped he would bring down the chimney, he'd hint that it might be something that would fit, like the orange and walnuts that were all he received when he grew up. As he would recount this, there was no sadness in his eyes; if anything, there was sadness at our focus on presents. Yet when I asked him about what he and his dad talked about when he grew up, he evaded the issue. When I pressed, he evaded again. When I later took an end run back to the issue, he relented, "My dad worked six days a week. By the time he got home, we were in bed. On Sundays, he either worked in the garden or attended political meetings. There was no time to talk."

"You and your dad didn't talk at all?"

"No."

My dad didn't say much more about that, but I knew this was one present he felt privileged to be able to give.

If we want our children to have a balance between their abilities to earn money and to show love, it will help if both their parents model that balance. Dads in the family are even more important than women in the workplace: The workplace *benefits* from women, but the family *needs* dads.

Obviously, family roles are a family decision—as long as no one is asking for government aid. But if the government is paying money to subsidize anything, it needs to give the greater incentive to involve the parent who has been uninvolved, while simultaneously training both parents in job skills, communication skills, and parenting skills. That's an investment in family unity and in future taxpayers. In contrast, programs like TANF (Temporary Assistance to Needy Families, formerly known as AFDC) and WIC (Women, Infants, and Children) subsidize the exclusion of dads. In effect, they create, as we have seen, future welfare recipients. Or tax spenders.

It also costs the taxpayer less to help two adults under one roof than to help two adults under two roofs. Some states have already recognized this and acted on it. For example, if a teenager in Wisconsin bears a child, she is paid more if the child's father marries her, as opposed to the usual method of paying her more if he isn't around. However, if they have a second child, her payments become less, not more. Again, the unmarried parent has no *right* to taxpayer money; but if taxpayers pay for anything, it should be for rebuilding rather than for destroying.

The Man-in-the-Family Plan helps solve four problems: (1) it gives children their fathers back; (2) it gives women more time to enter the workplace and develop a sense of workplace mastery; (3) it gives children the role model of a mother who takes economic responsibility rather than a mother who is "a man away from welfare"—or without a man and, therefore, *on* welfare; (4) it puts children and emotions and a reason for living back into the lives of men.

The Man-in-the-School Plan

Our inner-city children often go from a mother-only home to a female-only school system and back to a mother-only home, with female childcare personnel and female social workers serving as female frosting on the female-layered cake. **Men are the Rosie the Riveters of parenting: They're brought in only when needed, and considered disposable thereafter.**

The more a child is exposed to mother-only in the home, the more the neighborhood schools have a mandate to balance that exposure with male teachers. Especially male teachers who are comfortable with the male value system.

While many cities are now experimenting with giving black boys black male teachers, that misses the core of the problem. A black child who is already living with a black mother is missing men more than black. Among the males to whom he is exposed in school, there must be blacks, but having him be taught *only* by black males doesn't help him overcome the distrust he might have for white males at an age when that distrust can be melted.

It is not, of course, only the boy who needs male influence; so does the girl. Schools with mostly male teachers, then, should not be only for boys living with mothers, but also for girls living with mothers.

What does this have to do with fathering? The more our children see men loving children, the more they will expect men to love children as dads; **the more our children see men being paid to take responsibility for children, the more respectable it will be for men to do work compatible with their role as dads.**

How, though, do we not only bring more men into the school system, but bring in men who understand the male value system? The Male Teacher Corps is one example. . . .

The Male Teacher Corps / Female Work Corps Exchange

I recommend designing a Male Teacher Corps to bring men from the business community into the school system, and a Female Work Corps to bring female teachers from the school system into the business community and into blue-collar work. This means exposing children to men who work in white-collar and blue-collar jobs, and giving our female teachers time on a construction site, on an assembly line, in corporate management, and even in running a business from their home.

The Male Teacher Corps not only exposes children to men from a variety of professions, but exposes children to men with more risk-taking, entrepreneurial male energy and values, creating a balance between exposure to the male and female value systems. Conversely, it exposes a female teacher not only to men, but to the type of male energy and values that corporate executives, construction workers, assembly-line workers, and truck drivers possess—the type of male energy with which some of her male students will spend most of their lives.

The encouragement of women to consider alternatives other than teaching will help reduce not only the oversupply of females in teaching, but also the tendency for some teachers to treat teaching as their job and their turf. Teachers with multiple experiences are less likely to battle for singular turf.

Reinventing Fatherhood and Motherhood for the Twenty-First Century

Introducing a New Language—"Relationship Language"

In a Stage I survival-focused world, a father needed to be a problem-solver. He needed to "tough it out" by denying feelings. He needed to persuade, argue, debate, set rules, distinguish right from wrong without flexibility. These skills made him "eligible," they brought him a wife and children. In every sense of the word, these skills were his relationship language. Problem is, "toughing it out" fed his loved ones' mouths, but didn't nurture his loved ones' souls.

In a Stage II world, in communities in which survival is mastered enough to create a balance with self-fulfillment, we have the option of "relationship language" that nourishes the soul. Although our grammar schools are teaching a whole generation *computer* language to adjust to the technological needs of a Stage II society, we have neglected to teach this generation *relationship* language and conflict-resolution skills to address the social and psychological needs of a Stage II society. And when it is taught, in countries like Germany, although called "social competence," it focuses on workplace teamwork—still on survival, breadwinner-oriented work goals.[1]

What exactly are these skills? They are skills of not just expressing opinions (schools are now good at this: "Get the kids to express their opinions"), but of articulating the perspectives that others hold until "the others" feel completely understood; they are not just debating skills, but listening skills; not just skills in argument, but skills in empathy.

The first set of Stage I skills prepared us to win in conflict by defeating others; the new skills prepare us to win in conflict by understanding others. The first skills are win-lose; the second skills are win-win. The new skills should not replace the old, but add to them.

The poet Robert Bly explains that before industrialization, men communicated by working together, and this is how a man learned to be a man.[2] Now he must go beyond sharing instructions about how to *do* together to learning from women and others about how to *be* together—to make that transition from human doing to human being. Imparting to our sons instructions about how to perform better for others is very different than sharing feelings about life experiences that make us happy or sad.

It is difficult for men to communicate feelings of disappointment to their wives when men have all their emotional eggs in the basket of their wives' love. The vacuum of no support system is too devastating for most men. Relationship language will not find a fertile ground among men unless we create support systems for men. This is why I encourage every man to become involved in a men's group.

We have seen from the *Parade* magazine survey that fewer teenage children would be having children of their own if they were able to communicate more effectively with their parents. Relationship language requires parental involvement even more than computer language. With computer language, a child has the luxury of actually feeling good about knowing something about which his parents are ignorant; but if she or he is learning to listen in school and is confronted by shouting at home, it creates confusion. This implies outreach programs by the school systems to the parents, and support for the type of connection between sons and fathers that is encouraged by the work of Bly, the New Warriors, and fathers' rights groups.

Prenatal and Parental Education

Research is increasingly showing that our prenatal and first-year environments significantly affect our brain capacity and neural networks. For the government to *require* all parents to obtain prenatal education is more government than I am comfortable with; but if the government is already involved giving taxpayer money to the mother, it must take responsibility for establishing a formula to increase government funding the more the father is involved, and the more the parents participate in prenatal education and nutrition programs, in marital education to prevent conflict, and in marital counseling in times of conflict.

Many changes can occur locally. Besides obvious ones like local education efforts, look around town . . . does a hospital have a "maternity ward"? Or a "Women's Unit" or a "Women's Center"? Just as feminists accurately helped us see that a business club called "the Men's Center" would send women a message that they aren't invited, so a children's hospital called a Women's Center sends dads a message that they aren't invited.

Solution? When that portion of the hospital is instead called a "Birthing Center" then we don't send a message to the dad that his bonding with the child is secondary—that he is just a visitor. "Maternity Ward" prepares the couple, should there be a divorce, for the psychology of mother, child, and visitor. Being a "visitor" at birth is preparation for "visitation" later—not fathering forever. "Birthing Centers" puts the emphasis where it should be—on the infant and its birth. A father and child reunion begins with a father and child union.

When will we know the union is working? When the reunion isn't needed.

What Every Dad Can Do (and Mom, Too)

Prior to broader societal changes encouraging men to be fathers in the twenty-first century in a manner similar to the way we encouraged women to be workers in the twentieth century, what can dads do (and moms, too) that can make them better parents now?

When I see dads being most effective with children, it is usually when they have an intuitive understanding that, for example, **the car trip to and**

from the soccer game is potentially as important as the game itself.
How did the child handle things when someone else cheats, or hogs the ball,
or receives the position the child wanted?

In my own experience both as a stepdad and camp counselor (with the Y
in suburban Ridgewood, New Jersey and the Boys' Clubs in Newark, New
Jersey), I find that most kids open up much more easily when they have the
security of knowing I will listen for a while without judgment. Yet when I
only listen, I find I miss an opportunity to proactively encourage the child to
come up with her or his own solutions. I get the most enthusiasm when I ask
some questions and let the kids chip in with their own ideas. The end result
seems to be an increase in the child's confidence as to how to interpret the
world, how to make connections between a game and life.

Notice that the above example is one from team sports. Daughters are
especially deprived of good team-sports role models. For example, when I
speak with audiences, I will make a "bet" that no one can identify a female
team-sports hero or role model who will be recognized by more than half of
the audience. We can name dozens of nationally recognizable female *individual* sport heroes—female tennis players, gymnasts, ice skaters, track stars—
but not a female *team* sports hero.

Individual sports teach the girl to be dependent only on herself to win;
the positive lessons are self-starting, self-discipline, calling on internal resources without depending on others. The emphasis on herself is primary.
Team sports teach the girl to strike a different balance: She must know when
to shoot the basket herself, and when to pass it off to a teammate, but the
emphasis is always on making herself secondary to the team. Teen sports are
about striking the balance between cooperation and competition.

Individual sports are wonderful for the daughter who is socially dependent and not a good self-starter; team sports are wonderful for the daughter
who is entitled, self-centered, spoiled, or more comfortable with animals
than with humans.

Part of what a good dad can do, then, is to make sure that his daughter
also gets involved with team sports, and to help her with the lessons in life
that are innate to any team empowering itself.

Some dads tell me their sons respond much more positively to criticism
than their daughters—that their daughters seem to take it personally, to give
up. Why? Boys learn very quickly that if they perform, they will receive love.

Our sons are more likely to translate criticism, therefore, as helping them become good performers, perfect their game, and therefore gain respect, approval, and "love." In contrast, there aren't many high school boys trying out for cheerleader for the girls' basketball team (!), so our daughters are much less likely to see themselves getting boys' love by being a good performer.

So how can a dad prepare his daughter to do the type of winning in sports that they both want her to do in life? Start with helping her understand how sports are preparation for life, and encouraging her to help define for him how much she wants to improve and how much she wants to just play. However, her input should be a guideline, not a mandate. As mentioned above, single moms and dads are often especially fearful of making suggestions that their children might interpret as criticism—they are sometimes afraid of losing their children's approval. (Without a spouse, the children are often the only source the single parent has for feeling needed and loved.)

Dads are especially prone to interpret their obligation to be a good role model as always doing what is right. However, even if the dad could do what is right 99 percent of the time, he would be a *worse* role model than a dad who did fewer things right and acknowledged when he was wrong. **Since no one is always right, always *being* right is really a role model for his children feeling inadequate.**

In my personal life, I learned this lesson painfully. My brother was thirteen years younger than I was. I thought that by achieving well in school, being athletic, being student body president, etc., I was creating a good role model for him. In fact, he experienced scrapes with delinquency before he began to successfully achieve. One day, when he became a ski instructor at a very young age, he announced, "Finally, I can do something better than Warren." The fact that he could do many things better than I could is beside the point. The statement shocked me. It created one of those "clicks"—a flash of understanding that I could be a much better role model by sharing more openly with him my shadow side, my faults, my mistakes; asking him to be my teacher rather than being his.

I asked Wayne to teach me skiing. We set up a time in the fall. But it was too late. An avalanche buried my brother in the spring. He died before my plans were realized to become a better role model by being a better learner.

When a dad admits he is wrong or asks for help, he allows the child to see him- or herself as adequate even when she or he is also wrong. It encourages children to make suggestions and, therefore, to discover their creativity because they have a chance of making a contribution.

A father who is always right encourages children who are either imitators or rebels. He encourages children not to take risks for fear they will be wrong. The child who never learns to admit mistakes and say "I'm sorry" misses one of life's crucial lessons. For example, when dealing with a bureaucracy, it is usually more effective to do what needs to be done and then, if an error is made, say, "I'm sorry," rather than to ask permission.

Only when divorce occurs do many dads realize that more of their reading has been to improve the skills of their trade rather than their skills as a parent. From *The Five Key Habits of Smart Dads,*[3] here are some suggestions to help dads strengthen their connection with their children and reinforce their children's emotional security:

- If you have to go out of town, tape-record yourself reading bedtime stories for your children to listen to while you're gone.

- Switch places at the dinner table; have everyone sit in someone else's customary chair and behave like the person whose chair they are in.

- Read your kids' high school textbooks. You'll never be at a loss for a conversation topic.

- On your business card, under your title, insert the line "Father of" followed by the names of your children. The card will make your kids feel they get equal billing with your career.

In Conclusion . . .

Dad-deprived children are to this generation what money-deprived dads were to the Depression generation. Just as the Depression left a generation of dads feeling they never had enough money, so father deprivation is leaving a generation of sons and daughters with different psychic wounds.

Our daughters are often left with an insatiable need for male approval. This psychic wound can lead to a teenage girl being even more likely than most girls to be sexual to please a man rather than for her own pleasure. She can easily be taken in by men who promise a lot but deliver little. It is not uncommon for her to try to keep him by becoming pregnant, or to create a false bond by creating a drug high. Underneath it all, she is in search of a love high to fill her love void.

Sons deprived of their dads are left with a different psychic wound. If their dads are successful, they want to be like them, but don't know enough about them to know how. If their dads have been badmouthed, the sons internalize the inferiority. No matter how good a mother is, it is virtually impossible for her to fill the psychological hole in a boy who doesn't receive daily approval from the adult male version of himself. Thus many boys brought up without dads feel rudderless and rejected. Gangs are poor substitutes for dads.

In brief, sending a father-deprived child into the world and assuming everything is okay because the dad provides money is like sending a drunken driver onto the highway and assuming everything is okay because the gas is paid for. It doesn't mean that the drunken driver will not get to his or her destination. It just means that the risks are enormous. And the consequences of failure are forever.

I wish I could say that an individual dad who wanted to be with his children could do so. Unfortunately, millions of men around the world are prevented from being with their children because a mother unilaterally feels that the children are better off with her—and the judicial system makes it almost impossible for a father to share life with his child if the mother doesn't want him to do so. That's why, just as women needed the help of the law to enter the workplace in the twentieth century, men will need the help of the law to love their children in the twenty-first century. Part II explains just how deep this discrimination runs, and what we must confront unconsciously and consciously, politically and legally to bring our dads home again.

The Politics of Bringing Dad Home Again

Introduction

Imagine a famous male attorney. He works ninety hours a week. He has primary parent time. He is now involved in a case that will make or break his career. He is on TV worldwide every day.

His former wife, a fit mother, works forty hours a week. She feels he has no time for the children. She asks for primary parent time temporarily. Her goal is shared parent time. The male attorney refuses. He wants the children, though the world can see he has virtually no time to be with them—he's always on TV. On top of this, he wants child-support payments from a woman who makes a fraction of his income.

Now imagine the woman—a good mother—being refused temporary primary or shared parent time. In this case, I would support the feminists and the media criticizing this man as being an egomaniac with a need to control and a desire to bleed his poorer ex-wife's pocketbook, deprive her of the children, and deprive the children of their mother.

With two exceptions, this actually happened. The first exception? The "male" is a female—Marcia Clark; and the "female" is a male—Gordon Clark. Second, the media and feminists did *not* condemn the mother, who had no time, for wanting to deprive her children of a father who had time. Nor did they condemn a woman who made more in a one-hour speech than her ex-husband made in a week for wanting him to supply her with money rather than the children with love.

Instead, despite all the lawyer jokes, the most powerful female lawyer in the world at that time was painted as the victim. The world was told she should not be punished by being deprived of her children "just because she's a professional woman."[1]

The media committed two fundamental errors: First, they put the mother's rights before the children's rights. Second, they rarely mentioned that "deprivation-of-children" was Standard Operating Punishment for the "Working Dad." It was being protested only now that it was depriving a mother of children.

This attitude derived from feminism, but it is not the feminism that was. . . .

The Feminism That Was

Most American children suffer too much mother and too little father.
GLORIA STEINEM, AUGUST 26, 1971[2]

When Gloria Steinem made this comment, I was on the Board of Directors of the National Organization for Women in New York City. I supported NOW because mainstream feminists like Gloria knew that balanced children needed more of a balance between mother and father.

My first conflict with NOW erupted in the mid-1970s when NOW chapters increasingly rejected father involvement by rejecting shared parent time as the preferred arrangement after divorce. NOW wanted only mothers to have the choice of parent-time arrangement. But primary mother time meant more mother, less father, the opposite of what Gloria *had* favored. As both Gloria and NOW focused more on mothers' rights and less on children's, my ethical red flags popped up.

Meantime, fathers' rights groups were founded on Gloria's principle: "Most American children suffer too much mother and too little father."

Before I begin, two caveats. Most mothers want fathers equally involved, many want dads to be more involved than they are, and many do *not* expect child support from dads who are equally involved. *Father and Child Reunion* views these moms as part of the solution—the reunion planning committee. Conversely, many fathers have wronged their children. They are part of the problem.

Second, a father's right to a child must always be the secondary issue. *Primary is the child's right to both parents.* Whenever we focus only on fathers' rights, we eventually undermine fathers' rights because we lose sight of their primary purpose: children's needs. The same with mothers' rights. Both parents' rights must exist *primarily* to assist the parents in fulfilling their responsibilities. Primarily does not mean exclusively. When the virtue of focusing on a child's needs gets taken too far, it too becomes a vice.

Both parents' rights must be in balance so children can grow up with a balance between both parents. Part II focuses on fathers' and children's rights to each other for the sole purpose of bringing them in balance with mothers' rights—so children can grow up with a balance between both parents.

6

Men's ABC Rights

Men's ABC Rights and Responsibilities: Abortion, Birth, Caring

In the old days, a woman's biology was a woman's destiny. Not good. In this chapter it will become clear why, today, a woman's biology is a *man's* destiny.

If you want your adolescent son to be cautious about having sex, and you've been warning him about AIDS to no avail ("Come on, Dad . . . Mom, I don't know a single heterosexual who has died of AIDS, do you?"), have him also read this chapter. I will make it clear why I am not being hyperbolic when I say that today, when your son puts his penis into a woman's body, he puts his life in her hands. Here's why. . . .

This pendulum-swing from "a woman's biology as a woman's destiny" to "a woman's biology as a man's destiny" includes **women today having the right to abort or to sue for support.** It is due, in part, to three options that only women have generated, what I will call women's ABC Rights and Responsibilities:

1. **Abortion;**

2. **Birth-control method** (pill, diaphragm, IUD, etc.) and **Believability;**

3. **Caring arrangement** (adoption; invite dad to parent; parent alone; require dad to pay, but prevent him from parenting; parent alone without informing dad, but require dad to pay "after the fact").

In contrast, men have generated three "slightly different" options that are available to your son:

1. **Agree**

2. **Agree**

3. **Agree**

If we are to generate three equivalent options for your son, we might call them men's ABC Rights and Responsibilities—your son's R&R when he and a woman mutually consent to create a child—or mutually create a fetus by mistake.

It might seem strange to talk about your son's rights when we are more likely to hear some version of "A man can just have sex and disappear—a woman has to live with the consequences, right?" So before I outline why I believe he needs ABC Rights, let's take a look at the status of his rights today.

A Man Can Just Have Sex and Disappear, But a Woman Has to Live with the Consequences, Right?

Many women have said to me, "Women are more cautious about sex before marriage because a single man can just have sex and disappear; a woman has to live with the consequences." Is that true? No. In fact, as we have seen, a man cannot just walk away: He's legally responsible to support the child. His wages can be garnisheed—whether or not he would have preferred an abortion. It is the woman who can legally "walk away"—by getting an abortion.

A reality check: Name one real-life man you personally know who would walk away from a child which he and the woman *who was his choice for marriage* decided *together* to have? If you think you know one, have you asked *him* if the decision to have the child was also his?

Male responsibilities are built into *every* state law. Most states have some version of these Ohio laws that Planned Parenthood does a good job of explaining in a brochure to young men:[1]

Here is a summary of an *unwed* dad's *legal* responsibilities:

- If the *woman* decides to keep the child the *father must pay* for the child—for the next eighteen to twenty-one years . . . even if the mother prevents him from seeing the child.

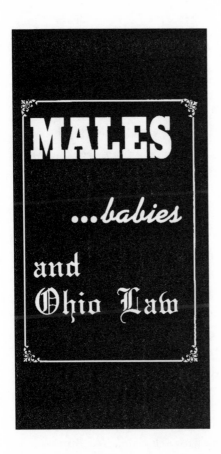

MALES

...babies

and

Ohio Law

- A mother can raise the child by herself and sue the man for child support *without ever even mentioning to the father that the child is his.* She can wait until the child is twenty-three and *then* sue him for eighteen years of child support. At that time, he must submit to a blood test and, if shown to be the father, he can be required to pay all birth expenses and child support since the child's birth.

- He must pay no matter what he earns, whether the mother is or was a good or bad mother, and whether or not the mother uses or used the support money wisely or on drugs.

In brief, a man can "have sex and leave" only if a woman lets him. In reality, it is the woman, not the man, who has the option to "have sex and leave."

How does this translate into everyday life, including the lives of men who are married and previously married? Just a few examples:

ITEM. A Wisconsin court ruled that a man's occupation didn't produce enough income to support two households—his and his ex-wife's. They ordered him to change occupations.[2]

ITEM. A father discovers he has been paying child support for a child that he had been fraudulently told was his. The child support was not recoverable.[3]

ITEM. Pennsylvania courts ruled that an estranged mother can be relieved of child support through college,[4] but also ruled that an estranged father cannot, even though the child "unilaterally renounced his relationship" with the father.[5]

Can a Man's Fatherhood Be Legally Denied?

A married woman had an affair with a single man, Michael Hirschensohn. Blood tests showed that Michael was the father. However, the court ruled that Michael did not even legally "exist" as the father—the woman's husband was declared to be the father.[6] Michael had no choices.

In contrast, the mother's choices ranged from having an abortion without informing either her husband or Michael, to having her husband support a child that he never knew wasn't his, to divorcing her husband and suing Michael for eighteen years of child support.

In brief, when a woman decides to have an affair, that's only the *first* choice she gets. Can you imagine a married man choosing between the child's real mother and his wife? Or *forcing his wife to pay so he can raise his mistress's child?* Or divorcing his wife and suing his mistress for child support? These choices are what makes it a myth that babies have less impact on fathers than mothers.

Are the Laws About "Choice" In Tune with What America Wants?

In a nationwide poll, 90 percent of married *women* said that women's reproductive rights have unfairly curtailed men's. How? Married women felt that a man had the *right* to know if his partner was considering an abortion. They felt he should have both the right to know at the consideration stage *and* the right to be given a chance to participate in the decision.[7] Two-thirds of the unmarried women felt this way, too.

Fifty-seven percent of married women also felt that *the man had the right to refuse permission for the abortion.* Unmarried women disagreed. Ironically, men were not polled as to their rights. But in a separate statewide poll in Ohio, 72 percent of men felt that a father had a legal right to demand that his unborn child not be aborted.[8] Note that this implies a desire on the part of these men to take responsibility, not abort responsibility.

Pro-lifers and pro-choicers have become so preoccupied with defining the rights of mothers versus the state and the fetus that everyone has forgotten the rights of the fathers. The interest groups have lost touch with what makes common sense to people who don't wear blinders for a living, and since only their voices have spoken up, they are the only ones legislators hear.

These examples are but the tip of the iceberg as to how we have made an unnoticed transition from the Era of Women's Biology as Women's Destiny to the Era of Woman's Biology as Men's Destiny.

Let's dig beneath the tip, looking at each of men's ABC Rights and the need for them, remembering that each of men's rights comes with a parallel responsibility: the responsibility to be a partner with the woman in choice of methods of birth control, abortion, or caring for the child—decisions not only about being a provider and protector, but about being a nurturer and connector, not only to the child, but to the woman with whom he created the child.

The resistance most often encountered to a man becoming a partner in the abortion decision is the belief that women have these rights to choose because it's a woman's body that's used. Is that, though, the real issue?

Men's "A" Right and Responsibility: Abortion, or the Fallacy of "It's a *Woman's* Right to Choose Because It's a Woman's Body"

> *Human rights have historically derived from the Constitution or from God; but the rights of fathers are derived from women.*
>
> SAM DOWNING, FATHER[9]

**OUR BODIES
OUR BUSINESS**

6

Ms. *Magazine, July/August 1989.*
This graphic was used to frame articles on abortion

Dear Ann Landers: . . . If a woman has the right to choose an abortion, shouldn't the man have the right to demand that she end an accidental pregnancy rather than pay $100,000 over the next twenty years to support a child he will probably never know? . . .

MEDIATING IN THE MIDWEST

Dear Mediating: . . . Since it's the woman's body we're talking about, she should decide what happens to it.

ANN LANDERS[11]

A woman's body *is* hers to control. When she chooses to share it with a man, she exercises that control. He makes a parallel choice. If together they produce a fetus, equality would dictate joint rights and joint responsibilities. **Male-female fusion does not create women's rights. It creates a fusion of rights.** It does not produce what German feminists call Reproduktionsautonomie, or reproduction *autonomy,* but reproductive *interdependence.*

The motto "It's a woman's right to choose because it's a woman's body at stake" implies that if a man's body is also at stake, he would share that right to choose.

Is a man's body at stake? Any time a man is asked to work to pay child support, he is using his body, his time, his life—not for nine months, but for a minimum of eighteen to twenty-one years. So the motto of the feminist with integrity is, "It's a woman's and a man's right to choose because it is a woman's and a man's body at stake."

A woman has no right to a unilateral choice that affects the rest of a man's life any more than a man would have the right to a unilateral choice that affects the rest of a woman's life. That's why, for starters, rape is a crime.

When only men could register to vote, we required only men to register for the draft. Today both sexes can vote, but only men must register for the draft.

We are at a unique moment in history—when a *woman's* body is affected, we say the choice is hers; but when a boy's body is affected, we say the choice is *not* his—the law requires our eighteen-year-old sons to register for the draft, and therefore to accept potential death-if-needed.

Even before the draft, the exclusive right of only men to vote came with the expectation that no woman was expected to die for what only men voted for. Women are the only sex or race having the right to freedom without the *obligation* to die for that freedom.

But . . . *is* the "woman's right to choose" really based on it being her body—or is that just the excuse? One man wrote me, "My doctor wants my wife to sign a consent form for my vasectomy, but she can get an abortion without my signature."[12] He couldn't understand why he couldn't even *prevent* a pregnancy without her permission, yet she could—without his permission—abort a fetus they had both created.

Moreover, the man with the vasectomy was being denied a decision about an organ of his body. Biologically, a fetus is more like a parasite than a body organ: it grows into a complete and separate human being, has an elaborate system designed to isolate its immune system from the mother's, including blood isolated from the mother's through the Eustachian tube and the placenta, is genetically unique, and has a mind of its own.[13]

Nevertheless . . . *if* the woman's right to choose based on the fetus being in her body really was the guiding principle, what decisions would you make as the judge in these frozen-embryo cases? . . .

The "Petri Generation": Questions Frozen Embryos Will Soon Be Asking

ITEM. Mary Sue Davis and her husband used their eggs and sperm to create embryos in a petri dish. Then they filed for divorce. In a battle for custody of the embryos, the judge awarded custody of *all* of them to the woman. The judge rationalized that although the embryos were only four to eight cells, they were "people."[14]

15

Had the judge considered the embryos property, everyone would have seen it as sexist to award them only to the mother; but the second they were ruled to be "people," we became blind to the sexism of awarding them only to the mother. We can see that **the slogan "Our Bodies/Our Business" is just a smoke screen since we still assume the mother gets the child even when her body has not been used.**

But it gets even more unbelievable. . . .

The excuse for the embryos being granted to the mother was that she wanted to create children from them. The husband objected to her using them. They weren't in her body; but she won. However, when both of them got remarried, *their positions reversed:* She no longer wanted to use the embryos to create children, but he did, because his new wife was infertile. Nevertheless, *he still could not get the embryos—even though he was in exactly the position that had allowed her to win the embryos.* There could hardly be a case that could more completely prove the totality of women's rights with regard to children—or anything that might ever become a child.

ITEM. Mr. and Mrs. Del Zio's sperm and egg had created an embryo in a laboratory petri dish, but the hospital mistakenly destroyed the embryo. Mr. and Mrs. Del Zio both sued for damages. The court awarded Mrs. Del Zio $50,000 and awarded Mr. Del Zio $3.[16]

When the embryo was in a petri dish, the woman's rights were still more than 15,000 times more important than the man's. She was awarded psychological damages, he wasn't. Why? Because the law is designed to protect women more than men. When it comes to parenting, about 15,000 times more.

So, in the future, when hospitals sponsor ads to "Join the Petri Generation," when demographers tell us we have a "frozen-embryo boom," and when pro-embryo feminists claim maternal custody is in "the best interests of the embryo," there are a few questions the Petri Generation will be asking. Questions like, "Why were daddies' rights frozen out?" Daddies will have a hard time explaining, "When I was a young daddy, we never even thought of fathers' rights. Fathers' rights were, well . . . in the embryonic stage, ha, ha." Perhaps the Petri Generation will try to understand the "In and Out Generation," but these are the questions frozen embryos will be asking.

How Women's Rights Are Creating Men's Rights

ITEM. When two lesbians fought for primary parent time, the woman whose body was *not* used was granted it. The feminist National Center for Lesbian Rights and the ACLU both fought for the parent-time rights of the woman whose body did not bear the child—calling their advocacy "cutting-edge."[17]

18

Lesbians' Custody Fights Test Family Law Frontier

By DAVID MARGOLICK
Special to The New York Times

Interesting. When the body *not* being used is a man's, feminists say that it's exactly because his body is not being used that he doesn't have equal rights; when the body not being used is a woman's, feminists declare that she should have equal rights.

Both sides of the contradiction are considered "progressive" and "liberal" for two reasons: A woman's rights are being championed, and feminists are doing the championing. The contradiction is not liberal, but hypocritical.

We saw this pattern (of men's rights being supported by women when their own interests were at stake) when second wives started fighting first wives when they believed first wives had commanded too much in child-support payments or alimony that was now depriving them of that income. We see this also when a woman who hires a surrogate mother suddenly finds herself in the man's position when the surrogate mother says, "My body, my child," as in the Baby M case. . . .

Why Surrogate Mothering Destroys the Argument That a Woman's Right to Choose Is Based on the Fetus Being in Her Womb

ITEM. In the Baby M case, the judge ruled that the woman who bore an infant and used her womb (the surrogate) had no rights. The rights were given

to Mrs. Stern, who used neither her womb nor an egg, but made the contract.[19]

Mrs. Stern was awarded parenthood of Baby M even though she contributed nothing—neither womb *nor egg*. At most, she contributed what a
man usually contributes—money (and some of that was likely produced by
her husband). She got custody because she—or she and her husband—created the contract. This has been the case in the 4,000 or so surrogate births
in the United States since the late 1970s.[20]

In surrogate-parenting cases, courts make it clear that a long-term commitment to a child is more important than the womb.[21]

Since men and women can equally commit themselves contractually,
this leaves them as equals. **Equality was what threatened the feminists.**
To such a degree that almost all feminist organizations are opposed to surrogate motherhood.[22]

Feminists saw that if a surrogate mother used her body and didn't have
"the right to choose," their whole argument—that a woman's right to choose
is based on the fact that her body is being used—falls flat on its face. They
saw that 99 percent of women were still using their own wombs, and that if
using her womb could be the basis of women's rights, this would leave, practically speaking, almost all women with all the power to choose, and men
with none. It is ironic that a movement that made its reputation championing the irrelevance of biological differences when those differences were
to most women's *dis*advantage immediately returned to biological deter-
minism when those differences were to most women's advantage.

It is also ironic that a movement making its reputation on a woman's
right to choose in the precise area of reproduction would oppose surrogate
motherhood, which allows a woman who has something wrong with her
uterus the choice to still have a child; which allows the woman who cannot
produce eggs to still have a child; which could allow the woman who feared
she would jeopardize career advancement by becoming pregnant to have a
surrogate mother bear the child, have her husband be the primary caretaker,
and herself be the primary breadwinner. All the feminist ideals of expanding
women's options would seem to be enhanced by surrogate motherhood.

Is all of this, then, a contract fight? Precisely. The right to choose is not
based on the womb, but on the intent of the contract. When a woman and a

man contribute a sperm and an egg to sex, they are the ones who created a contract of equal responsibility and equal rights. The fact that it is the woman's womb being used does not increase her rights any more than it increases the surrogate mother's rights. As the female author of a book on surrogate mothers puts it, "If female hormones can be used as an excuse to break contracts, we will never have a woman in the White House."[23]

When a couple is dating, their implied contract is short-term. A woman who has a fetus in her womb does not have the right to change that short-term contract any more than the surrogate mother has the right to change the contract.

We would not think of allowing a man to determine a woman's life merely because a fetus he helped create was in her womb; why then would we allow a woman to determine a man's life merely because a fetus he helped create is in her womb? Any law that allows this double standard violates the Fourteenth Amendment's provision for equal protection of both sexes under the law. And a law that allows either sex to unilaterally change a short-term contract into a long-term contract breaks contract law.

Why Surrogacy Cannot Be Prohibited . . . Even by Feminists

Surrogacy differs from abortion in that it increases options by creating life rather than increasing options by destroying life—or potential life. Therefore, it will be harder to stop it than to stop abortion, or even birth control. It is also harder to stop surrogacy because it provides such a crucial option for a woman whose uterus is damaged, or for an infertile couple. If the state makes a law against it, it will merely drive the couple to another state. If the federal government makes a law against it, it will merely drive it underground to be done among "friends." Laws against surrogacy will make criminals out of couples who want to create families. In brief, prohibiting surrogacy is ineffective at best; dysfunctional at worst.

The right and responsibility to be involved in a decision about whether to have an abortion implies rights and responsibilities to decide what to do if the decision is *not* to have an abortion—or to care for the child. That's the "C" right and responsibility: caring. But men cannot be equal participants in that decision until they have equal rights and responsibilities to prevent the process from even beginning—or birth control.

Men's "B" Rights and Responsibilities: Birth Control and Believability

Some people say men have their equivalent of a birth-control pill: a condom. First, both sexes have condoms. If the pill were to be eliminated because women have condoms, women's justified outrage would make it apparent that the condom is no pill. If the condom were a substitute for the pill, the pill wouldn't be selling to women.

Of course, a couple *can* put a condom on a man even if a woman uses the pill. But in practice, both sexes are often hesitant to interrupt the flow and spoil the romance and buildup of passion with finding a condom, opening the package, unraveling the condom, and putting it on a penis that might be shrinking as fast as the condom is expanding.

For both sexes, condoms are a "should," and a "should" mixes with passion like oil mixes with water. For some couples, condoms are to intercourse what putting latex over one's lips and tongue would be to kissing. It mixes with passion like, well, like condoms mix with sex! Condoms do make rational sense, but in love, we often do what does *not* make rational sense—including, ironically, the decision to have children!

To be fair, though, the hesitation of men is often greater than women's even when women already know whether or not they are using birth control. Why? For many men, intercourse with a condom feels like showering in a raincoat. And disconnection of physical feelings means disconnection of emotional feelings. He feels less intimacy. And men, with less permission to be intimate with each other, crave intimacy from women.

And there's something deeper going on. . . .The first time he has intercourse with a woman is often the end of about 150 risks of rejection (between eye contact and intercourse). **To him, intercourse is the woman finally saying, "I accept you."** He fears that any interruption in the flow will lead to the woman changing her mind, thus returning him to his fear of rejection and his status of being not-yet-accepted. This is one reason sex is more to men than just sex: It is acceptance . . . or the end of the period of rejection.

Once sex is understood from this perspective for the man, it becomes

more apparent why many a man's penis turns soft during the process of condom finding, package opening, condom unraveling and condom fitting . . .
the fears of her losing her passion, changing her mind, and his being rejected
are registered by his penis, which thus retreats before the condom arrives.

No matter what the reasons, though, the birth-control pill is something
millions of women would be unwilling to discard for a condom. The birth-
control pill has been said to have freed women's lives more than any other
single factor; this was never said of the condom. If men had a birth-control
pill and women didn't, well . . . that's a political impossibility.

The existence of a female-only pill is politically possible partly because
of the second of those two "Bs" in the Women's ABC Rights—Believability.
We have socialized men to trust women, and socialized women to expect
this trust. If you are a woman, you can get a sense of the power of this trust
by imagining there being a birth-control pill only for men. The man says,
"Don't worry, I'm on the pill." Would you trust him?

Most women of whom I ask this question say they would laugh.[24] Once
they get to know a man, that changes, but men are socialized to trust women
until evidence to the contrary surfaces; women are socialized to be suspicious of men until an individual man earns trust.

Underlying the second "B" is **the unconscious assumption of the
moral superiority of women**—that men can trust women to tell the
truth more than women can trust men; that a woman would never consciously or unconsciously become pregnant to get a man to marry her and
support her and the child, yet a man would lie to a woman because he "can
just walk away." So if she says she's on birth control (and doesn't have her-
pes, etc.) and he still reaches for a condom, he is violating the unwritten
code of women being inherently worthy of trust.

Suppose she says she's on the pill but doesn't say anything about sexually
transmitted diseases (STDs). Why do some men not use a condom to prevent STDs? For some men, it's because they know they can urinate afterward to minimize the risk. For others, an STD is a risk many men are willing
to take with at least some women at some times. But a man who chooses to
risk an STD should not be required to risk a lifetime of supporting a child
when, as we will see below, the technology of a men's birth-control pill is
within reach this decade should we choose to prioritize the research.

It is difficult—almost impossible—to feel empathy for almost any negative consequences a man experiences in connection with sex. Why? Think about it. We'd rather allow our children to watch a Western with two people killing each other than an X-rated movie with two people having intercourse. When we have this "I'd rather have my kids witness murder than sex" attitude toward sex, and then make it the responsibility of boys to initiate it, we are setting up our sons to be the less-trusted sex. We are setting ourselves up to feel hardened toward any negative outcomes a boy or man experiences after pursuing sex. When we feel, "men, sex, that's all they're after," and "men will do anything and say anything to get sex," we are not exactly setting up men for either empathy or believability.

When all these factors work together in our psyche, and almost no man can express any of them to a woman (although most men recognize each of them once articulated for them), they make us want to offer our daughters every possible option even as we overlook our sons.

None of this implies that the great majority of women are not trustworthy—so this trust *is* almost always warranted. But "almost always" is not always. . . .

The "Trick and Sue" Law: Female-as-Kryptonite

Dear Ann Landers: . . . My twenty-one-year-old sister is three months pregnant. "Lisa" is not married and doesn't want to be. She has had several miserable relationships and despises men, but she wants a family. . . . When dad asked if she knew who the father was, she said, "Of course. I picked him out. It was no love affair. He thought I was on the pill." . . . Set me straight, Ann. . . .

SAM (SAN JOSE)

Dear Sam: . . . She needs to know that the baby's father is legally responsible for child support, even though she deceived him. . . .

ANN LANDERS[25]

Frank Serpico (commemorated in the movie *Serpico*), was able to successfully untangle the complex web of corruption in the New York City Police Department virtually single-handed. Yet, when a woman acknowledged lying that she was using birth control in order to purposely trick him into fathering her child, her legal rights to trick him and sue for a mother subsidy were so secure that she was eventually able to accomplish what all the corrupt New York City police could not—getting Serpico out of New York. Here's how she did it.

After being shot by fellow officers afraid of having their corruption exposed by Serpico, Serpico was handicapped and receiving a disability pension. The woman was allowed to have the child, keep the child, and get $945 a month in child support, virtually all of Serpico's disability pension, forcing him to flee the country because he couldn't afford to pay the child support.[26] In so doing, he left the one place he knew—New York City—where he had repeatedly risked his life and had become a hero.

Frank Serpico learned that finding proof of police corruption helped lead to its partial defeat, but even the woman's own admission that she had lied led not to her defeat, but his. And her lies were not called corruption, they were called motherhood. This corruption of motherhood was sanctified by law: what I call the "trick and sue" law. Superman should meet such Kryptonite.

Superman didn't. But Jack Kent Cooke was no Clark Kent, and he did. He was only the owner of the Washington Redskins. When his womanfriend got pregnant, he agreed to marry her. But only on the condition that she sign a prenuptial agreement and abort the first-trimester fetus she was carrying. She agreed to do it before the wedding. But after the wedding, she told him she had kept the fetus and wanted the child. He insisted that she end the pregnancy; she refused and, *four weeks later,* they separated. She carried the infant to term.

Suzanne sued for $15 million, plus $18,000 a month in alimony and child support.[27] She received a $75,000 annual stipend, a Jaguar, and the use for five years of Jack's corporate apartment in the Watergate complex. For each day of marriage, then, she was paid roughly a half-million dollars. That's what she got. What did he get? A broken contract. A child he contracted not to have. A broken marriage. And, perhaps, a shorter life—he died nine years later.

Rulings like this also hurt women. Cooke soon disinherited all his former wives.

This is an international problem. In Israel, fathers are suing mothers for having children unilaterally, without consideration for the father's desires.

On their 1987 honeymoon, Jack (about to leave for Bel air
with his bride) was unaware that Suzanne was still pregnant.

The men call themselves Fathers by Force. A frequent complaint is that the women have "lied and said they were using contraceptives when, in fact, they were planning to have a child all along. Then, they successfully sued for paternity and child-support payments."[29] However, the main focus of the Israeli fathers is not on issues of deceit, but on taking legal measures to recoup the financial and emotional damages they incurred when the women with whom they were involved decided unilaterally to have a child.[30]

When a government requires a man to support a child he was tricked into creating, that government subsidizes fraud. No, it is worse than that: It subsidizes the woman using a man's body for eighteen to twenty-one years without his consent.

Fortunately, there is a solution that allows the father to take responsibility for preventing that from occurring. That is, it is finally profitable for private industry to develop a men's birth-control pill, a process the government could jump-start by providing more substantial incentives, as it has in the human genome project.

Here's why it's possible, and why the most commonly stated objections are either outdated or soon will be . . . if there's a will.

Is a Men's Birth-Control Pill a Viable Solution?

Nothing freed women more than the women's birth-control pill. And, because most women are trustworthy, the female pill also gave considerable freedom to men. Nothing will free men more than a men's birth-control pill. And a men's pill also frees a woman, from being the only one subjected to hormone manipulation. It allows a couple to rotate taking the pill, giving each of their bodies a rest. As men share this responsibility, the woman experiences him more as a partner from the moment of conception—or a partner in preventing the moment of conception!

A men's pill is far behind a woman's for many reasons. Drug companies have felt women wouldn't trust a man to actually be on the pill just because he said he was. And they've felt men wouldn't take the pill because they don't perceive birth control to be their responsibility.

There are also technical concerns. When I taught in the Department of Reproductive Medicine at the University of California in San Diego back in the 1980s, I saw how many medical doctors thought the development of a male pill would be so much more difficult than a female pill because a female pill required stopping only one egg per month while a male pill required stopping millions of sperm every day.

It's difficult for a lot of us guys to understand that millions of sperm aren't that much more powerful than a single egg! (This was before I wrote *The Myth of Male Power!*) I'll get to the serious side of those technical concerns in a minute, but first the psychological concerns, starting with trust. . . .

Trust *is* a problem before a relationship has begun, especially toward a less-educated, transient, younger man. Once a man and woman are in a relationship, though, as the most recent multicultural study (2000) finds, only 2 percent of women do not trust men to tell the truth about being on birth control.[32] So, aside from one-night stands, trust is not an issue. And for one-night stands when trust *is* an issue, many *men* will want to take the precaution of a birth-control pill, especially if the man has income. For these men, of course, a pill is a highly affordable insurance policy.

What about the concerns that men won't take the pill because they don't perceive birth control to be their responsibility? Despite the enormous drawbacks of condoms and vasectomies, the Population Center for Research in Reproduction at the University of Washington finds that "approximately one-third of contraceptives in the USA are used by men."[33] One-third of the responsibility is extraordinary when we consider both that only women have the pill and what I mentioned above about the reasons men are more reluctant than women to use condoms. And besides, to the degree that men are not taking responsibility, the pill's convenience creates an appealing transition.

The market for men whose everyday lives have been completely altered by not having a men's birth-control pill is huge. There are three groups of men, each a market of millions, whose lives have been thus affected. First, millions of men are paying child support, sometimes for children they cannot see, and usually for children for whom they have second-class-citizen-type rights. These men will deliver a powerful message to their sons about the value of birth control potency. And their sons, with hormones making them impatient with *condom interruptus,* will become a market for a pill's *anxiety reductus.*

Second, one of the best-kept secrets I uncovered in the process of starting hundreds of men's groups around the U.S. is how many men said "Me, too" once one man in the group was brave enough to volunteer something like this scenario, from Kit:

> My wife and I had an agreement to not have a child, although we both knew it was me who didn't want one. She said she was on the pill, but suddenly she became pregnant. She admitted she had forgotten to take the pill, but the look in her eyes—both afraid of my

disapproval and hopeful of my approval—and then her letting me know it was "meant to be," that she couldn't bear getting an abortion, she could "feel it inside" her, her hormones were being triggered, I'd be a great Dad, she'd be devoted, it would bond us, we'd work it out. . . . Well, by the time she'd finished, I found myself unable to destroy her with my truth. Not only did I agree, I tried to seem enthusiastic.

What struck me was that, in many groups, this did not come up at all in the first six months or year. But yet, once one man spoke up about this, other stories poured out of the woodwork, each man asking for reassurance that this would never slip out beyond the group, that there be no jokes at social functions. . . . The other men felt relieved not being the only one, although anger and helplessness also surfaced. It reminded me a lot of the way women in many of the first women's groups responded when they shared first stories of sexual harassment, rape, incest, and date rape. Among what must be millions of these men is an enormous market for a men's birth-control pill.

Third, when random DNA tests are taken of babies, about 10 percent turn out *not* to be the child of the father the mother declared.[34] Since one father often has two or three children, this implies that about 15 to 20 percent of all fathers are spending their lives supporting at least one child they were deceived into thinking was theirs. The level of emotional betrayal can be felt only by a woman who imagines herself working for years at a job she didn't like but kept because it earned more, retiring later than she wants, only to someday discover it was another woman's child and her husband chose her to raise it because she could best supply the income. If it is even just 15 percent of all fathers who have this experience, once this other "best-kept secret" is revealed, it implies a huge market for a men's birth-control pill.

Is part of the problem that some of these facts are not known to men? Yes. But pharmaceutical companies advertise, and men learn. Every month men absorb new facts about computers, cars, and sports. And increasingly, men are also showing interest in Viagra, Rogaine and all sorts of, er . . . "personal growth." More seriously, though, when *Men's Health* magazine is read by enough serious male consumers to attract enough advertisers to make *Ad Weekly*'s list of the top ten hottest publications of the 1990s, that's the pharmaceutical companies' green light.

Now for the technical concerns—that a female pill has to block only one egg every month versus a male pill blocking millions of sperm every day. To make an extremely technical discussion readable, what scientists are now working on is some combination of hormones and compounds that, together with testosterone, suppress sperm without creating a man who's too horny. The idea is to prevent the sperm from being born, so to speak.

The problem of the power of the 20 million to 250 million sperm, then, is solved by not letting them even become sperm. But obviously, every basic solution has consequences. The process works in most men, but not all men; it works more effectively in Asian men than Caucasian men, most likely because of Asian men's less-fatty diets.[35]

Is it possible to stop sperm that crash the party, especially those stubborn little sperm that survive suppressants? Yes. Prevention is not the male pill's last stand. For example, the drug nifedipine has recently been found to be able to prevent sperm from binding to a woman's egg. And nifedipine is no untested drug—it's been around for years, playing hero to people at risk of heart attacks.[36] It's a calcium blocker. Many prescription drugs—from calcium channel blockers like nifedipine to antidepressants—can inhibit either sex drive or reproduction in one way or another.

So there you have it—so many sperm, so many enemies. Where are all these enemies when we need them? Well, they're getting closer.

The most advanced form of men's birth control as of 2000 requires injections every three to four months—a lot better than it used to be (every couple of days). But the actual pill won't be available to the average consumer until drug companies get involved. Scientists do the basic science, drug companies package the formulation in pill form.

Until about the year 2000, drug companies were almost uniformly male-pill shy, in part out of fear of male-pill-buying shyness, and in part out of fear of male-pill-users' lawsuits. However, drug companies such as Bayer, the makers of the nifedipine drug Adalat, are taking a second look.[37] And the European drug companies Organon and Schering, producers of female birth-control pills, have just committed to investing in a male birth-control pill.

Will their lawsuit fears materialize to the point of making them back off in the future as they have in the past, when they looked at the lawsuits resulting from the female pill and breast implants? I predict not. As a rule, men are less prone to sue as long as they know the risks ahead of time and no woman or child in their family is hurt. The government can help by creating a ceiling on the size of lawsuits.

The government can also help by funding basic research, paving the way for pharmaceutical and universities' research opportunities. Currently, the World Health Organization has conducted successful trials and the National Institutes of Health is providing funding. The pursuit is central enough to every family's freedom to create the family they wish that it is justifiable to initiate on every level, in every avenue.

A men's birth-control pill adds to women's options (to take or not take the pill), protects women's bodies (by allowing men to share the risk), and begins the Era of the Multi-Option Woman and the Multi-Option Man, as opposed to our current era: the Era of the Multi-Option Woman and the No Option Man. It allows men to share both responsibilities and rights, ending the era of telling a man he must pay without a vote in what he's paying for.

Men's ABC Rights and Responsibilities involve men's right to a vote in the birthing process from the beginning, and men's responsibility to share the burdens—from the beginning. The current system is like denying a woman the vote but requiring her to pay the taxes. Its effect is not just that a man who puts his penis into a woman's body puts his life in her hands, but that a woman who puts her body around a man's penis puts choice in her own hands.

In a democracy, a government's policies are rarely questioned until the underlying assumptions that create them are questioned. The female-only pill is grounded in assumptions that appear contradictory: on the one hand, the assumptions of women's rights and options being the ones most worthy of funding; on the other hand, the assumptions of birth control being women's responsibility, grounded in the assumption of children being women's responsibility and women's biology as women's destiny.

In reality, the female-only pill gives women the right not to have children, thus wiping out the entire mandate of responsibility. However, by keeping the *appearance* of responsibility, the territory is ceded to her should she want it. This is like saying men have the right not to produce income, but if they choose to, the territory is theirs should they want it.

Once a man is in on the ground floor with rights and responsibilities for birth control, he has an investment in the process we want him to have an investment in—being a partner in nurturing the fetus to become a child, if that is his choice, and caring for the child of his choice. To see whether that's viable for the future, let's start with what's happening now. . . .

Men's "C" Right and Responsibility: Caring

If a Man Wants to Love a Child, Does the Woman
Have the Right to Abort It?

ITEM. A state judge in Indiana issued an injunction to prevent an unmarried eighteen-year-old woman from having an abortion because a twenth-four-year-old man said he was the father and wanted the child. But the woman had an abortion anyway.[38]

Women's "A" right is to abort. Men's "C" right is to care.

Before men can exercise their "C" right, a woman must always have what I call "The Five Rights to Choose": to choose whether or not she has sex, with whom she has it, when she has it, and whether she uses birth control, and to choose abortion *if there is no alternative* for a wanted child.

The moment a man provides an alternative—a legally notarized commitment to care for the child for eighteen to twenty-one years, both emotionally and financially—her unilateral rights end and shared rights begin.

Shared rights? Yes. The father's right to care and the fetus' right to become a loved child. They must be shared with the woman's "Five Rights to Choose."

A father's "C" rights begin with his "C" responsibilities: volunteering both a womb of love and a womb of financial security. Then, shouldn't the right of the fetus to live and be loved exceed the woman's right to kill it? If a man provides two "wombs" for eighteen years, cannot a woman provide one womb for nine months?

A child is also wanted when a father takes responsibility to find an adoption agency that has parents who want the child. The Internet has made adoption a much easier process. When a woman's choice blocks the father from taking this responsibility, then pro-choice is again being used to prevent wanted children. And, ironically, to prevent fathers from taking responsibility.

When a father or another family can love a future child, then the degree to which women's instincts for birth are stronger than her instincts for aborting its birth is the degree to which she would choose to allow that future child into the world.

If we care about the female-only right to abort, then let's be up-front about it.

But suppose a child could be wanted? We won't know until we give the father the *right* to be informed of the pregnancy *early enough* to determine whether he can give the child a good home and love. Otherwise we might be giving the woman the right to abort a *wanted* child.

How a Woman Can Put a Child Up for Adoption Without Informing the Father . . . And Why He Can't Stop Her

Ed McNamara[39] shared with me this story of him and his womanfriend having a lovely dinner in a San Diego restaurant after some months of not seeing each other. As she caught him up on the past months, she told him that she and he . . . "just had a baby."

"What?!"

"I've named her Katie."

Ed choked on his fork. "Where *is* Katie?"

"I've put her up for adoption!"

"Adoption? *Our* daughter?!"

"Yes. And guess what? She's been adopted! I thought you'd like to know."

Ed was paralyzed. But not for long. . . .

Ed filed for custody of Katie when Katie was only *five weeks old*. But by the time the case came to trial, Katie had been with her adoptive parents for five months. Ed was a contractor's estimator and the judge evaluated Ed as "a good parent who could provide a good, loving home for the child." But the judge ruled that the child had already bonded with the adoptive parents. Ed appealed the case all the way to the U.S. Supreme Court.[40] Increasingly, the courts' hands were tied. Why?

Although Ed filed as quickly as he could, by the time the case came to trial, the court had to deal with the issue of whether taking it away from its adoptive parents would disrupt the child's stability and its ability to bond.

When a woman is not required to immediately notify a man of their pregnancy, the time that lapses forces the court to choose between hurting the child and giving the child to its dad. **The woman who does not immediately notify the father of her pregnancy is, in effect, blackmailing the court by preventing it from connecting the child and father without hurting the child.** By delaying informing him, she has hurt both the child and father, depriving the child of its natural relationship with its dad—a deprivation that can never be recovered.

The Ed McNamara case helps us see the *legal* need for a woman to immediately notify a man of her pregnancy, but it doesn't help us understand how this would also serve the woman's and child's *emotional* needs. The "five-day rule" does.

Should a Woman Be Required to Notify the Father as Soon as She Discovers She Is Pregnant?

When Mary Lou became pregnant, she discussed her feelings with her parents, a counselor, two of her closest womenfriends, a minister, an abortion-clinic adviser, and her doctor.[41] She went through periods of delight, tears, self-blame, a desire to be married to Andy, deep doubts about Andy, and a desire to get an abortion. Finally she decided she wanted to get married. She then announced to Andy her pregnancy—and her desire to get married. Andy went through periods of delight, tears, self-blame, a desire to be married to Mary Lou, deep doubts about Mary Lou, and a desire to have Mary Lou get an abortion.

Mary Lou was deeply hurt about Andy's doubts. She had unconsciously expected Andy to skip the "working through" process, to reach the same conclusion she had reached, and to do it in less than a tenth of a second: "I didn't want to see that look of hesitation and confusion that I saw in his eyes in the first tenth of a second after I told him I was pregnant. I wanted Andy to be delighted." By the time she had made up her own mind, she had forgotten about her own hesitations and confusion—including her doubts about Andy. By working it through first and then presenting it to Andy with unrealistic expectations of total delight, she set herself up to be disappointed in Andy, to "reinforce her deepest doubts." Andy learned that there was no safe place to express any feelings except the positive ones. She said she wanted Andy to be honest, but really she didn't—honesty requires a reasonably safe place to share *all* emotions.

Our current belief is that Mary Lou should have the time she needs to work through her feelings and options, and choose when and how—even if—she tells Andy. I believe it would be helpful to both Mary Lou and Andy to **expect Mary Lou to tell Andy of her pregnancy virtually as soon as she finds out—so they can generate options together, support each other through whatever mixture of emotions they experience together, and share the hard times. This is what love is about.** Love is not about a woman being isolated or isolating a man. No woman is an island.

Our tendency is to object, "Suppose Mary Lou is traumatized . . . suppose she needs time?" *Both* sexes need time. Equal time. We expect men to express feelings and then expect men to adopt the woman's feelings. We all recognize that it takes men longer to get in touch with their feelings— maybe the doctor who discovers the woman is pregnant should call the man first, give him a few days to get in touch with his feelings, and then give the woman and the man the results together. (I'm not really suggesting this, but in many ways this timing would give a woman more support and give the man a *psychologically equal* amount of time.)

Suppose Mary Lou is hesitant because she was afraid Andy might not be the father. Fortunately DNA tests can now tell her who the father is as soon as she determines she is pregnant.[42]

If we expect men to be psychologically involved, we need to give men equal psychological time. If we expect men to be *legally* responsible, then close-to-equal time needs to be a legal right. If a man is to be held legally responsible, it is fair for the law to require the woman to make every reasonable attempt[43] to notify the man of her pregnancy within, for example, four to five days.

The intent? Equal decision-making for equal parenting. Which starts either with the doctor informing *them,* or with her informing him *before* she informs others. (Equal parenting does not mean both sexes will play the same parental *role.* They can play different roles and still be equal parents.) But equal decision-making starts with who both of them decide to consult, when, and whether they talk with others together or separately. There is no reason the woman—especially an unwed teenage girl—should be burdened by these decisions in isolation.

To legally require a man to support a child without giving him a say in the decision is like *legally* requiring a woman to move with a man to his new job without giving her a say in the decision.

This approach empowers women because it assigns the psychological and emotional burdens to both sexes, not just women. It also sends the message that men are not just wallets, but parents. The job of parenting consumes time, money, emotions, and judgment in huge chunks. Equality demands that both sexes be required to give equally in each of these areas unless both parents agree to do it differently. Few things produce more humility or eradicate self-centeredness more quickly than being an involved parent. If we want men to be less self-centered and more nurturing, we can start by getting them more involved—from the start. Equal parenting begins with equal parenting.

Equal parenting will not begin, though, if men know that the investment of their heart will be treated with contempt by the law. . . .

How the Attitude and the Law Create the "Dad-Time Catch-22"

> You have never seen a bigger pain in the ass than the father who wants to get involved; he can be repulsive. He wants to meet the kids after school at three o'clock, take the kid out to dinner during the week, have the kid on his own birthday, talk to the kid on the phone every evening, go to every open school night, take the kid away for a whole weekend so they can be alone together. This type of involved father is pathological.
>
> JUDGE HUTTNER, NEW YORK STATE
> COMMISSION ON CHILD SUPPORT[44]

ITEM. Patti Shamp had already asked her ex-husband to care for their son. Then she had a stroke. She was paralyzed, unable to talk, and required full-time assistance. Her ex-husband felt it would be better for their daughter to also be cared for by him. Patti still wanted to care for their daughter. The court appointed an independent investigator. It was felt the father could do the best job for the daughter. The judge ruled in favor of the mother.[45]

We can feel for how Patti might have needed the daughter, but isn't the issue supposed to be "the best interests of the *child*"? Frequently, when the mother's interests conflict with the child's, the mother's supersede the child's. The unstated assumption is that whatever is the mother's interest *must* be the child's. Isn't that matriarchy?

ITEM. A study conducted by the Drake University School of Law found that when parents contested parent time, mothers won 92 percent of the cases.[46] Similarly, in New Hampshire, mothers also received primary parent time in 92 percent of all contested cases.[47]

Does this mean that if a man wants primary parent time, the children have only an 8 percent chance of being primarily with their fathers even when their fathers want them? No. It is worse than that. A dad who is economically poor has virtually no chance of being an equally involved dad without his ex-wife's permission. So he loses without a contest. A father with some money soon learns investing in a court case against an unwilling mom is like buying a lottery ticket for $100,000 and seriously hoping to win. So he too loses without a contest.

Sometimes a dad's sense of powerlessness makes him withdraw. We call him a deadbeat. It's usually more accurate to call him deadened.

Everyone would agree with a woman's right to choose if it didn't interfere with other rights. Which usually means the right of the fetus to live. But a woman's right to choose also turns out to interfere with a child's right to have a fully involved father. And a father's right to be an equal partner in his child's life. **When only the woman has the right to choose, it leaves everyone else with the right to lose.**

For most dads, the loss begins before the battle has begun. If he feels he *can* afford to "buy" dad time, he must then confront **the "Dad-Time Catch-22": If he cares enough about his children to fight for them legally, he cares enough not to want to put them through a legal battle.**

As his psyche deadens with that dead-end, he experiences another case of the "Multi-Option Woman and the No-Option Man": The Multi-Option Mom and the No-Option Dad. Her multi-options are:

1. Primary Parent

2. Equal Parent

3. No Parenting

Most dads feel their three "options" are the three I mentioned above: Agree; Agree; Agree. He can, of course, fight the system to gain options. A man fighting for shared parenting time after divorce today, though, feels like a woman fighting for the right to be sexual on her first dates during the fifties—it's a theoretical option, but you'd better be willing to sacrifice a lot if you plan to exercise it. And even if he wins shared parenting time, a mother who is angry can wreak havoc on its reality. . . .

ITEM. When Dr. Robert Fay, a pediatrician, had shared parent time with his son and daughter, he was nevertheless unable to obtain copies of his children's school records either from his ex-wife or from the school. When he finally won the right to the documents, the school refused to mail the documents even if Dr. Fay paid for the mailings. The entire appeals process cost Dr. Fay $30,000 of personal money and six years of time. He was reimbursed $1. The backward state? New York.[48]

The pattern? To become equal to women, we require a man to "compensate for his inequality." His three options for compensation?

1. Paying (lawyers, etc.)

2. Fighting

3. Putting his children through court

If Dad appears to be overcoming all three barriers, Mom can virtually guarantee he fails by dropping the nuclear bomb of the Parent Time Wars— accusing him of sexually abusing their children. As we saw in Part I, *94 percent of false accusations are made by women* and 96 percent of those who were falsely accused were men.[49] Most accusations are made during parent-time battles, and that is the time when they are most likely to be false. More on that later.

Meantime, what are the consequences if we ignore men's ABC Rights and Responsibilities? The next generation will not be Mars and Venus loving each other, but Mars and Venus fighting each other. Not quite "Star Wars: The Next Generation,"[50] but "Bar Wars: The Next Generation."

Some Conclusions and Solutions

"I Feel Like a Slave. . . ."

The first consequences of ignoring men's ABC Rights are our sons' fear of ABC Responsibilities. It is only the fear of *responsibilities* that catches our attention and feeds our editorials. But it is the lesser problem. Underneath our sons' fear of responsibility will be their fear of women, sex, and commitment.

What feeling is behind these fears? One I frequently hear from men is "I feel like a slave." Problem is, a dad doesn't feel comfortable discussing this with his children—he doesn't want them to feel guilty. So it leaves his children feeling rejected: his daughter suspicious of men; his son with fears (of women, sex, and commitment) that are not clear enough to discuss even with a therapist he trusts.

Among which dads is this feeling most common?
I hear "I feel like a slave" *most frequently* from:

- Dads making high mother-subsidy payments *without* access to their children

- Dads making high mother-subsidy payments *with* access to children who are being told negative things about the dad

I hear this feeling *most angrily* from:

- Men who are spending eighteen to twenty-one years supporting a child he thought was his, but discovered was another man's

I hear it *coupled with confusion, ambivalence, anger, and guilt (for having the feeling)* from:

- A dad whose wife or womanfriend said she was on birth control, but later acknowledged she had "forgotten" to take the pill. If he also believes he and she had an agreement that she would get an abortion should birth control fail, his feelings of being a slave are intensified.

Of course, the feelings of being a slave do not come from taking a job he likes less to support a child he *chose* to have, but from taking a job he likes less to support a child he did not choose to have. And, often, at being tricked into supporting a wife to boot. Most of these dads feel a betrayal of the trust they invested in women—a betrayal of "the contracts of their private conversations."

To many men, the unwritten partnership contract accompanying a child is like the unwritten partnership contract accompanying sex. If either partner says "No," it's okay to try to persuade the resistor, but if the hesitant partner still says "No," then it's "No," and going ahead anyway is what he feels is rape. Someone who does not heed an unchanged "No" goes from partner to enemy. **When he feels the government is forcing him to work for his enemy, he feels like a slave.**

When we made slaves out of African-Americans, we discovered the more they worked, the more the master benefited, the sooner the slave died. When we create circumstances by which dads feel like slaves, we make it dysfunctional for dads to work.

Won't they work if we shame them (*e.g.,* "deadbeats," "Most Wanted" posters in post offices), catch them and imprison them? Maybe. (Although it's hard to be that productive in prison.) Truth is, when we force people to do labor that benefits someone else almost exclusively, and punish them if they don't, we create people who *pretend* to be working. Thus many dads become experts at hiding money.

But Dad's emotions are complex: he loves his children, even if he has problems with their mom. His underground earnings are distributed in accordance with this complexity. Money appears where there is hope for freedom (attorneys) or love (new woman, or attorneys [to get children to love]), but disappears for his ex. His money follows his emotions. He's trying to become a human being, not a human doing. Not a slave.

Fortunately, it is not the primary purpose of the government to extract free labor from a dad; the primary purpose is to protect children. So is there a way of keeping dads from feeling like slaves?

Yes. Working on each of men's ABC Rights. Among the most important are support for a men's birth-control pill and opposition to the government giving women incentives to have children out of wedlock (even as it tells women to not have children out of wedlock). When a woman's decision is to raise a child without a man, the government can respect the woman's decision as hers, but not subsidize her any more than she is already subsidized both by paying lower taxes on her lower income, and still lower taxes by having a child (thus increasing her tax-deductible dependencies). This still gives her more of a tax break than she would have if she had a husband who earned money, but it does not supply her with a substitute husband of government-sponsored supports.

A second series of solutions involves giving men equal protection to women under the law. . . .

"Bar Wars: the Next Generation"

Once we understand that the use of the woman's body is an excuse for a much more deeply-seated sexism—"*mom*ism"—we free ourselves for the solution to equality in parenting: Any embryo, fetus, or child created by two people is the responsibility of both in every area—from care to financing—and whatever rules apply to parent time apply equally to both sexes.

The sexism of "momism" will embarrass us as more and more eggs are fertilized in petri dishes rather than wombs and nurtured to life in the wombs of strangers, leaving the bodies of the mothers and fathers equally involved. It will embarrass us to deny rights to surrogate mothers after claiming that a woman's right to choose is based on the fetus being in her body; and it will embarrass feminists and the ACLU to be to be claiming that a lesbian mother who did not have the fetus in her womb has equal rights but a father who does not have a fetus in his womb has no rights.

Ironically, until dads demand rights, dads' rights will often be "by-product rights": a by-product of which woman wins the most rights to the child—the surrogate mother who used her womb, or the contractual mother who didn't; the lesbian who used her womb, or the one who didn't.

The first answer to the question "What are men's reproductive rights?" then, may be "The same as a woman's whose womb is not used." Until at least that step is taken, lawyers will confront a legal system with two sets of rules: one for moms, one for dads—creating the twenty-first century's "Bar Wars: The Next Generation."

If dads have only by-product rights, though, children will have only by-product dads: dads whose involvement is determined by Mom.

So, what do men want?

A "Shared Choice" Movement

Most men want a "women choose, men choose" system; in their eagerness to protect women, what they see they have helped create is a system that might more accurately be called "women choose, men lose." To men it feels like "all pay, no say." A male pro-choice movement does not want the reverse of a "women-only pro-choice" movement; it wants, rather, to *share* the choice—the choice to abortion, birth-control method, and childcare arrangements.

A "shared choice" movement sees the fetus as the genes of a woman and the genes of a man; the flesh of the woman, the flesh of the man; the responsibility of a woman, the responsibility of a man; the rights of a woman, the rights of a man. It desires a transition to equality.

If women have the choice as to whether or not they want their bodies to be used to make children, then equality means men having the choice as to whether or not they want their bodies to be used to make money to support those children. Today, when a female makes the unilateral "choice" to raise a child, the man loses his "choice" not to raise money. When the government interferes with a woman's desire to abort a fetus, the government is seen by many as wrong because it is interfering with her rights; when the government interferes with a man's desire to keep the fetus alive, the government is seen by many as right because it is expanding her rights. Motherhood is sacred even when it includes disposing of the fetus; fatherhood is disposable even when it includes keeping the fetus.

Giving only a woman the power to decide what a man will do with his life—but not the other way around—is giving her the power of a slave-keeper. Forcing a man to do "100 percent pay, but no say"—under penalty of being put in jail—is the modern-day equivalent of slavery.

Discussing only the "right to choose motherhood"—rather than the "right to choose parenthood"—is sexist. Equal Rights to Choose—in abortion, birth-control method, or caring arrangement—are men's ABC Rights and as fundamental to men as are the ABCs.

Saying "pro-choice" and really meaning "women-only pro-choice" is like saying "American citizens vote" and really meaning "only male Americans vote."

Women-only pro-choice is like men-only business clubs. Business clubs were "men only" when only men took all the responsibility for supporting women and children; we could theoretically have women-only pro-choice if only women wished to take responsibility to support the children. But, in practice, the children need both parents, and the children's *needs* should not be legislated away for a woman's preferences.

To let men get involved with children only on terms dictated by women—when women want them to, and then only in the ways women want—is as chauvinistic as laws that would let women earn money only when their husbands consented, only in jobs their husbands or menfriends allowed, and require them to put most of the money into "Mortgage Support." If we want a transition in responsibilities, we need a transition in rights.

A major obstacle to this transition is the belief that divorce makes women poorer and men richer—and if that is the case, special protection for women after divorce is warranted. Let's see if that is the case. . . .

7

Does Divorce Make Women Poorer and Men Richer?

Dear Ann Landers: . . . Something is wrong when a woman tells
the judge that her spouse was "a good husband and an excellent father," admits her own infidelity, and still gets custody of the child,
ownership of the house, and a generous portion of her husband's
salary. . . . Something is wrong when the adulterous wife makes
$1,000 a month more than the child's father, but the court says she
is entitled to nearly one-third of his salary.

A VICTIM OF THE SYSTEM

Dear Victim: . . . It is a matter of record that the vast majority
of women end up much poorer after divorce, while their ex-
husbands' standard of living improves.   ANN LANDERS[1]

Since the late 1980s, the "feminization of poverty" has increasingly been
assumed to be a reality. Its credibility heightened when a feminist named
Lenore Weitzman reported her findings that women who were divorced
suffered a 73 percent decline in their standard of living while their ex-
husbands experienced a 42 percent rise in their standard of living.[2]
**We interpreted women's alleged decline in income after di-
vorce as an example of how women suffered after divorce, never as
an example of how men subsidized women during marriage.** Never-

theless, were this true, it would be cause for serious concern. We can cele-brate the fact that it is not true. Here's why.

First, I will address the larger picture of women as the more-likely-to-be-poor. Until 1991, the Census Bureau published statistics comparing the net worth of women who are heads of households to that of men who are heads of households. But when the women came up wealthier (with net worths from 104 percent to 141 percent that of men's), those statistics ceased to be published.[3]

Frequently throughout this book, we shall see this censorship of data when it does not conform to the woman-as-victim image. Back to the image painted by Weitzman's book: At that time, the net worth of women was 141 percent that of men.[4] If women who were divorced became 73 percent poorer and men became 42 percent richer, it would be difficult for female heads of households to have a net worth 141 percent of male heads of households. At the very least, it paints a different picture.

The Weitzman study looked at just the *first year* after divorce; only at people living in the San Francisco and Los Angeles areas; only at data from 1968 to 1978 which was never updated (about a phenomenon as much in flux as divorce). And here's what got left out:

Economists such as Duncan and Hoffman, who looked at a nationwide sample, a larger sample, and a more recent sample, also looked at the first *five years* after divorce.[5] They found that during the first year, women did ex-perience a decline in income—but of 9 percent, not the 73 percent claimed by Weitzman. However, **they found that by the end of the second year, women's standard of living is equal to the standard they had before divorce** (due mostly to remarriage). And that by the end of the fifth year, women were 10 percent *ahead* of where they were before divorce. Yet, the popular media ignored this more updated, national sample.

The fathers in Weitzman's study grossed $41,261 annually after di-vorce. Quite different from a *national* sample showing $20,555—half of Weitzman's figure (both in 1984 dollars).[6]

Weitzman was ultimately forced to acknowledge that she had "miscal-culated." But before her acknowledgment, it was possible that the econo-mists were wrong and the feminist was right. Why did we not hear about both so we could judge for ourselves? Instead, the "feminization of poverty" became an unquestioned fact, creating an atmosphere from which judges felt it their duty to become the divorced woman's first substitute protectors. However, the protection of women actually boomeranged against women and children. How?

It encouraged especially the 40 percent of women who do not work at all when their children are young, and the 20 percent who work part-time, to argue for sole or primary parent time (to obtain more child support) rather than to share custody and put the extra time into building up work skills, thereby creating for themselves a *genuine independence from their ex-husbands and an ability to choose a next husband because of love* rather than because of his ability to provide an economic security blanket.

How do the large child-support payments hurt children? The payments are awarded as a result of the very primary mom time that deprives the children of their dads; and that primary mom time also hurts the dads by depriving them of their children.[7]

We still haven't proven that Weitzman's study is less accurate than Duncan and Hoffman's. Doing that helps us understand the experience of divorce from both sexes' perspectives. Some examples:

- Who has the family home? Weitzman does not calculate the value of the family home, which the mother with children almost always receives and lives in. She does not figure out what it would cost the woman to rent that home in that neighborhood and add a percentage of that to her income. Until we add that and subtract from the man's income the amount it would cost him to have an equivalent residence in an equivalent neighborhood, we do not have a fair assessment of the "masculinization of poverty."

  And until we calculate the psychological cost of being uprooted from his home and neighborhood when he is most in need of support and psychological stability, we do not understand the "masculinization of loneliness."

- Twenty-one percent of women remarry within *one year* after they have divorced.[8] These women do not remain poorer. And the ex-husband still pays child support. Duncan and Hoffman found that the standard of living of women who remarry was equal to what it was before they had been divorced.[9]

- By the end of five years, more than half the divorced women had remarried, with their income levels returning to what they were before they were divorced.[10] This is why looking at only the first year after divorce ignores the income jump of all the women who eventually remarry. (Women who di-vorce often *do* lose their source of income, but to look at only the first year after divorce to calculate the long-term impact would be like looking at only the first year after the job loss calculating the long-term impact of losing a job.)

- Twenty to thirty percent of men paying child support are also helping to subsidize the children of a new woman in their lives.[11] Weitzman does not calculate the degree to which a man's income is reduced by helping to support his new wife's children. By mea-suring only the first year after divorce, Weitzman misses almost all these men. She also misses the "Two-Male Subsidy" received by many remarried women.

- Feminists often discuss women having two jobs: work and chil-dren. True. But no one discusses those divorced and remarried men who have three jobs: work, and two sets of children to nur-ture and financially support.

What About Women and Men Who Do *Not* Remarry?

- The year after divorce, a woman might resume her education, en-ter a training program, or enter the workforce at beginner's pay.[12] By measuring only her income during this year of training and not the income that results from the investment in that training is like measuring a doctor's income by his or her income during medical school. Yet **Weitzman used the women's "training year," or "reentry year," to represent their entire post-divorce expe-rience.**

- In contrast, the year after divorce typically finds the man putting in an abnormal amount of overtime to prevent himself from thinking of his loss, as well as to pay for the alimony and child support obligations and to save up for a new home.[13] **To use the extra income a man makes from his attempt to minimize his psychological trauma to tell the world he is the benefactor of divorce is at best a bit of a ruse.**

- The man will commonly be advised by his lawyer to defer raises and bonuses in the year prior to divorce so as to limit his child-support and alimony payments. This makes his income *appear* to go up far more the year after divorce than it actually does because the year after is when he gets all his deferred raises and bonuses (plus his normal ones).

- The expenses incurred by fathers visiting their children during "dad time" were not subtracted by Weitzman from the father's income.

- Just as in the year after divorce a woman loses the man's income, which can be legally compensated for by alimony and child support, the man loses the woman's tendency to cook meals and, therefore, often increases his expenses by eating out. These expenses are not subtracted when Weitzman says the man's standard of living goes up 42 percent.

- When a divorced woman goes out with a new man, he typically pays; Weitzman does not ask the woman who dated to add free dinners, tickets, etc., as part of her income; similarly, when a divorced man goes out with a new woman and pays, Weitzman doesn't subtract this socially-expected expense from his income. Nor does she account for how the very loneliness he experiences after divorce, especially if the children are turned against him, leads him to asking out women a lot during this first year; his need for respect leads him to asking out younger women who typically pay less. None of these expenses are subtracted from his income.

Are We Underestimating the Woman's Contribution During Marriage?

Feminists have helped us appreciate how much women's labor in the home is worth—not only to the family, but to the man's future career—what Weitzman calls his "career assets." Weitzman did not subtract *anything* for the man's loss of the woman's contribution. Isn't this an insult to the woman's contribution? To have alimony but no "husbandimony" suggests that only the man had something to contribute.

Weitzman suggests that a man's future earnings or career assets be shared with the woman after divorce. He is expected to continue his contribution to her; she is not expected to continue her contribution to him. Shouldn't the man be compensated for the time it takes him to cook his own meals, clean the house, do laundry, and whatever else she provided that allowed his career assets to grow? **If the value of his career assets are to continue to support her, then the value of her contributions must continue to support him.** Either they both continue to contribute to each other, or neither does.

No matter how much she contributes to him, the man's losses can never fully be repaid. The check a man writes can do something to compensate for the "feminization of poverty," but no one can legislate that a woman write a check to continue giving female love to a man to compensate for the "masculinization of loneliness." Which leads us to psychological poverty.

Psychological Poverty

Real poverty is also psychological poverty. Although the "feminization of poverty" is magnified, the "masculinization of loneliness" is invisible.[14]

The masculinization of loneliness may begin with the mother badmouthing the father to the children. As we have seen, the mom is more than four times as likely to badmouth the dad as the dad is to badmouth the mom (according to the children).[15] This isolation from those who love and need him most is often compounded by isolation from the neighborhood and friends.

When Lynette and Gene divorced, Gene was psychologically disconnected—not only from the children, but from the neighbors he considered to be his support system. When Gene returned to pick up the children, he felt the neighbors looking at him through a negative filter. He found out Lynette had revealed to them "the things I could never tell you when Gene was around." Gene didn't feel comfortable keeping the kids waiting while he told the neighbors *his* side of the dirty laundry. Soon, the people he considered his support system saw him as a jerk living in an apartment and dating "some young thing." Neither Weitzman nor the economists calculated this immeasurable psychological poverty.

How Men Lost Their Children Because They Were *Not* the Primary Parent, and Lost Their Money Because They *Were* the Primary Breadwinner

I am often asked why I was so supportive of the feminist movement during the 1970s but so critical of it since the 1980s. Did I change? Or did the movement change? The answer can be seen in what happened to the movement between the 1970s and 1980s. In 1974, when I wrote *The Liberated Man* (a book explaining to men the value of the feminist movement and of independent women), feminists like Lenore J. Weitzman were writing that "The current preference for the mother in custody cases . . . is so pronounced that it might *deny fathers* equal protection. Fathers who would like to have custody and *who might make better custodians* face such an uphill battle that *many are discouraged from trying.* In addition, **children might suffer when the real 'best interests of the child' are ignored or undermined by this automatic preference for the mother.**"[16] (Emphasis mine.) This concern for *sexism*—no matter which way it cut—was why I was so supportive of the early feminist movement despite its male-bashing.

By the late 1980s, though, the same Weitzman joined other feminists[17] to argue both that divorce hurt women more than men and that divorced women should have the option to be the paid parent if they had been the primary parent. The first point was misleading at best, and the second point, the "Primary Parent Theory," said that if the woman was the "primary parent" before the divorce, it would be in the best interest of the child if she were the primary parent after the divorce. But if that is true and the child's benefit is the issue, she would have the *obligation* to be the primary parent after the divorce. But she was demanding the *option*—*her* choice, not the child's benefit.

The Primary Parent Theory not only gave her the option to be at home, but to force her former husband to pay for her to be at home, *thus controlling not just her own life, but his life, too.* Which is why babies have as much impact on him.

In essence, he would be *required* by law to become her "mandatory employer"—to pay for her to do the job of mother if she so chooses. This would be like saying that a husband who was the primary breadwinner before divorce should have the first choice as to whether he wanted to be the primary breadwinner after divorce *and force his wife to be at home with the children.* No one would support forcing the woman into a role while giving the man a choice. After a divorce, both parents must have equal opportunity to both the workplace and the homeplace. If they *both choose* traditional roles, fine; but the starting place must be one of equal opportunity. I soon saw that feminists who supported the "Primary Parent Theory" were not in favor of equality of opportunity, but of unequal opportunism.

Men for whom divorce means walking out of their children's lives except when *they choose* to see the children are the male equivalent of the adolescent feminists: men who want options without obligations. Morally, they have no *right* to walk out. A law that allows that is similarly immoral. "Primary Parent" laws are just such laws.

The irony of primary-parent laws is that on the one hand **feminists were arguing** *for* **women's equal rights to jointly created career assets that emanated from the male financial womb, but arguing** *against* **men's equal rights to jointly created children that emanated from the woman's childbearing womb.**[18] Few seemed to care that reducing a man to visitor to his children on alternate weekends would be like reducing a woman to visitor to the home they bought together—while she lived in a slum. In practice, he was usually an alternate-weekend visitor to the children they had jointly created, who were living with his ex-wife in the home they had jointly created.

In brief, she is the partner to what primarily he creates; he is the visitor to what primarily she creates.

To me, this wasn't equality.

As feminism made this transition from equal opportunity to unequal opportunism, I made my transition from supporter to critic. But in my inner psyche, there was no transition: I went from supporter of equality to supporter of equality.

Legislators bought the "primary parent" theory as a basis for women getting primary mom time, but they would never have bought a "primary breadwinner" theory as the basis for a man having primary "dad time" with the income for which he was primarily responsible. When these two theories combined to become standard judicial practice, they became the "let's have our cake and eat it, too" laws of liberation. Again, politics prevailed over equality.

The feminist theory of "It's-a-Woman's-Choice-Because-She's-the-Primary-Parent" soon became the nouveau version of biology-as-destiny, but in feminist clothing. It forced the woman's husband to become her employer, but with no say as to whether or not he wanted to be her employer, no say as to whether she should remain hired or be fired, and no ability to do performance evaluations. He had an employer's obligations, but no employer's rights; he had fewer rights than the employee.

The theory called "It's-Women's-Choice-Because-She's-the-Primary-Parent" is the equivalent in the custody stage to what the theory called "It's-Women's-Choice-Because-It's-Her-Body" is in the abortion and birth stage. Both theories rationalized women's choice and men's obligation.

How did this happen? Because men said nothing, legislators heard feminists—the squeaky wheels. Politics became more powerful than equality. Both theories were part of the feminist movement's transformation from advocating equality to advocating the multi-option woman and the no-option man. The *incentive* for the Primary Parent Theory was child support; the *politics* was made possible by the belief in the deadbeat dad. . . .

Is Child Support Helping or
Hurting the Family?

I write to my ex on the back of my checks.
FROM A MICHAEL FRANKS SONG

Are We Giving Women Incentives
to Break Up the Family?

Wives initiate divorce twice as often as husbands.[1] Why? Husbands doubt-less do as much as wives to create the relationship problems that lead to a partner wanting a divorce, but if divorce were so beneficial to men, it is un-likely that women would be twice as likely to initiate it. By giving the woman the option to the children, child support and the family home, are we giving women a financial and emotional incentive to initiate the breakup of the family? Yes. **In states that adopt shared parent time, divorce rates drop within a few years.**[2] That is, women initiate most of the di-vorces in part because they know they can get the children and the income; when they don't know that, they're more likely to hang in there.

Put another way, her option to "fire" her husband from his role as father and then require him to subsidize his own "firing" (mother-subsidy pay-ments) might be thought of as an incentive for women to initiate the breakup of the family. It would be like giving an employer the option of fir-ing an employee and requiring the employ*ee* to make monthly "employer support" payments because of the additional burden experienced by the em-ployer (now forced to hire and retrain someone else). If we gave employers this incentive, no one would have any trouble predicting massive firing of employees.

From a Child Deprived of Dad to a Dad Deprived of Child: One Man's Story

This is one man's story of the impact of separating Dad and child. The impact has now reached the second generation.

> My father was the best father a child could hope for and he desperately wanted to raise his own children; my mother was incompetent and irresponsible . . . but the divorce judge granted her request to raise all four of us children. . . . My mother was unable to support four young children, so rather than letting my father support us, she married the first man she could. He was a cowboy recently released from prison for murder; he drank, smoked, swore, gambled, and was often violent.[3]
>
> Predictably, I hated this man, not so much for his vices, but because he was displacing my father, to whom I was strongly attached and who had none of this man's vices. I rebelled against my stepfather in every way I could, earning me a childhood of merciless beatings, devoid of love.
>
> . . . As a teenager, I became antisocial and borderline juvenile delinquent. . . .
>
> Fortunately for society and me, a retired German scientist took me under his wing and gave me the moral guidance that the state would not allow my own father to give. . . . I began to put my shattered life together. I did not get very far before I was drafted into the army and sent to Vietnam to fight and, perhaps, to die, ostensibly to defend the freedoms that my father and I were so cruelly denied. . . .
>
> . . . I went to college, established a career, married, and had a wonderful child. . . .During the first year of my daughter's life, I did everything I could to be a loving, involved father; and, to that end, established a very strong bond with my daughter.
>
> My wife began showing signs of emotional instability during that first year, so I encouraged her to join me in seeing a marriage counselor: she flatly refused. . . .

When my daughter was one year, one month, and seventeen days old, my wife kidnapped her and moved in with her mother. She then went to Judge Isabella Grant of the San Francisco Superior Court; requested—and, to my dismay, got—temporary custody of my daughter, limiting me to infrequent visits and placing terrible emotional stresses on the infant. My wife gave no reason for her request and Judge Grant asked for none. Judge Grant would not even consider my arguments against my wife's unilateral acts.

The court assigned my wife and me to a Family Court counselor for mediation. The counselor had taken *her* children from their father through divorce and, to my dismay, used that as an example of acting in "the child's best interests." I then began worrying that my daughter and I were in real trouble. My suspicions became stronger when the counselor freely admitted to be "working at the pleasure of the judge" and said she could not afford to risk her job by acting contrary to what she knew Judge Grant wanted. When I asked the counselor what Judge Grant wanted, she told me, with a straight face, that Judge Grant normally awards sole custody to the mother if the mother does not agree to joint custody and, furthermore, I would save everybody a lot of trouble if I would simply agree to what the judge would almost certainly order anyway.

Judge Grant went on to "award" my child to my now ex-wife. . . . As if that were not enough, Judge Grant, in effect, ordered me to finance the abduction and abuse of my own daughter, cynically calling it "child support." . . .

. . . I later discovered that [my ex-wife] had, for a long time, been secretly receiving free legal services from a feminist organization helping her plot divorce. This feminist organization receives funding from the City and County of San Francisco and the Bar Association. They then use those funds, among other ways, to help women take children from their fathers.

Should "Child Support" Be Renamed "Mother Subsidy" (or "Father Subsidy")?

It's hard to think of anything more cynical than using the term "child support" to connote a payment of money, usually by the dad. We sometimes hear "Child support is more than monetary support; it's also emotional support." True, but it's an insult to parenting—and, therefore, to traditional women mostly—to limit the words "child support" even to a combination of money and emotional support.

If child support can be reduced to any few words, they might be "For better or worse." Today, "For better or worse" is far more applicable to parenting than to marriage vows. But child support cannot be reduced to a few words. More than money and emotional support, child support means a tolerance for being taken for granted and made wrong, gobs of time chauffeuring, refereeing, never being sure that, no matter what decision you make, you won't end up paying a therapist to tell your child that's why she or he has been emotionally abused. It requires teaching, listening, mentoring, motivating, medicating, being a friend but not being a friend, tying shoelaces, cooking, cleaning, and wiping up when *you* feel like the rag. Calling child support a payment reinforces the father feeling that a payment is him taking care of his share.

A few weeks ago, I was flying to Ireland on an overnight flight. A dad turned the two seats next to him into a bed, his lap into a pillow, and leaned over to kiss his daughter good night. I didn't have anyone next to me. So I leaned over, held my pen, and wrote Paul Simon's "Mother and Child Reunion" in slightly different form. . . .

Father and Child Reunion

I heard Mommy say that Daddy
Wasn't the hubby she wanted him to be
But Mommy never asked me
If Daddy is my daddy to me

Chorus:
> *The child support check doesn't say "I love you"*
> *I can't play "horsey" on its back*
> *The child support check doesn't kiss me goodnight*
> *Or tuck me in the sack*

Mommy makes turkey for Thanksgiving
She thanks God for our fam-i-ly-y

But while she's praying, I'm a-cryin'
"Daddy's missing, and it's lonely to me"

(Repeat chorus)

Mommy prayed in church she'd win me
But to me, the victory was a sin
I want mom and dad to love me
I want a father and child reunion

(Repeat chorus)

Paul Simon, where are you when I need you?

Are Mother Subsidies Really Designed to Give Women a Special Break?

Is it possible for child-support payments to both *under*pay the mother (mostly) and discriminate in *favor* of the mother? Yes. It is rare for child-support payments to pay a parent more than minimum wage for the hours put into raising a child. And that parent is usually the mother.

Yet, when Alice McKnight Fitzgerald, a medical doctor who earned $120,000 a year, saw how much her former husband, who earned $30,000 a year, was receiving (according to child-support guidelines the U.S. Congress requires all fifty states and the District of Columbia to draft), she was shocked. She challenged it and won, which forced a reexamination of the guidelines in the District of Columbia from the perspective of a woman earning more. The guidelines were overturned—after only one woman victim fought for her rights.[4]

Child-support payments are not tax-deductible for the father; yet they are tax-free for the mother receiving them. Previously, a father paying child support could declare the child as a dependency exemption; since 1985, the mother gets the exemption for having the child and the father loses it.[5] It is another incentive for the mother to keep the child.

Killing the Goose . . .

Darrin White was ordered to pay $2,071 a month in Canadian dollars for child support and alimony. He was earning only $1,000 a month. One thou-

Darrin White: Dad Who Was

sand of the dollars was for alimony payments. His wife, with the same job qualifications, was allowed not to work, although it was Darrin who had been on stress leave. The first $2,071 was due immediately. Darrin disappeared. His body was found in woods near the University of Northern British Columbia.[7] He had put a noose around his neck and allowed its closing to explain to the world he felt he had no way out.

Now Darrin's children have neither a dad nor his money. According to Health Canada statistics, suicide in younger men has risen dramatically over the past forty years, but there has been little if any research to find out why.[8] As we've seen, men who are divorced are almost *ten* times as likely to commit suicide as divorced women.[9]

Darrin's wife received the children and the home. When we demand a dad give child support and wife support, then take away his children and home, we kill his soul, his reason for earning, his reason for living. Even if it *isn't* more than he earns or she deserves. When we drive him into a dead-end, he becomes a deadbeat, dead broke, or just dead. As a dad's death is forced upon him, with him dies his family's soul.

When Responsibility for Children Is Equal, Who Pays More?

Full-time dads are much less likely to receive money from Mom than the other way around. Fifty percent less likely.[10]

When dad does receive money, it is less.[11] Is this because the mother earns less? Sometimes, but **even when the full-time moms and full-time dads earn the same amount, mothers are ordered to pay only 80 percent of what the fathers pay.**[12]

Almost every week, though, I receive letters from dads who care for their children full-time. For example, in one I received today, the dad had lost a parent-time battle, but when the mom could no longer handle the older son, she said, "you want him, take him." He wrote:

> She voiced alarm that I was not sending her "her" child-support money. I pointed out that the support money was not hers, but for the child, and since the child was living with me, why on earth would I be sending it to her? It gets worse. My ex had started a business and by this time had thirty employees. . . . I could not get one nickel of child support from her. As soon as the boy turned eighteen, she sold her business and retired. I never had the stomach to take her to court. . . .[13]

The point is not that there are deadbeat wives—both sexes have their deadbeats—but how rare it is for a full-time father to take a deadbeat mother to court. Thus it appears that any given deadbeat mom is less likely to be found—to become a statistical "deadbeat mom." Despite this, the statistics still reveal that moms are less likely to pay, and more likely to pay less.

Which Sex Is More Delinquent about Paying Parent Subsidies?

ITEM. When children were living with their *dad* and the court ordered the mother to pay a father subsidy (usually because her income exceeded the father's), the mothers paid an average of 33 percent owed; fathers paid an average of 62 percent owed. It took a Freedom of Information Act request to get this data from the D.C. Office of Paternity and Child Support Enforcement.[14]

ITEM. The same request revealed that 13 percent of fathers *overpaid* mother subsidies; not a single mother overpaid father subsidies.[15]

In brief, when *dads* have the children, mothers are far less likely to be ordered by the court to pay mother subsidy, are ordered to pay less, are less likely to pay it, and never overpay.

We will see below that when women fail to pay, they are far less likely to be found in contempt of court and be sentenced to jail.[16]

If a Dad Doesn't Pay His Mother Subsidy, He Goes to Prison; if a Mom Doesn't Pay Her Father Subsidy, She . . .

ITEM. Bobby Sherrill was making his mother-subsidy payments on time . . . until Iraq invaded Kuwait. But Bobby, working in Kuwait, was kidnapped and taken hostage for three months in Iraq. Although his dad had paid some of the money while he was held hostage, he hadn't paid it all. When Bobby returned to the United States, he was arrested, put into handcuffs, and taken before a Magistrate.[17] Bobby tried to explain his situation to the Magistrate, asking, "Is there any way I could be released to make the payment?"

The Magistrate reportedly replied, "Only if you make the payment."

Bobby volunteered a check; the Magistrate demanded cash. It was at night and Bobby had no access to cash. He asked, "Is there nothing I can do to postpone this until regular business hours?"

The Magistrate replied, "Not unless you can get someone to get hold of the Chief District Court Judge."

The article commented that the arrest had devastated Bobby's *mother*— it "really wrecked her" when they "threw the handcuffs on him and dragged him off just like he shot somebody."

ITEM. Ralph Limon was sentenced to more than a year in a California state prison for failure to make mother-subsidy payments. His failure landed him on the county's "10 Most Wanted" posters (you know, the ones you see in post offices).[18]

While almost no measures are taken against moms who deny children to the dads, dads who don't pay mother subsidies are now commonly placed on these "Most Wanted" posters in post offices. And, as a careful look at the poster indicates, the one mother who was delinquent was not arrested.

The only debtors who can go to jail are debtors for alimony or child support.[20] In practice, that means almost exclusively *male* debtors. *Even in bankruptcy,* neither child support nor alimony debt is dischargeable.

When debtors' prisons were a reality in England, their descriptions in Charles Dickens's *David Copperfield* shamed the English and shocked the world. Yet more than a century later, a supposedly more-advanced country still has them, in effect. For men only. Debtors' prison is a male-only club. For some reason there are no protests.

What few people questioned about Dickens' England was that when the *family* was in debt, the *man* went to prison. On the surface, this was based on the assumption that the man had responsibility for raising money, the woman for raising children. But, **if only the father goes to jail for a**

delinquent debt, should not only the mother go to jail for a delinquent child? Dickens would have had a "pen-fest" with the imagery of a father and children in front of a fireplace on Christmas Eve while mom is behind bars in a damp prison cell awaiting tuberculosis.

In Delaware County, Pennsylvania, the male debtors are displayed 300 times a week on cable television and once a month in full-page newspaper advertisements.[21] In some areas, when police arrest a man, TV stations are notified and they broadcast the father on the news as he is being taken off to prison. The public sees fathers-as-criminals, but doesn't see as criminals the mothers who deny children their fathers, or the possibility that the dad who was arrested was unemployed.[22] Because the dads don't have equal access to the children to begin with, and because the laws against mothers go comparatively unenforced, this one-sided persecution of only the dads is unconstitutional and sexist.

Is it fair to call this a modern-day witch hunt? There's a difference. Witches rarely had children; the dad's children can see their dad being "burned" on TV without a trial. That image will be forever etched in their memories.

The justification for not putting women who fail to pay child support in prison is that they are needed to care for children. Yet men with the same children go to prison. This is a breach of the Fourteenth Amendment's "Equal Protection Under the Law" clause. It is unconstitutional. It is also unwise. How can we ask men to be more involved with children when we put them in prison, deprive them of equal access, and require them to pay more?

Him: No Money, Prison; Her: No Money, Social Services

Thousands of fathers in Iowa missed child-support payments after being demoted or fired. Or becoming sick. The collection agency notified credit agencies that the fathers' credit was no good. Often the court had already awarded the father lower payments (because of his having been fired, etc.), but as the left arm of the bureaucracy had the lowered support order, the right arm was sending out delinquency notices to credit agencies. Still other fathers were in the process of seeking lowered payments.

The collection agency would have discovered this had the men been granted due process, but the men were not given trials, and the collection agencies had the support of federal law, which requires Dad's wages to be garnisheed and credit agencies notified if the father's payments are delinquent.[23]

The reasoning behind automatic notification of credit agencies is that "when we're delinquent with car payments, credit agencies get notified. So why not with child-support payments?" Here's why: A person who cannot afford a car has the option of selling it to avoid delinquency. A father cannot sell his child to avoid delinquency.

When this program was implemented in Iowa, although it was one of the best years in the decade economically for Iowa, the Iowa suicide level among men soared.[24]

In brief, when a man fails as a wallet, we put him in prison; when a woman fails as a mother, we offer her social services. We're taking a criminal approach to men, a social-services approach to women.

Why We Think of Dads More as Deadbeats Than as Dead Broke, Deadened, Dead-Ended, or Dead

MYTH. *Few men pay mother subsidies (child support), and even fewer pay it in full or on time. Even the Census Bureau confirms this.*

FACT. The headlines we read telling us how little men pay are based on Census Bureau figures. All these Census Bureau's figures are *based on the reports of women*. And only women. Yet, even among these women, 51 percent acknowledge receiving the full amount of child-support payments, and another 25 percent say they received partial payments. Overall, of the 14.6 billion dollars awarded to women, ten billion dollars (over two-thirds) was paid.[25] But this is based on women's *recollection*.

Only recently did the government commission a special survey including men. The men reported paying almost 40 percent more than the women reported receiving (between 80 percent and 93 percent of what the court ordered),[26] plus more payments in full and on time.[27]

It would, of course, be as fallacious to run headlines saying "Men Pay 93 percent of Child Support" as it has been to run the "Deadbeat Dad" headlines. But here's the big question: Why haven't we seen any "Men Pay 80 to 93 percent" headlines? Well, suspiciously, as soon as the men's perspective was discovered to be so different, Wayne Stanton of the Family Support Administration had the study *discontinued*.[28] This is part of what constitutes the "lace curtain" or the tendency of government, the media, academia, and the helping professions not to print anything that makes a woman look like less of a victim than the public consciousness holds her to be, a concept I develop in *Women Can't Hear What Men Don't Say*.

MYTH. *Fathers don't pay mother subsidies for one of two reasons: First, the father just plain refuses to pay; or, second, he runs away and the mother cannot locate the father. Even the Census Bureau confirms these two reasons.*

FACT. These "two reasons" are the *only two options listed* by the Census Bureau![29] Second, once again, the Census Bureau asked *only women* why fathers don't pay child support!

CURRENT POPULATION SURVEY

> 54. **What was the main reason you did not receive these payments regularly, was it because** ▉
> *(Read categories)*
> The father refused to pay? ◯
> You were unable
>   to locate father? . . . . . ◯
> Or was there
>   some other reason? . . . ◯
> ▉ *(Specify in notes)*

The problem with this? The *main* reason fathers don't pay *isn't even asked*. That is, all three major studies that have looked at why men do not pay have discovered the same thing: *The man's income level is the most important sin-*

gle determinant of whether he pays, how much he pays, and how regularly he pays.[30] (Each additional $1,000 in annual income is associated with a $301 rise in the annual award level.[31]) *Yet "inability to pay" is not even shown as an option in the Census Bureau question.* The result? We read in newspapers that the two main reasons men don't pay is because "they refuse" and "they can't be located." We are not told that these are the only two options listed!

Asking only women why men don't pay is like asking only men why women refuse visitation. Imagine paying taxpayer money to ask only men:

---

54. What was the main reason you did not receive visitation privileges regularly, was it because (Read categories)

- The mother refused?   ____

- You were unable to locate mother?   ____

- Or was there some other reason?   ____

  (Specify in notes)

If the Census Bureau asked only these questions and newspaper headlines read "Census Bureau Finds Mothers Refuse Visitation and Disappear with Children," I would quickly label that sexism. However, when we ask only women why men don't pay and give them two choices, both of which blame men and neither of which is the main reason, newspapers cite it as fact and virtually no one even questions it, much less calls it sexism.

Aren't there other reasons men pay or fail to pay child support? Yes. Regular payments in full are highly correlated with weekly visitation,[32] with a friendly relationship with the mother,[33] with shared parent-time arrangements,[34] residence in the same state,[35] a higher education level on the part of the mother,[36] the father being white.[37]

Fathers paid less when a formula was used to determine the award level,[38] when support was court-ordered , when he had to pay through a public agency (as opposed to directly),[39] when he was black (even when his income level and the number of children were identical to the white father's).[40]

Note that the Census Bureau offered none of these options, and thus headlines neglect to tell us that when a dad is allowed to see his children, he usually does, and when he sees them, he pays.

How Mom Can Get Dad to Pay

Dads who see their children pay for their children. When fathers were given access to their children, the default rate in mother-subsidy payments "dropped from as high as 70 percent (default) all the way down to 7 percent."[41] Another study found that contact with a child led to mother subsidy payments increasing from 34 percent to 85 percent.[42] A father who cannot love does not pay. Out of sight, out of wallet. Withholding payments is his only leverage to get love.

Do mothers really deny fathers contact with children? And, if so, why? Almost 40 percent *of mothers* reported they had refused one or more times to let their ex-husbands see the children, and acknowledged that "their reasons had nothing to do with the children's wishes or the children's safety, but were somehow punitive in nature."[43] Even more of the fathers—53 percent—said they had been denied "visitation" one or more times. The percentages were this high just within the first two years after divorce. This study was conducted by a woman, under a grant from the National Institute of Mental Health.

Other studies find that dads without shared parent time feel they do not withdraw from children's lives but are, instead, driven out.[44]

When dads (mostly) don't pay child support, the government steps in—it spends $3.4 *billion* on child support enforcement. When moms (mostly) deny dads access to children, the government backs out—it spends only $10 *million* on "visitation" enforcement. In essence, the government spends $340 disciplining dads for each dollar it spends disciplining moms.[45] But that's not the half of it. About 80 percent of the government money spent to enforce dads' access is given to agencies *without* access enforcement programs![46] Rather, they are given to agencies with programs that *limit* a dad's access—that is, programs that require his access be supervised. The money is still used to discipline dads, not moms. In reality, then, the spending is about $1,000 to discipline dads for each $1 to discipline moms.

The crime is that it is precisely Dad's access to children that leads both to children's emotional health and mom being paid. Few men want to pay mother subsidies to a woman—or to children—who have turned against him, any more than would a mother. Most dads want to be nurturers. They will pay to nurture.

But many dads resent the law requiring them to pay for children they did not father, or when they are tricked into making the woman pregnant, or when they are never informed they are a dad until the child is an adult, or are suddenly told the mother is moving so they'll have to fly 1,000 miles to see their child. Can fathers be forced to pay under these conditions? Let's start with men being forced to pay for children they did not father.

Can a Man Be Forced to Pay for a Child His Wife Conceived with Another Man?

ITEM. It was eleven years before an Indiana man discovered he was paying mother subsidy for a child that was not his. Yet the court did not allow him to stop paying—*even in the future.*[47]

ITEM. My phone rings. A San Diego woman named Sue is furious. "John, my new husband, is being sued for thirty thousand dollars of child support for a child who he's recently discovered is not his, but he can't even take a DNA blood test to prove that unless his ex-wife agrees—and she won't agree. Besides, he'd still have to pay child support even if he *could* prove the child wasn't his. I don't think this is fair. I am a law student and I want to fight it. DNA blood tests weren't even available when he signed the divorce papers, but when he signed divorce papers saying he had a child, he lost all his rights."

Note that it is Sue—and not John—who is so ready to do battle with John's former wife. Ironically, **the greatest advance in men's rights will probably occur when women's rights conflict with women's rights**—in this case, Sue's right to share her new husband's $30,000. It is when the rights of the former wife are depriving the current wife of rights because of men's lack of rights that we suddenly care about men's rights. (Of course, we are really just caring about women's rights.) Nevertheless, the women who fight for "men's" rights invest in good karma for themselves—as long as "men's" rights stop at fairness.

The solution? Making "paternity tests"—or DNA blood tests—routine upon the discovery of a pregnancy. A DNA blood test can be made a prerequisite for a birth certificate. In this way both the maternity and paternity are confirmed.

Why routine? If blood tests were not required before a marriage, each partner would fear "getting the marriage off to a bad start" by asking the other to take one. Similarly, a father feels caught between requesting a paternity test and preserving a happy marriage. (A husband cannot greet his pregnant wife with "be sure to take a DNA blood test before I decide whether to celebrate your pregnancy.") Making blood tests routine would help men know they are raising their own child just as women know they are raising theirs.

Are Paternity Tests Part of a Father's Constitutional Right to Life?

When a man has children, he is much more likely to take a job in the "death professions" to support them; he is more likely to work overtime; and more likely to take a job he likes less because it pays more. A man who is doing this to support a child which is not his has been subjected to a fraud that

48

The judge gave her everything—the kids, the car, even the house!

IS CHILD SUPPORT HELPING OR HURTING THE FAMILY?   185

might deprive him of life (the death professions), liberty (working over-time), and the pursuit of happiness (taking a job he dislikes). DNA blood tests can prevent that. Making such tests a prerequisite to a birth certificate is part of a father's right to life, liberty, and the pursuit of happiness.

Dads Still Pay When Moms Move Away

ITEM. A mother who had primary mom time with her two children remar-ried and moved with her children from California to Oklahoma. The father was unable to find the children for seven years, until they contacted him. The father stopped paying child support only when he could no longer con-tact his children. Yet the California court required the father to pay child support for all the years the children were, in effect, kidnapped from him.[49]

A colleague of mine—a father who could contact his child—described the pain he felt each time he put his son on a plane to fly halfway across the country to where his mother had moved: "Putting my seven-year-old boy on an airplane for the trip back home alone, and watching the tears roll silently down his face, was like dying a little."[50]

Fathers' Rights today is at the level of "Taxation Without Representa-tion."

9

"Visitation" Is for Criminals

Introducing . . . "Parent Time"

Most Mothers Want More of Dad in Their Children's Lives

Most mothers want *more* of Dad in their children's lives, not less. Perhaps the most taboo discussion for books on divorced parents is the mother and father *both* saying, "It's *your* turn to take the children"—each parent wanting *less* child time. Not because they don't love their children, but because divorce spreads *both* parents too thin (the woman, via her juggling act; the man, via his intensifying act: working fifty to seventy hours a week to meet the divorce's intensified financial burdens).

SAN DIEGO UNION-TRIBUNE   Thursday, April 25, 1996   1

(Steve Kelley is on vacation)

Raising children was not designed for single parents. (Which is why divorce was such a taboo prior to birth control.)

If we penalize mothers for denial of "visitation time," we must also penalize fathers who don't show up for "visitation time." The issue is not fathers' rights to visitation time, but both parents' obligations to their children. The issue is how to make both parents real parents despite what parenting was never designed to deal with—divorce.

"Visitation Time" Versus "Parent Time"

The word "visitation" accurately reflects a system that does almost all it can to reduce one parent to a visitor—to an "ex."[2] But while a spouse can become an "ex," a parent cannot. Any family in which both parents are alive is a two-parent family, even if the parents are divorced.

Our children are better served by speaking not of "visitation" *versus* "custody," but of "parent time." When we speak of Mom winning custody or of Dad getting visitation time, we speak of someone winning, someone losing. When we speak of Mom or Dad spending "parent time" with a child, we speak of two parents, not a parent versus a visitor.

Why worry about words? Less because they reflect reality than because they influence it. "Visitation" reflects the era of the absentee father; "parent time" influences the reemergence of the involved father. "Visitation" reflects the destruction of the family; "parent time" influences the reconstruction of the family. "Parent time" influences an era that understands that as either parents loses, so the children lose.

"Parent Time" as Psychological Child Support

ITEM. Forty-two percent of all children of divorce who are living with their mothers say their mothers tried to prevent them from seeing their fathers after the divorce. Only 16 percent of children who are living with their fathers reported that their dads tried to prevent their mothers from seeing them.[3]

When a parent denies a child its "parent time," that parent is denying the child its child support—its psychological child support. In many languages, such as Spanish, when "child support" is translated, the connotation is just that—psychological support. They understand that child support is *primarily* love. A child can't say, "Hey, Dollar Bill, I had a nightmare last night."[4]

The Child's Social Immune System: The Case for Denial of Parent Time as Child Abuse

A child might be thought of as possessing a *social immune system*. We now know that time with *both* parents strengthens the child against juvenile delinquency, drug addiction, damaged verbal and math skills, damaged intelligence, sexual confusion, mental instability . . . (Other than that, a child without a dad does great!)

A check can be written to compensate Mom for a delayed mother-subsidy payment; a dad can never experience the first words of a son once those words are missed, or the first steps of his daughter, or his children's first day of school, or even the humbling of the rebellion process. Nor can the child recover a memory of his or her dad reading bedtime stories that he never read, of cuddling he never did, of a school play he never attended, of a Little League game at which he never cheered—or even the memory of unwanted advice before a first date . . . a memory that ripens into knowing that his dad cared.

Denial of parent time is one of the deepest forms of child abuse exactly because stepping into a child's life is like stepping into the proverbial river that is never again the same. Fortunately it is a form of child abuse that can be stopped by preventing the abuser from receiving alimony and parent subsidy until the behavior changes, fining the abuser if the behavior doesn't change, and eventually removing the child from the abuser's home as we would from any abuser's home—once the abuse is verified. The alternative—requiring a father to finance the destruction of his children—combines mental cruelty to the father with the destruction of a generation that will pass on its destructive patterns to the next.

Why Automatically Assigning Moms the Children Usually Hurts the Mom, the Child, and the Dad

The expectation that women have the children after divorce is self-defeating for most women. Divorcing women rank finances as their single biggest worry.[5] The divorced woman is served best by building bridges away from economic dependency, toward economic autonomy. A woman with the children and without economic autonomy often "father hunts" and gets too quickly involved with a man she only convinces herself she loves; her economic dependency makes her feel like a prostitute to her new husband and a menace to her new husband's ex-wife. Reflexive maternal time, then, shoots women in their two Achilles' heels: security and love.

Reflexive maternal custody defeats men because, when men divorce, their primary area of desperation is lack of emotional connection. He has fewer same-sex friends; all his emotional "eggs of intimacy" are stored in the basket of his wife; thus his children take on a new importance—and are lost to him the moment they do. As a husband, he typically spent more time with his wife's family than with his own parents,[6] a family from which he is often isolated after divorce; conversely, she is much more likely to ask her family for both emotional and financial support after a divorce.

Children lose because the children pick up the strange combination of anger toward men and dependency on their money that is so strong among women whose divorces catalyzed feelings of economic helplessness rather than placing them in the workplace where they can gradually transform those feelings into a sense of mastery. If the mother is open to building an economic base independent of her former husband, she is frustrated by having no one to partner with her as a parent.

This leaves children shot in their two Achilles' heels: isolation from time with mother and/or psychological and physical isolation from father.

Reflexive mom time, then, shoots women, men, and children in their Achilles' heels just at their most vulnerable moment. The solution? Equal Opportunity Parenting.

Do Dads Really Care? Or Are Most Fathers Who Say They Want More Time with Their Children Just Trying to Reduce Mother-Subsidy Payments?

> . . . I had been in jail and on a hunger strike for eleven days—no food, just two cups of water per day. I had an undeniable fear that I was not going to make it out of there alive. . . . I saw my children being denied access to me, the judge ordering visitation and, then,

his resolute refusal to order sanctions against Sandra, my ex-wife, for continually violating his orders. There was the shame and the guilt and the impotence and the self-disgust. If I allowed my children to be involuntarily taken away from me, if I didn't resist this injustice by every means available, if I didn't force the court to listen, how could I look myself in the face, maintain my dignity, be a good man? . . . Like a rape victim, I knew I could not live with myself unless I fought back. . . .

DR. MAURICE SMALL[7]

After a divorce, men's biggest fear is, typically, losing their children (women's is poverty).[8] This doesn't ring true for many mothers because many fathers who don't seem to be very focused on their children when they are married suddenly become focused on their children after divorce and, as mentioned above, this makes many ex-wives suspicious that the fathers are claiming to want time with their children only to cut down their financial-support obligations. Of course this can be true, but we judge too quickly if we don't understand the divorced father's postpartum blues.

The Divorced Dad's Postpartum Blues

A father often feels that providing a financial womb is his sacrifice in return for which he receives a child's love, watches her or him grow, imparts his values, grows himself, and experiences life through his child's eyes. Divorce often means he remains a financial womb in return for whatever his ex allows. *Her* discretion. He is struck by the meaninglessness of a life without love, and by the realization that, when he divorced, his children became his only source of love and meaning. This creates the divorced dad's equivalent of the mom's postpartum blues.

If divorce makes dads aware of their need for love, why do some men in fathers'-rights groups sometimes seem angry, hurt, and bitter? Because it is also at this time that many fathers have the first sneaking suspicion that all along they've been used as a wallet so their wives could get their children's love. This generates anger. It is also the time many fathers wonder whether their wives ever really loved them. Which is hurtful. Then, when they reach out for their children's love, they discover they're not really theirs; they're hers—except when it comes to money. This generates bitterness. Many women, seeing the anger, hurt, and bitterness, understandably miss the genuineness of the love.

If dads really do care, why do many fathers seem to neglect their children the moment a new woman comes along? For Doug, it was like this: Divorce gave Doug the male equivalent of the woman's postpartum blues, but it also forced Doug to work an extra fifteen hours a week (to pay mother subsidy, mortgage, and rent for his own apartment). When he met Bonnie, she made him promise "a weekend for just the two of us." He promised. But then, his ex asked him to take the children that weekend. Doug knew that if he put the children or work before Bonnie again, Bonnie would walk; and Bonnie was the only one he could talk to about his problems with the divorce. However, Doug's ex saw only Doug's fudging about the weekend with the kids, so she felt his statements about how much he wanted to see the children were less than genuine. Doug felt caught between the two types of love he most needed—a problem every mother who is single should understand.

When men feel caught between two sources of love, they know how to pursue . . . as Gandhi pursued independence, and as Dr. Maurice Small pursued his children.

Why Mothers Deprive Fathers of "Dad Time"

While many women want their former husbands to spend more time with the children, some don't. What's going on in those cases? Sometimes it's the desire for mother subsidies, but usually something else is going on as well. These are the women most likely to see their children as both their primary job and their primary identity.

From a woman's perspective, sharing parent time feels like what a man might experience if his ex-wife came to his office and shared his career. He might claim the sharing is not in the best interests of the employer. But what he really would be caring about is the affront should his ex-wife do as well as he did at his own job. While the fear is understandable, the difference is that his career is his, their children are theirs.

The fear is not just that the estranged father will share in her identity, but that "dad time" will give the dad a chance to align the children against her, which will make her feel incompetent in the area of her primary identity. That feels to her like it would feel to a recently divorced man to see the colleagues at his office be aligned against him. So she might take the offensive and align the children against the father, helping her "prove" to herself that *he* was the one worthy of rejection—not her.

The more the woman is dependent on her former husband's mother-subsidy payments, the more she fears "dad time" might mean Dad picking up the children and spotting evidence for a trip she is taking or seeing new possessions that might provide documentation for him to make a case for lowering mother subsidy. Or evidence she is living with a new boyfriend and that her ex-husband will either burst into a jealous rage or protest in court that he is "paying money to have his children see their mother sleep around." Women who protest that "dad time" is just an excuse for her ex to continue interfering in her life are often feeling these feelings for these reasons. If, on top of this, her ex is at all critical of her parenting, the feelings of interference are likely to increase geometrically.

A father experiences these same fears every time his ex has the children. It is important for mothers to know that *and* it is important for men to know why her fears are often more threatening to her than his are to him, to the degree that children have become her primary identity.

Fathers often feel they are being denied "dad time" out of vindictiveness. This is most likely to happen after a divorce in which the woman felt like the rejected party. When rejected by someone we love, we feel "killed"; instinctively it is natural to want to "kill" what "killed" us. In Euripides' version of the classic Greek myth *Medea,* Jason leaves Medea for a beautiful princess. Medea seeks the ultimate revenge. She vows, "He shall never see alive again the sons he had from me . . . this is the way to deal Jason the deepest wound."

For the woman, the killing instinct also surfaces with an attempt to "kill" those things that allowed him to reject her (*e.g.*, his money, status, reputation, independence) and, second, to deprive him of everything she was offering him (emotional support, sex, children). Depriving him is her way of "killing" him—of making him miss her contribution—and of reaffirming to herself her own value.

What does *he* "kill"? Him*self.* Remember that he is ten times more likely than a woman to commit suicide after divorce?[9]

Whether as in the Medea myth, or in the aphorism "Hell hath no fury like a woman scorned,"[10] it is not coincidence that a woman's anger is at its most intense when she feels replaced by someone who has the beauty she used to own, which she fears will never be hers again. Thus, when Elizabeth Broderick was rejected by her husband for a younger woman, she eventually killed both her husband and his younger wife while they were in their bed.

In brief, a court cannot assume a mother has no motivation to deny a father "dad time." The motivation is understandable, but playing to it is rarely in the child's best interests.

Denial of Parent Time Is Not Only Unconstitutional . . . It Is Taxation Without Representation

Both parents have Constitutionally guaranteed rights to see their children. Depending on the period in history and the context, it has been protected by their right to "life, liberty, and the pursuit of happiness";[11] by the Fourth Amendment's "unreasonable seizure" clause (in which a child cannot be taken from a parent without "due process"); or by the Equal Protection clause of the Fourteenth Amendment.[12]

The problem for fathers has been that tradition runs thicker than equality. When the law must choose between the tradition of motherhood or equality, tradition wins. Tradition ignores equality, runs around equality, creates conflicting laws, and depletes incentive to enforce judgments that favor equality if they are in tension with tradition.

To pay child support and be denied time with a child is taxation without representation. Yet when a woman denies a man his parent time, judges often feel in a bind: They cannot punish the mother by denying her financial support, because that also deprives the child of financial support. Nor can the judge put the mother in jail, since that deprives the child of a mother.

But there's a problem the judge neglects: A mother who denies a child its father is committing one of the most documentable forms of child abuse.

How Any Mother Can Deny a Child Its "Dad Time"

Although the majority of mothers want father-child contact, it is currently almost impossible to stop a mother who doesn't.[13] She can align the child against the dad, move out of the area, send the child to relatives, make phone contact with the father almost impossible (thereby frustrating arrangement-making and maximizing misinterpretations via messages), withhold information about the child's progress in school, or claim *she* had been abused by him.

Perhaps the most potent form of preventing the father from seeing the child is exemplified by the tale of the two Elizabeths: Elizabeth Morgan and Elizabeth Broderick. Elizabeth Morgan claimed her daughter was sexually abused by her dad; Elizabeth Broderick claimed *emotional* abuse. The tale of the two Elizabeths has another thing in common: Without evidence of the mother's claim, neither father ever saw his children again once the Elizabeths were done with them.

A child's report of taking a bath or shower or cuddling up in bed together in the morning followed by "strange behavior" can create legitimate concern. It can also serve as an excuse to have the dad investigated, knowing both that he will be damaged no matter what the outcome and that the child's report is enough to protect her from being accused of making a malicious or false accusation. More than a few fathers have told me that when they wanted to pay less or get more "dad time," their exes merely threatened to "report you and Cindy being in the nude together." Almost all these fathers feared the consequences and backed off. Practically speaking, a woman who wants to keep a dad from a child is currently a power with no checks or balances.

When the *New York Times* ran a guest editorial by a feminist on the deadbeat dad, a woman with a different experience took her to task:

> My friend went to see his children every Friday for twenty-four months. Half the time the house was dark, and no one answered the door. The other half, though the children's mother was nowhere in sight, the oldest child answered the door, shouted some insults and accusations, echoed by his two siblings standing on the stairs behind him, and sixty seconds later the door slammed in his face.[14]

Yet if you were to ask them and his former wife today if he ever visited them, they would all solemnly swear he had never been there once, never sent the cards and letters that were returned in 1,000 tiny pieces, never cared for them, never sent the $22,000 a year he has sent in child support and alimony for the last seven years. And your reporter would be deeply sympathetic and swallow every word, because women never lie about such serious matters, and men, as we all know, are swine.

When, oh when, is the real truth about the human condition going to come through in our post-feminist world?

JANE JAFFE YOUNG, NEW YORK, IN LETTERS TO THE EDITOR
The New York Times, JUNE 28, 1990

Most denials of father time, though, do not involve the father knocking on his ex-wife's door and finding that she has absconded with the children. *It involves the ex-wife not allowing the child to leave the home.*[15] This is the most common complaint, registered by almost 70 percent of the more than 6,000 fathers who called various hotlines. The problem is that the mother who prevents the child from leaving the home can be technically obeying the court order (she is allowing "*visitation*").

Parents who completely deny their children access to the other parent are, in essence, kidnappers. Theoretically, they should be prosecuted under the Federal Parental Kidnapping Act of 1980. However, this is rarely done when a mother kidnaps a child—but quickly done when the dad does.

Should Women with Children Have the Right to Move?

Should women with children have the right to move? Yes. Should children have the right to both parents? Yes. Should both parents have the right to their children? Yes.

We all want women to have the right to move, children to have the right to both parents, and parents to have the right to their children. But when the woman's right to move away means that the father and children will become strangers, then the woman's right is no more a unilateral right than is the children's or the father's right to each other's love.

The solution? A Divorced Parent Move Law that would make it illegal for a mother *or father* to just take the children and move away without attempting to work out a mutually agreeable arrangement with the other parent. If they agree, no problem. If they don't, they must seek mediation. If mediation fails, then the issue can be settled in court. Under no circumstances, though, can a parent move away without going through at least the first step.

What percentage of time did the fathers complain that the mother had falsely accused him of sexual abuse (as a way of denying the child its "dad time")? Thirteen percent.[16] The accusation allowed the mothers not to be seen as disobeying a court order by denying parent time. It allowed them to get the order reversed.

In the past, when a mother abused a child by depriving it of its father, he could retaliate by withholding funds, and the law generally let them fight it out themselves. Until recently, this battle contained at least some semblance of balance. Now the mother can legally get sole mom time, legally have his wages garnisheed, and legally—with an unproven accusation of child abuse—deny "dad time." The father has none of these protections (except theoretically). When accused of sex abuse, he has lost even the basic legal right of being considered innocent 'til proven guilty. He is beaten dead by the system. I would estimate that for each "deadbeat dad" there are three "beat dead dads."

Toward Some Solutions

The Balanced Parenting Act

The solution is not fathers' rights—it's balanced parenting. It is unconstitutional to deprive either parent of his or her child, but it is immoral to deprive a child of either parent. For reasons that hopefully became apparent in Part I, the starting assumption of divorcing parents, mediators, and courts needs to be "children need both parents—let's make that happen." That will not happen unless fathers have equal rights. But equal rights is a means, balanced parenting is the goal. And a Balanced Parenting Act[17] should make that clear. Which is why organizations that care about fathers' rights are increasingly using names like National Council for Children's Rights—because their goal is the children, not the fathers.

If Women Have an Equal EMPLOYMENT Opportunity Commission, Why Don't Men Have an Equal FAMILY Opportunity Commission?

We have seen that when divorce occurs, we demand that the man reimburse the woman for economic losses, but not that the woman reimburse the man for family losses—loss of contact with his children and his wife's contributions to the family. Our institutions reflect this sexism: Women who are denied equal access to employment can seek help from an Equal *Employment* Opportunity Commission; men who are denied equal access to children cannot seek help from an Equal *Family* Opportunity Commission.

An Equal Family Opportunity Commission would assist dads who were deprived of parent time, who couldn't make mother-subsidy payments, who felt falsely accused of child abuse. A father can contact a local commission if he feels his "dad time" has been denied; the commission can hold his mother-subsidy payment in escrow. After the commission's investigation, the payment is disbursed accordingly. Holding the payments in escrow gives the father no incentive to falsely accuse the mother of denying him "dad time" in order to have an excuse not to pay the mother, and discourages the mother from denying her child "dad time" because she also knows she will jeopardize her payment.

If it did nothing else, the Equal Family Opportunity Commission could save the country billions of dollars by investing millions to create a nationwide network of counseling centers for divorced dads. How?

The Men's EEOC (Equal EMOTIONAL Opportunity Commission)

When divorce makes everyone feel "not needed," at least a mother feels needed by children. A father often feels needed by no one—emotionally. For a mother, the isolation of divorce is at least buffered by her *increased* emotional connection to the children. His isolation is compounded by *decreased* contact with his children. In brief, he experiences a second emotional divorce. Were we to start an EEOC for men, the second "E" might stand for "Emotional"—an Equal *Emotional* Opportunity Commission.

A divorced father who loses his children often feels "fired" from the family. He does not feel good about writing monthly checks to the person who "fired" him. A woman can empathize by picturing how it would feel to give severance pay to an employer who fired her. He feels he is paying to be rejected.

Men who are paying money to the person who fired them from their children feel like they are being asked to do their old job (breadwinner) without the old benefits (children). This might be fine for men who don't want contact with their children, but for the majority who *do*, it feels like "no say, just pay"—or "open wallet, shut mouth" . . . or "taxation without representation." And that's fodder for a revolution!

A divorced man most often misses the emotional grounding he once experienced when he returned home to people he felt needed him. If his wife was genuinely emotionally supportive, he also misses her, not just her role. When divorce occurs, we leave men with an emotional deficit that leads them to seek emotional support from financially needy and immature women. It ropes him into a needy woman both trapping him and making his ex-wife think, "What a jerk. . . . Maybe I was too easy on him." As for the new, needy woman, it keeps her financially dependent, sets her up to fight with his ex for their competing needs, and sets up his children to hear bad things about Dad from Mom. Might it be cheaper for our society to give him some emotional support?

For many men it goes even deeper. A man often feels he is the object of his ex-wife's contempt—a contempt that can be turned into law. That is, she can make him the only man in the world who is specifically prevented *by law* from spontaneously seeing his children without her permission. This feels to many dads as if their children have been killed. But . . .

He must deal with more than this "killing" of his children—he must deal with their "deaths" without a mourning—because they are never acknowledged as dead. When my brother was killed in an avalanche, no one in the family could sleep well until we found his body. Why? Because finding his body and burying him, although excruciating, nevertheless allowed us to begin the process of mourning and healing. When a dad's child is dead to him, but still alive, he can never begin the process of mourning; he can never heal. We feel this unhealed hurt and bitterness when we meet dads who are denied their children.

For some dads, even the analogy to his not being able to mourn over a child's "death" is inadequate. Female-conducted studies show that 50 percent of moms are still talking negatively about dads a year and a half after the divorce (versus 20 percent of dads). When we multiply this times the ten-to fifteen-times-greater likelihood of a mother to be with the child, we can get some feel for many dads who, when they see their children, see the anger of their ex-wife in their own child's eyes. For many dads, hearing "I love you, Dad" turn into "I hate you, Dad," just weeks after his separation, feels like knives of anger stabbing him in his heart while he's reaching out to seek an ounce of love at a time he needs it the most.

How does a dad defend himself against a child who has been turned against him by an angry mother? He steels his heart. He becomes afraid to call. Afraid to visit. Afraid to be a dad. Sometimes even afraid to be. When asked to pay child support, he feels emotionally dead—like a man being asked to send a check from the grave.

What can an Equal *Emotional* Opportunity Commission do? Something as simple as refer him to a support group or a masculinist therapist (specializing in male issues after divorce); set up men's coffeehouses; train ombudsmen to communicate with ex-wives; network with other men and children in similar positions via camping or sports; car pool; take each others' children for weekends; plan joint trips with groups of women, or, if worse comes to worst, refer him to a book to read! It would cost us all a lot less than suing each other.

The worst form anger can take is that of a parent who feels her or his chance for "winning my child" is enhanced by "ruining my ex." The law has given the most vindictive parent an invitation to play the "abuse" card. This is the Great Temptation.

10

Playing the "Abuse" Card

As I discuss in Part I, abuse is not parenting, but poisoning. And sexual abuse is especially insidious. Sexual abuse is most frequent between stepfather and stepdaughter. Because the problem is both so real and frequent, virtually everyone is afraid to question any accusation or hint of accusation. However, when the fear of questioning an accuser overpowers due process and the assumption of innocence until proven guilty, families and children can be abused in the following ways. . . .

Sex Abuse Charges: True or False?

An Overview

ITEM. Douglass Tarrant, an assistant superintendent of schools in Florida, was accused of committing a lewd and lascivious act. He did not know that his fifteen-year-old accuser had recanted her story two days earlier.[1] He made a videotape proclaiming his innocence. Then he shot himself.

ITEM. Eighty percent of child sex-abuse accusations are determined to be unfounded.[2]

ITEM. In Florida, 92 percent of child-abuse cases appealed (*after initial guilty verdict*) were found to be false or unsubstantiated.[3] All 1,200 of the people appealing had previously been listed by the Human Resource Services as "confirmed" child abusers. Had they not appealed, they would have remained on the Department's computer files as confirmed abusers for fifty years.

ITEM. Approximately 80 percent of people accused of child abuse *who are eventually found innocent* nevertheless lose their jobs or suffer other employment problems.[4]

ITEM. There has been a 2,000 percent increase in *sex*-abuse allegations in the past ten years.[5] (Author's note: All child-abuse allegations have increased, but sex-abuse allegations have skyrocketed.)

Some charges of sexual abuse are neither "true" nor "false," but a matter of interpretation. A child told that nudity is filthy who then sees her or his parents walking around in the nude might experience trauma, but a child who is told that nudity is natural might be more traumatized by a parent slamming the door when the parent sees the child walk by as the parent is dressing. One family's healthiness is another's abuse. **What is traumatic or abusive to the child is very much related to what is consistent with the family's belief about what is moral.** This does not mean the family's belief should overrule the law, but that failure to first speak privately to a family—and with an *innocent*-until-proven-guilty approach—prior to taking legal action, results in experiences like this. . . .

From Norway to America, Soviet Style

Four days before Christmas, Margaret and Steve Gran and their family were all having family dinner together in their home in Minneapolis.[6] There was a knock on the door. A cadre of police presented the Grans with a warrant for the emergency removal of their children. The children were hysterical. An officer picked up one tiny daughter and the other ran and hid under the bed and cried until the mother persuaded the child to come out so the police could take the children away. The police took the children away for sixteen days to a "Home Away for Tots."

How did this happen? According to the *Wall Street Journal,* a "tip" on the part of a neighbor—that Mr. Gran had sexually abused one of his children—led, without investigation, to the children's removal. Upon investigation, it was concluded that the suspicions were unfounded.

By the time the youngsters were returned home, "they weren't the same children," the *Wall Street Journal* reports Mrs. Gran as explaining. "They were traumatized."

Six years after this experience, Mrs. Gran reported that their children are still afraid of the police and are still constantly fearful of losing their parents. When the Grans sued the county for removing the children prior to an investigation, the federal judge ruled that the county enjoyed qualified immunity from lawsuits. The Supreme Court refused to hear an appeal.

This is not, though, a phenomenon limited to America. 'Round-the-world headlines told us recently of a Norwegian man, who had been charged with rape, holding up thirty-five hostages at gunpoint, including women and children.

Behind the headlines was another story. The man had been granted primary parent time with his children. His former wife responded with a rape charge.[7] Without investigation, his children were immediately taken from him. He was allowed no contact, doubtless leaving the children with only their mother's version of why the police had to remove them and why he couldn't contact them.

In May of 2000, his son turned thirteen. His pleas for his son to call him fell on deaf ears. Without the ear of social workers or police, he snapped. But not in the way the headlines led us to believe. . . .

He immediately told the hostages he would not hurt them. He only wanted a half-hour of TV time to explain his case, to get someone to listen. If he couldn't get it, he would hurt only himself—he might commit suicide. He released all but seven hostages. He got the TV time. He immediately told the police and public the only person at risk was himself. A panel of psychologists listening on TV (you know how the media brings in us expert-types to make everyone feel they're having a sociological experience watching their local version of Cops versus Daddies) asked what drove him to such desperation. He explained about not being able to call his son, not being able to be heard, and concluded, "When you have been so unfairly treated by the social services and the police, there is nothing left . . . many would kill themselves because they couldn't handle it—I have nothing to lose."[8]

Whether in America or Norway, when we don't remove children from someone charged with abuse, yes, we leave the children at risk. But when assumptions of guilt precede assumptions of innocence, and thus action precedes due process, the children are not put at risk, they are *guaranteed* to be damaged. In twelve ways. . . .

How a Charge of Possible Child Abuse Can Create the "Twelve Guarantees of Child Abuse" . . . Even if the Charge Is True

There are one million *investigations* of *possible* child abuse each year by child-protection agencies in the United States. Of these, only 150,000 are substantiated enough to get to court. Of these 150,000, *only 8 percent represent alleged sexual abuse*—and only half of these are substantiated by the court.[9] Put another way, only six out of every 1,000 child-abuse investigations (just over half of 1 percent) end up being *substantiated* cases of *sexual* abuse.

What is the role of the *natural* father in child sexual abuse? Only one of four of the substantiated cases of sexual abuse is by the natural father.[10] Thus we can see that **only 1.5 out of 1,000 child-abuse investigations end up being a *substantiated* case of *sexual* abuse by the *natural* father.**[11]

How does this relate to the accusations made about Steve Gran? The chances are about one and a half out of a thousand that they were accurate. For that chance, the kids were exposed to a guarantee of at least a decade of trauma.

Emotionally, I understand this. My own emotional response to hearing that a child might be home with an abusive parent is, "We can't risk leaving that child with an abusive parent for one more minute." Were someone to push me on the issue, my gut response is "it's better to falsely accuse a parent than fail to protect a child."

When I think about it, though, there are two possibilities. Abuse; no abuse. If there is abuse, it could be one-time, or ongoing. If the abuse is a *one-time* thing, then "one more minute" is not a crime as long as the child is informed that the investigation proceeded at an emergency rate of speed; if the abuse has been going on for years, one more minute is not going to alter the child's fundamental psyche, again, as long as the child is informed that the investigation proceeded at an emergency rate of speed. Those are the abuse possibilities.

On the other hand, if there was no abuse at all, then the emergency separation creates a trauma—and therefore guarantees abuse (where none existed before). How? The moment a parent is prohibited from seeing a child because of *possible* sex abuse is the moment we subject that child to a *guarantee* of abuse.

How a Charge of Child Abuse Creates Twelve Guarantees
of Child Abuse

1. The child's image of his or her parent is transformed—from parent-as-trusted-loved-one-and-protector to parent-as-possibly-untrustworthy-criminal-and-abuser;

2. There is a loss of innocence;

3. A filter of suspicion and mistrust is created through which that child will view all men (or women)—often for years;

4. The child undergoes repeated interrogations by police, psychologists, and welfare agencies, in which a child saying she or he was not abused is seen as in the "denial phase" or being "unaware that 'touching like that is abuse.'" The child feels caught between parents and "authorities," unable to please both;

5. The child is given a never-to-be-forgotten image of his or her mother and father as each other's enemy;

6. The child is played off by one parent against the other;

7. The child feels personally responsible for driving the family apart, and lives with the image of being someone who not only cannot be loved, but who destroys love;

8. The child's dad and/or mom spend approximately $75,000 for lawyers, psychological testing, and expert witnesses; this can lead to anything from money conflicts to poverty, and often Dad is fired;

9. The child feels powerless to prevent his or her own stability from being undermined;

10. The child's dad or mom, who used to provide touching, now deprives the child of touching, responding to the child more with fear than love;

11. The child feels that neighbors and schoolmates think of his or her mom or dad as a criminal, often at a time in the child's life when peer-group pressure rules; and

12. The child is given a sense that she or he can get the parent into legal trouble any time the parent does something the child does not like, which undermines the ability of the parent to discipline, thus depriving the child of a real parent.

We have to balance these *guarantees* of abuse with the *possibility* that we are preventing an even worse form of abuse. We must be quite certain that the form of abuse we might prevent is worse than these twelve layers of abuse combined.

The Legal Dilemma

The probability of this occurring is increasing as states are passing laws that subject teachers, healthcare workers, and daycare operators to up to a year in prison for failing to report any mention of anything that could be potential abuse. Teachers who hear a child saying, "Daddy spanked me" fear being put in prison themselves should they fail to report it.

The underlying legal problem is that in normal criminal proceedings, defendants have the right to confront their accusers during trials and preliminary hearings. In these family-law cases, these rights of the defendant virtually disappear—which in practice means the police can literally knock on the door and take the father or the children away, as we would envision in a nightmare about the Soviet Union.

Is the Fear of Being Labeled an Abuser a Form of Psychological Sterilization?

When charges of child abuse result in any action that is apparent to the public or the children *prior to* a thorough investigation and private interviews with the person accused, a problem is created that runs even deeper than another form of child abuse. People become afraid to become parents.

I can predict that whenever I am doing a workshop in a community where sexual-abuse charges have been in the newspapers, more than a few men who have not yet had children will say something like, "All my life I looked forward to being spontaneous, cuddly, tickly, loving, comforting with my children. I would die if I were ever accused of sexual abuse because my daughter told someone about the way I played with her or touched her and some adult decided to report that as sexual abuse. It makes me scared to be a parent."

This fear of becoming a parent because of fear of being labeled an abuser leads to a new type of sterilization—psychological sterilization. Sexual abuse, like walking across a dangerous street, can create serious problems. And so can overprotection to the point of depriving our children of love and play.

Child Protection as Parent Abuse as Child Abuse

ITEM. Missouri reports 109 false or unconfirmed reports of child abuse *per day*.[12] This amounts to one out of every fifty-two households in Missouri *per year*.[13]

Think about this. If a Missouri couple has three children, they have perhaps twenty-eight years during which they are raising those children— about a 90 percent chance of being accused of child abuse during one of those years. Obviously, if they go through a parent-time battle, those odds increase; if one is a dad, those odds increase yet again.

ITEM. When people are accused in Florida, they are not told that a charge has been made.[14] They are placed in a child-abuse registry and remain there for seven years *even if they are found innocent* and are, therefore, really themselves victims. Many of these people are parents reported anonymously by children.

Most people can understand why a charge would remain on the books for a few years even if the person were innocent—if a person has been accused seven previous times, it's helpful for a judge to know that. But when 80 to 90 percent of reports are unfounded, then we know that seven years on the books is a setup for character assassination.

Teachers in Florida have become afraid to be strict for fear of having a student register an angry call.[15] For example, a student who gets a bad grade can tell a teacher, "Give me an F and I'll phone in an anonymous tip that you molested me—and you'll be listed as a sexual abuser for the next seven years. And if you talk your way out of it the first time, I'll call up again next week, then the week afterward. In other words, *if I fail, you're in jail.*"

Which of us would want to be the parent reported by a neighbor for abuse after we had spanked or slapped a child, and discover we already had three accusations on record? When a person contemplating having a child knows one mistake can give her or him "a record," she or he can become afraid of having a child.

The child's ability to get the parent into trouble with the law can give the child more power than the parent. Power without responsibility. To give the child no protection is a mistake, but to give the child the ability to summon the police to cross-examine parents without first asking to speak over the phone to the parents, without inviting the parent and child to see a counselor first, is to tip the scales in the opposite direction—and, in the long run, to hurt the child.

This woman put it succinctly: "Until a parent can be a parent and the child not run the household, I would not be a parent again."

Teachers and parents are increasingly telling me stories like the following:

> Maria was fourteen, on the verge of dropping out of school, and had "a mouth as foul as a lake of rotting fish." Well, one night she agreed to be home by six for dinner and homework. She and her boyfriend drove up after midnight—no call, nothing. I looked outside and saw Tony and Maria making out in the car, his hands under her blouse. When Maria finally came in, she didn't even bother to tuck in her blouse—or to button it. I was livid, but tried to make believe I hadn't seen her in the car and was just concerned that she had gotten into an accident. My hands were shaking, but I microwaved her dinner, and put it on the table. She ignored it. I asked if everything was okay—what had kept her out late. Her response? "Fuck off—get off my case."
>
> "I've told you a dozen times—no swearing in this house." . . .
> My stomach was turning. She'd gotten worse and worse for months now. I felt helpless, but I decided I'd stop hollering and make a peace offering. "Here's your dinner." She spit in the dinner, saying, "Take your shit and shove it." That was it. I lost my cool, went over

and slapped her. She spit in my face. I felt this gob of wetness and contempt dripping from my eye and nose. She sneered with a mocking smile, as if to say, "Fool." She swung her hair back then just walked away as if to say, "I finished you off, you little nothing." I couldn't take it any more. I turned her around and slapped her again, but this time hard. Her lip was a little cut.

She calmly walked over to the phone, dialed 911, and then suddenly, when the police answered, she feigned a child's fear: "Help me, please, my mother's hitting me all over the place." . . . She even pretended to be too distraught to remember her address . . . for a second. When she hung up, she smiled a victorious smile. She pointed to her eye and challenged, "Hit me here, that'll look good—come on, right here—come on, you afraid?" I was so furious that I did. She kept challenging, "Try the lip again." I could imagine the police about to drive up so I stopped. Within minutes, the police arrived and cross-examined me like a criminal. It was 12:30 in the morning and lights were going on in our neighbors' homes, people standing in the street. To this day everyone in the neighborhood looks at me differently—like I have a scarlet "A" for "Abuser" or something.

But that's the least of it. The police didn't take me away, but now I have a record of being reported for child abuse. I'm afraid to touch her again—or even to be strict. She's let me know in no uncertain terms she'd have no second thoughts about hitting herself, ripping her clothes, calling the police, and telling them I did it. Even if the police believed me, another scene like that would be a nightmare. I'm taking Valium, waking up in the middle of the night, wondering what I've done wrong. But most of all, I worry how my inability to set boundaries and enforce them will affect her life. I'm hurt *now*. She's the one who's going to be hurt for life.

Big Brother or Family Privacy?

The child-abuse laws in many states now define child abuse to include any type of *potential* child *neglect*. Martin Guggenheim, a juvenile-law scholar and professor at New York University Law School, finds the law written so broadly that virtually every parent is guilty of child abuse several times each week. Poor people even more so. This wastes the resources needed to zero in on protecting children who are genuinely abused. It has led to credible evidence of abuse being found after investigation in only one-quarter of the cases in New York State.[16] And to others, it has also led to our worst nightmares of Big Brother intruding on the privacy of family life.

What can we expect if we don't stop "the overprotection trend"? In Australia, sexual abuse of a child has been expanded to include "looking at the child's genitals for too long a period of time" as interpreted by the mother. If the father bathes a child and the mother feels the father is looking at the child's genitals for too long, she can accuse him of sexual abuse. The opposite cannot occur.[17]

In Australia, the man can be accused of "putting the child at risk," which means merely that the mother *fears* that the father could be a threat to the child. "Putting the child at risk" requires no evidence that the father has ever done anything that has, in practice, put the child at risk. The mere accusation makes judges back off from giving primary dad time—even shared parent time—to the father.

How Innocent Men's Lives Are Ruined by Unsubstantiated Abuse Charges

By the time Gary Emerson's wife dropped charges of child sexual abuse and Gary retained primary parent time of his three children, legal bills forced Gary into Chapter 13 bankruptcy.[18]

Gary's family had lived in Traverse City for a century, but, in Gary's words, "When people start reading your name in the paper for bankruptcy hearings and hearing your name on the radio for child molesting, you find out who your friends are. . . . Guys I used to go hunting or fishing with, I don't hear from them anymore. You call them and they're too busy."

Adult Morality Versus Children's Needs

Some years ago, I worked as a camp director at a camp attended by both adults and children. In a session with parents, a few divorced mothers expressed concern about having men sleep overnight in their home, particularly if they weren't serious. In a session with the children, I asked them how they felt. I got blank stares. Finally one of the girls said, "It depends. I love it when Mom has David over, but the other guys—uh, so-so. David always plays with me and *all* of us go to the movies and on trips together, so it's great. But the others just pick up Mommy and then I don't see Mom 'til the next day."

The adults' concern was sex. The children's needs were attention. The parents and children had a different "morality."

A number of the parents found it useful to see how their desire to protect their children had led them to become so preoccupied with projecting adult morality onto their children that they neglected to even ask their children about their real needs—for attention, respect, and love.

Cross-culturally, sexual abuse is very much a function of interpretation. Children's textbooks in Holland, Sweden, Denmark, and Norway frequently picture children and adults in the nude. In books to which parents allow their children access, pictures of people making love are considered part of sex education, not pornography. Crimes of rape and sexual molestation in those cultures are much lower than in the U.S.

I believe that one of the twenty-first century's most difficult "questions of introspection" will be: "Have we become a nation so preoccupied with projecting our adult morality onto children that we are *creating trauma* by creating taboos while simultaneously ignoring our children's real needs— their needs for attention, playfulness, discipline, touching, and love?" Protecting our children is a virtue, but every virtue, taken to its extreme, becomes a vice.

Sex-Abuse Education or Bedwetting?

While sex abuse education in the schools makes children more aware of genuine abuse, it also scares children and gives some the message that they can get attention by reporting touching as abuse.

A study in Berkeley found that about half of preschool children who had gone through a sex abuse program were more likely to see being tickled or given a bath as worrisome.[19] Another study found that sex-abuse programs led pre-schoolers to be frightened if they had to ride home from school with anyone but their parents.[20] Many parents report their children having nightmares and wetting their beds after exposure to these programs.[21] Yet more than half of elementary school children go through them.[22]

Real-Life Examples

A Law for Men, A Law for Women: New York

ITEM. An anonymous caller reported that a father in Schenectady County, New York, sexually abused his two toddlers and infected them with a venereal disease. The father immediately passed a lie-detector test and took an examination proving he had no venereal diseases. Despite the evidence, social-service officials recommended he be denied the right to see his children. A family-court judge agreed. (Under New York law, a social worker needs only "an indication" or "some credible evidence" to have a child placed in foster care.) The nightmare lasted a year and a half before it was revealed that the mother's live-in boyfriend had the same venereal disease as the children. Even then, the father was allowed to see his children, but only under strict supervision.[23]

ITEM. A mother named Marybeth Tinning in Schenectady, New York, killed several of her children. Officials didn't even suspect her—it was labeled "coincidence." It was only when she murdered her daughter, Tami Lynn, in a similar and unusual manner that she was tried and found guilty and became a suspect in the murder of *seven* of her other nine children.[24] This is the same Schenectady, New York, where an anonymous tip led to a father and child being denied the right to see each other.

A Law for Men, a Law for Women: Michigan

ITEM. Grace Geer of Michigan testified that she saw her husband David sexually molest their three-year old daughter.[25] Only one expert witness—a medical doctor—testified to the accuracy of the sexual-molestation charge, yet the twelve-person jury returned a guilty verdict. David was sentenced to between six and fifteen years in prison. While David was in prison, a lone detective remained unconvinced that justice had been served. He continued his investigation and eventually Grace Geer admitted to him that she had never seen David abuse their daughter.

When David was found innocent, the prosecutor, whose job it is to be suspicious of everyone until a suspect is convicted, said, "Mrs. Geer is *not* a suspect in this crime. And we're convinced that she does not know who molested the girl. She has no guilty knowledge of this crime."[26] Let's take a closer look at this statement.

David and Grace had been married nine years. Over those nine years, there was never any incidence of physical abuse between Grace and David. Grace, though, was involved in a couple of affairs and left David almost thirty times in their nine years of marriage. She would take the child and move in with a girlfriend or boyfriend. Could Grace's abuse charge of David be a way of Grace "covering her rear"? Maybe yes, maybe no. But the prosecutor will never know until someone has the guts to inquire.

Under the circumstances, convicting David while never investigating Grace tells us much about our willingness to ruin men, and our readiness to protect women.

When the original decision was made to find David guilty, two members of the jury were in tears, sensing they were making a mistake punishing David, feeling that Grace was lying, but desperately wanting to "do" something. Men's surface appearance of strength makes men the perfect victims for scapegoating.

One of the common mistakes made in sexual-molestation cases is proving the enlargement or reddening of the daughter's genitals or anus, then assuming the enlargement was due to molestation, then assuming it must be Daddy—or Mommy's boyfriend—who did it. A parallel process was quite common during the Spanish Inquisition: "This person has been accused of creating social disorder. Yes, social disorder does exist; it must, therefore, be caused by the accused; execute him."

Scapegoating, although destructive, is understandable. It helps a society send the message that the crime will not be tolerated. But when the scape-goats are almost all one group within the society, it tells us everything about the contempt and anger we hold for members of that group. And in sexual-abuse cases, the scapegoats are almost always men. They are not the only ones accused, but the ones most likely to be held in prison for months be-fore a trial and treated as guilty until proven innocent. If Jews were similarly singled out and then given unfair trials, would we tolerate it?

When a Dad Put Medicine on His Daughter's "Hiney" . . .

Janet Singer had ordered more than 1,000 tranquilizers in the year prior to slashing her wrists in a suicide attempt.[27] She was admitted to a mental-health clinic, and primary parent time of her daughter was given to the baby's father, Cecil Smith. After Janet recovered, she went to a lawyer's of-fice.[28] Following a visit to her lawyer, she reported to a social-work agency that her husband, Cecil, had abused their daughter, Amanda, by putting medicine on her "hiney." While at the agency, Janet obtained a Human Re-source Services (HRS) manual on techniques of abuse detection, and then, it was revealed in court, trained her daughter to play with dolls in a manner which HRS would consider indicative of abuse.

Janet then took Amanda to a therapist, claimed the child seemed de-pressed and disturbed, and hinted at abuse. The therapist told Janet that if she did not report the child's father to the HRS, then he would be forced to do so. Janet proceeded to report the abuse to both the HRS and the local sheriffs. The HRS interviewed the child, who pointed on the doll to the area of her "hiney" on which her dad had put the medicine and said it had hurt. An inexperienced caseworker concluded it was abuse.

In fact, Amanda's dad had put medicine on her "hiney" after his daugh-ter complained it hurt and after his parents recommended that he do that. But the conclusion of abuse was reported to Florida Judge David Harper who, also without interviewing Cecil, authorized the sheriffs to arrest Ce-cil. *Without a trial,* Cecil was thrown into maximum security prison with rapists and murderers. He was prevented from seeing his daughter.

As an alleged child molester in maximum security, Cecil was at "the bottom rung of the ladder" among prisoners, even below murderers, meaning the most subject to being anally raped. Cecil got away with having his throat grabbed and being choked. After five weeks he was switched out of maximum security, but kept in prison for an additional half-year. The charge against him was capital sexual battery, which carries a mandatory penalty of twenty-five years to life.

Cecil had never been in prison before, had good community ties, had taken primary responsibility for ten years for Janet's two children from a previous relationship, was considered a devoted parent, and yet was given an initial bail of a *half-million dollars*. His attorney filed three motions for a speedy trial, all of which were turned down for technical reasons.

After seven months in prison, Cecil got a trial. He was found innocent. He can now visit his daughter. Although the judge chastised Janet for manipulating the system, he concluded that since Amanda had been in the custody of Janet recently, it was best to keep Amanda in a stable place. So Janet accomplished her goal—the return of custody.

When I interviewed Cecil, I could tell he felt beaten, frustrated, and depressed. He had some hope that talking about it and exposing the system would help others, but when CBS's *48 Hours* called him for an interview, Cecil said a "gag order" was placed on him. But the straw that broke his back, he said, was learning that *Janet was now tutoring her best friend on how to get primary parent time of her and her husband's children*; that her friend is even going to the same social worker, even the same doctor.

Daughter Denies Abuse, So Why Is Dad in Prison?

Raymond Hunter, like Cecil Smith, was caring for his children while his wife, Brenda, was suffering from mental illness.[29] Brenda Hunter had been under regular psychiatric care for the past fifteen years and lived in Atlanta with her mother; Raymond lived with their two children in Dayton, Ohio. One day Brenda approached her mother with the accusation that Raymond was doing "something" with their daughter. Her mother placed a call to Children's Services of Dayton (CSD), who in turn contacted the Dayton police department.

Raymond's daughter and ten-year-old son were immediately taken from him and placed in foster care by CSD. From that day forward, he was denied all contact with them, even though charges had not been filed, and weren't filed for over six months.

This all happened despite the fact that —

- Raymond passed a lie detector test;

- He had been the primary care-giver for his family for years;

- His daughter, when approached separately by the police, the child services agency, and the prosecutor's office, denied all allegations and continued to deny them for four days, until the woman from the prosecutor's office drew graphic pictures for the girl which portrayed her father as a lustful animal, thus coercing an "admission" from her.

Raymond Hunter is black. He was tried by an all-white, predominately female jury. He was found "guilty" of rape. This was despite the facts that:

- Judge Brown found Brenda Hunter to be incompetent to testify at the trial because "she did not know the difference between the truth and a lie."

- His daughter placed twenty-four telephone calls to her paternal grandmother during the month of July, 1988, and stated each time that the accusation against her father was totally fabricated.

- Dr. Mary Pryor found the girl's hymen to be totally intact and without signs of sexual molestation. The fact that the daughter's vaginal opening was slightly enlarged was used as evidence of sexual activity, even though Dr. Pryor acknowledged this could happen by simply inserting a tampon.

Would Brenda be in prison for "five lifetimes" if Raymond had accused her of sexual molestation and the daughter had consistently denied it, and Raymond had suffered from mental illness and was judged too incompetent to even testify?

A Law for Women Only

ITEM. When Jane Johnston of Minneapolis was accused of sexual child abuse, she sued her former employer for defamation of character. When the charge could not be proven, Ms. Johnston was awarded $30 million.[30]

To my knowledge, no man has ever collected money for defamation of character or punitive damages for an unsubstantiated charge of sexual abuse. I am unaware of a man collecting this even for charges discovered to be *purposely* false (with the motivation of gaining primary parent time, as in the Cecil Smith case). In fact, I am unaware of a man even getting back pay when false allegations led to his being fired.

Women Who Sexually Assault, and the Teachers They Become

"I just gave your sons a sex lesson," a young woman planning to be a school-teacher boasted to two fathers of three young boys during a party. "I showed them my breasts, my vagina, and had them touch my breasts."[31]

Both fathers reported the woman, but charges were never filed by the police, the community service, or the fathers. One father explained, "I didn't want to ruin her career."

Imagine a man who was about to become a teacher having girls touch his penis and not being reported so that he could continue to pursue teaching?

Why Do Women Accuse Men of Sexual Abuse?

ITEM. Men are about nineteen times more likely than women to say they have been falsely accused of sexual abuse. About 85 percent of these abuse allegations are made by women during battles over parent time, during the throes of divorce, or when a live-in situation is failing.[32]

If a man had just lost a promotion to a woman and accused the woman of "sleeping her way to the top," would we take him so seriously as to fire her from her job and investigate later? That's what we do when we take men away from their children first and investigate later after he is accused by a woman of sexual abuse during a parent-time dispute.

Allegations of sexual abuse are most likely to be false during disputes over parent time. From the woman's perspective, an abstraction (equality) is competing with an emotion ("children mine"). Biologically it's her territory—and her territorial defenses go to the jugular. Men's equivalent is in the area of promotions. When her territory is threatened, we fail to view her allegation with the same suspicion that we would view his allegation when his territory is threatened.

But are there other reasons women in the throes of divorce are much more likely to accuse men of abuse than the other way around? Yes. For example, although both women and men feel divorce's rejection, men have learned through team sports to lose and move on without making the other team "wrong" for defeating them; and through the male role of taking sexual initiatives, men learn that almost every relationship with a woman involves plenty of rejection. In brief, one reason men are less likely to falsely accuse women of sexual abuse or child abuse is that they are more accustomed to handling rejection without blaming.

Men are less accustomed, though, to handling children. And women less accustomed to letting men do it *in men's style*. And it is exactly men's style—especially as viewed by the mother—that is a setup for accusations of sexual abuse.

Fathers tend to be more physical and more casual about bodies and sexual talk. A child's simple language might distort to her mother, for instance, the account of the father bathing her (and washing her body) or jokingly explaining about bodies and/or sexuality while taking a shower together. If this account is accompanied by any fear or reluctance from the child to revisit the father (from, for example, fearing the father will make the child go to bed earlier than Mom tells her to), this can be genuinely misinterpreted by the mother as sexual abuse.

Mothers falsely accusing fathers of child sex abuse, then, can be a reflection of the extreme differences in attitude that women and men often have toward nudity and sex. When a child comes home and says, "I took a shower with Dad," and mom gets anxious, the child who senses Mom's anxiety might wonder, "Is Daddy doing something bad to me?" A woman brought up to think of her body as something to be covered might genuinely fear abuse is taking place and, even if she says nothing, her fear is conveyed via her body language to the child—which leads the child to fear the dad and thereby eliminates the foundation for dad-to-child intimacy. Thus the chicken-egg effect (or is that the "rooster-sperm" effect?!).

Just as fathers are getting used to childcare without the mother around, so mothers are getting used to not expecting men to care for children in women's style—but, instead, to value the male sexual openness as his contribution.

Is the False Charge of Sex Abuse the "Nuclear Weapon of Domestic Relations"?

Thou shalt not bear false witness against thy neighbor.

EXODUS 20:16

Little did God know that He or She would have to warn, "Thou shalt not bear false witness against thy spouse."

When we call sex-abuse allegations the "nuclear weapons of domestic relations,"[33] it is because a sex-abuse charge—even if false—often costs the father his job, his health, his friends, his reputation, and his relationship with his child. He is forced to be witness to the loss of his child's trust in men even if he is proven innocent. And his legal bills frequently run in excess of $75,000. Why? Sex-abuse charges normally involve three separate court systems: the divorce court (family court), the juvenile court, and the criminal court. From the perspective of the accused, it feels like a three-ring circus.

MYTH. *Only a tiny fraction of divorce-related accusations of sexual abuse are false.*

FACT. Of the 80 percent of child sex-abuse accusations determined to be unfounded, divorce-related accusations are much more likely to be unfounded.[34] But no one can honestly say what percentage are *purposely* false.

FACT. In the early 1980s, a mother accused a father of sexual abuse in about 10 percent of all parent-time battles; by the late 1980s, *mothers accused fathers of sexual abuse in about 30 percent of all parent-time battles.*[35]

The percentage of unsubstantiated accusations is more remarkable the more one understands the system. For example, a father often confronts a male prosecutor who, if he is politically ambitious, often has blinders on— he knows that an image of protecting women is more likely to make him a hero than protecting a man who might turn out to be an abuser. In divorce or family court, the mother's accusations do not have to undergo the same burden of proof. In criminal court, it is proof beyond a reasonable doubt, which is a lot stiffer than the burden in divorce or family court—proof by a preponderance of evidence. All of this is in the context of a system in which a mother who is angry at a father is more likely to live with the child, enabling her to coach the child by making the child fearful of losing her approval.

If a Child Claims Abuse, It's Abuse; If a Child Denies Abuse, It's "Denial"

Before a case gets to court, the child will usually be interviewed by a female social worker at a child-protection agency. Dr. Elissa P. Benedek, a child psychiatrist who specializes in sexual abuse,[36] says, "We have been told repeatedly by children that authorities will not allow them to go to the bathroom or eat until they tell what really happened. . . ." **Therapists have concluded that a child was abused because the child adamantly denied anything happened.**

I am struck by how often, when I speak to social workers or listen to panels on child abuse, female social workers mention that they were attracted to the area of child protection because they themselves were molested. Finding new children to save—and punishing the men who have hurt them—can be a type of therapy and vindication for a social worker with a history of being abused. But this very history often makes her see abuse in everything and creates a missionary zeal that can blind her to the possibility of the man's innocence and to the havoc she might be wreaking on the life of an innocent man. As a rule, this woman has little sense of the "Twelve Guarantees of Child Abuse" that result from her well-intended attempt to protect a child. (See the preceding section titled **How a Charge of** *Possible*

Child Abuse Can Create the "Twelve *Guarantees* of Child Abuse" . . .
Even if the Charge Is True.)

A therapist in this "Mission Mode" sometimes operates like this: **If a child says he's abused, it's labeled "abuse"; if a child says he's not abused, it's labeled "denial."** Among all therapists, very *few* are this way, but the few who are tend to expand the definition of abuse so they can feel as if they are saving everyone.

The therapist with a need to find a victim is often unaware, for example, that when three girls in a "treatment" group have just revealed "What my daddy did to *me*," the next girl has a choice: She can either tell a story— "What *my* daddy did to *me*"—and *belong*, or say nothing and feel left out. When a therapist encourages the girl, "Now tell your story, Sue," Sue's need to belong is magnified by the need to please an authority figure. Telling the truth is an abstraction for a child who fears not belonging and not pleasing.

The Politics of the Medical Report

ITEM. Two separate studies have found that medical tests showing that a girl was sexually abused were wrong 25 to 30 percent of the time.[37]

This means that perhaps tens of thousands of men have had "scientific" evidence falsely "prove" them to be criminals. A loving man was called "Dad" one day, "criminal" the next. Overnight, the recently divorced man's children—his one source of love at an all-important moment, is ruined— based on false evidence. If he is eventually vindicated, it might be after he has had an ulcer or a heart attack, or found a gun. Based on false evidence.

Dr. Robert Fay recalls that a therapist brought to him for evaluation a girl who, the therapist said, had "disclosed that her daddy abused her."[38] Dr. Fay revealed that he felt he wanted to *protect* the child, not evaluate the child; and found himself looking for "proof" of abuse—or at least evidence of abuse—not the truth. He remembers finding in one girl some abnormalities that could easily have been used as "evidence of abuse." Just as he was about to prepare the documentation that would have led the court to conclude that there was "concrete evidence" that the girl had been abused, he decided to ask the girl a few questions. "Was there any other possible way she might have been hurt in this area in the past couple of months?" To his surprise, the answer was "yes." She had had a bicycle accident, gone to the doctor, and, fortunately, the traumas Dr. Fay was planning to use as "evidence of sexual abuse" had already been documented as related to the bicycle accident.

Dr. Fay realized that had the girl not gone for an exam and had those traumas documented, or if he hadn't asked questions that led to the child recalling the accident, the court would have had "concrete evidence" that the child was abused by the dad. This scared Dr. Fay . . . enough to interview the girl himself. His impression was that the girl didn't seem to feel she had been abused. So he asked the referring therapist if he could sit in while the therapist talked with her, only to witness a "therapist-with-an-agenda" trying to get the girl to say her daddy had touched her "down there." From this, the therapist assumed abuse. Dr. Fay had only to ask what Daddy was doing to get the answer that Daddy touched her "down there" when he bathed her, and used to do it when he changed her diapers.

How Public Opinion, the Lace Curtain, and the Law Work Together

Who's Right? Dr. Elizabeth Morgan or Dr. Eric Foretich?

When we think of Dr. Elizabeth Morgan—the woman who hid her daughter from her dad and spent two years in prison so her daughter could not be seen by her father—and Dr. Eric Foretich, who do we think of as being accused of child abuse? Most people think of Foretich, and their central question is whether or not Eric Foretich is guilty. In fact, *both* have filed claims that the other abused the child. Only Elizabeth's claims, though, have gotten credence, despite the facts that only Elizabeth's claims have been thrown out of the Superior Court in Washington, D.C., three times; only Elizabeth has had to withdraw claims of child abuse against someone else (both of Eric's parents);[39] and only Elizabeth fits almost perfectly the profile for false allegations of sexual abuse discussed in the conclusion to this section.

With Eric declared innocent by the court after unusually thorough investigation, Elizabeth defied the court order to let Eric see their child, essentially kidnapped their daughter Hilary from her dad, was put into prison for contempt of court, hired a PR firm, appeared on numerous national TV shows, got a contract for a fictionalized book called *Custody*,[40] had an ABC movie made based only on her side of the story,[41] and got the entire U.S. Congress to *unanimously* pass, and the President of the United States to sign, a law on her behalf.[42] How did one woman do this? And what does her success tell us about our system?

Elizabeth started by getting pregnant only a few months after she and Eric started dating, then flew to Haiti to marry Eric, then left him right away, with their daughter-to-be still in her womb.[43]

Elizabeth and Eric fought a long parent-time battle after Hilary was born. Elizabeth won. But as soon as Eric received even partial parent time ("visitation"), Elizabeth accused Eric of abusing Hilary (then two and a half) and also accused *both* of Eric's *parents* of abusing the child for almost two years. (Only when this last accusation began to backfire—and was also without evidence—was it dropped.)

It was at this point that the court found Eric innocent and ordered Elizabeth to allow him to see the child, and that Elizabeth defied the court order, kidnapped the child, and was put in jail for contempt of court. But . . .

While in prison, Elizabeth Morgan hired a public-relations firm and conducted a campaign from her cell. By 1989, a *USA Today* survey found that 69 percent of the public believed her; 9 percent believed Eric.[44] Among women, 81 percent believed Elizabeth versus only 2 percent who believed Eric. Elizabeth had won with publicity what she lost in court—the assumption that she was innocent and that the father was guilty. Exactly how?

The public-relations firm was able to succeed in part because of the receptivity of the media to female-as-victim stories, a concept that I develop in *Women Can't Hear What Men Don't Say*, but that we can see a touch of in this *Time* magazine coverage:

Trial by "Lace Curtain"[46]

When *Time* magazine reported on the Morgan and Foretich case, its headline read "Doing Time for No Crime."[47] In fact, Elizabeth Morgan was doing time for effectively "kidnapping" her daughter—concealing the child from its father in defiance of the court's order to reveal the child's whereabouts, and depriving the child of its dad. Yet *none* of these were mentioned as violations in the article in *Time*. To the contrary, the headline said there was *no* crime.

Included in *Time* was a sympathy-provoking picture of Elizabeth Morgan behind bars ("doing time for no crime"). *Excluded* was Foretich's perspective—excluded to such a degree (not only from *Time,* but

WASHINGTON

Doing Time for No Crime

Behind bars: Morgan in jail

46

from almost all of the media) that the following shocking facts never became part of the public's consciousness:

- The Virginia Child Protective Services labeled the allegations against Eric as "unfounded" and closed their files with a recommendation: "No further action."[48]

- When Elizabeth Morgan wouldn't accept the findings of the Child Protective Services, *she* took Hilary to Dr. Joseph Noshpitz, author of *The Basic Handbook of Child Psychiatry.* After Dr. Noshpitz met with Hilary for nine months in therapy, he concluded that Hilary was not a victim of sexual abuse, but suffered from "adjustment disorder" due to all the divorce-related hassles. He said that during play therapy, Hilary had imagined herself as "the thing that was being passed back and forth between [her parents]."[49] Despite the finding that Hilary was suffering from the hassles resulting mostly from Elizabeth Morgan's accusations—and not from abuse by Foretich—Elizabeth continued the accusations. Was this not child abuse by Elizabeth?

- The former president of the American Psychiatric Association, Dr. Elissa Benedek, examined Hilary and concluded there was no evidence of sexual abuse by Dr. Foretich, and that Elizabeth "had no understanding that any of Hilary's current disturbance might be related to the parental separation and divorce, separation from her father and grandparents, loyalty conflicts, her [Elizabeth's] overprotectiveness, and her rewarding, consciously and unconsciously, Hilary for making accusations."[50]

- Dr. Foretich passed three separate polygraph tests.[51] He has successfully won his case before twenty-eight judges.[52] He has lost his case before no judges. Why was the case so rarely discussed from the perspective of *his being harassed,* or his being deprived of rights, or his loss of his child's love, or the child's deprivation of her dad as an unforgivable form of child abuse (because it can never be undone).

- Dr. Catherine DeAngelis, Deputy Chief of General Pediatrics at Johns Hopkins University School of Medicine, was hired as an advocate for Hilary. She had seen thousands of children with vaginal complaints. When shown nude pictures *Elizabeth* had taken of Hilary inserting crayons and spoons into her vagina, she said the crayons could easily have caused the increased diameter of Hilary's hymen, and had she originally seen the pictures, she would have looked no further.[53]

Why did not *Time* mention all these facts and thus allow the reader to consider whether Elizabeth might be the real child abuser?

This type of "lace curtain" coverage created the atmosphere that motivated the entire U.S. Congress and the President of the United States to do an end run around the court's decision and rush through a bill to, in effect, free Elizabeth. (The bill limited prison terms for contempt in parent-time disputes, but the intent of protecting mostly Elizabeth is clear from the fact that it would expire eighteen months later [called a "sunset law" as in "expiring at sunset"]). This "Elizabeth Law" was passed *by unanimous consent,* then signed by President Bush.[54] (And then the country wonders why it takes so long to solve the deficit.) All to rescue this *one woman* who had committed at least two crimes: contempt of court and the "kidnapping" of her daughter.

The significance of this? First, some perspective: The U.S. Congress did not even agree by unanimous consent to enter World War II against Hitler.

What did Elizabeth have going for her? The public's propensity to believe and protect a mother more than a father; relatives—from a brother who is both a former federal prosecutor and a former Democratic candidate for governor of Maryland, to a fiancé who is a federal judge; a political atmosphere—ranging from feminist groups to Christian evangelical groups all allied in their assumption of a woman's innocence and a man's guilt. A woman capable of orchestrating all of this and channeling it to her ends was able to convince all of them she was incapable of protecting her child without their help.

These legislator-protectors of women are both liberals and conservatives, both men and women—they are everyone. Which is why the bill was passed unanimously—despite there being no evidence that Elizabeth was protecting her daughter, and despite there being plenty of evidence that a daughter without a father is much more subject to every abuse in life from delinquency to drugs.

Perhaps most astonishing is that this form of child abuse is being called liberalism and "progressive." At least when the Nazis burned books, no one thought of them as progressive.[55]

The Larger Picture

A larger picture is emerging which allows us to see that the law is being used to support three things we might regret. First, Elizabeth appears to fit almost perfectly the profile of a woman who makes false charges of sexual abuse:[56] her propensities for publicizing rather than downplaying the sexual abuse; employing "hired gun"-type expert witnesses and her own therapists and then not believing them when they disagreed; her willingness to flout the law with the assumption that she has a monopoly on the truth; the initiation of the accusation during a battle over parent time. The second misuse is the perpetration of the twelve forms of child abuse discussed above. But the third might be the most dangerous: supporting a woman who might be using a child for her own ends. How so?

When U.S. District Judge Sporkin saw the tapes of Hilary that Elizabeth had supplied to the media, he likened her action to the way "a child pornographer . . . goes out and abuses a little child."[57] (He was comparing Elizabeth to the pornographer.) He ruled against Lifetime Cable showing the BBC program on grounds that portions would cause Hilary "irreparable harm." He saw that Hilary felt so private about what were supposed to be private videotapes that she didn't even want the therapists to see the tapes—she asked them to leave the room. Elizabeth, though, wouldn't agree to the judge's refusal to make public the tapes of Hilary. On appeal, Elizabeth got her way, and supplied the tapes to the media. Columnist Howard Rosenberg of the *Los Angeles Times* points out that it is hard to believe that a mother is interested in her child's best interest when the child asks for two therapists to leave the room, and her mother chooses to let the whole world into the room via TV.[58]

Meanwhile, Elizabeth sold her movie rights to TV producer Linda Otto, who produced not "A Child's Right," or "A Family's Right," but "A Mother's Right: The Elizabeth Morgan Story" for ABC television. However, Linda Otto is a child-molestation victim herself "who has focused her producing career on documentaries on stories about children as victims."[59] Otto has spent long periods with Elizabeth, but plans *not to even interview* Eric Foretich.

One of the most convincing pieces of evidence against Eric Foretich came from the videotapes made by Elizabeth. They showed Hilary becoming hysterical when Foretich showed up for his court-authorized "visitation" with Hilary. Elizabeth released these tapes to CBS for *Saturday Night with Connie Chung*. Millions of viewers felt "something must be wrong" with Eric when the tapes showed Hilary being so upset at seeing her dad. But few people asked if Elizabeth had told Hilary, "Daddy is going to do something terrible to you" or "Daddy is going to take you away from me forever after he takes you from here."

Here is a case in which no one knew at the outset who was right. Yet we can see how our instincts to believe women and disbelieve men support the media's lace curtain, which in turn supports the instinct, which in turn creates a law that supports the woman.

Sex Abuse Charges: Toward a Solution

When Should the Law Reach into Our Homes?

There are some underlying questions that need to become part of the national dialogue before we give the law too much permission to allow an anonymous phone call to deprive children of their parents.

- Is our unwillingness to clamp down on false charges of sex abuse our unconscious way of scaring men off from being involved with their children? Is it also pushing women back into the homemaker role?

- Why is this happening at exactly that point in history when men are gaining some rights to the children?

- Are we using female social workers and female teachers to impose upon fathers a female version of sexual morality? Should we not be balancing male socialization about sexual openness with female socialization about sexual caution? Might we learn from countries that have lower levels of sexual crimes and greater levels of sexual openness, such as Scandanavian countries?

- Are we letting the community's most sexually-closed persons control the community's sexuality? For example, John and Nancy considered it healthy to cuddle up in bed with the children on Sunday mornings and to tickle, massage, or play together as a family. When John and Nancy divorced, both continued the Sunday ritual. But when little Sally went to nursery school, she joyfully shared this with a classmate and the classmate told her own mother. The mother made an anonymous phone call that led to John being investigated, and John prevented his children from jumping into bed with him the next Sunday. Are we thus *allowing the most sexually closed persons in the community to control the entire community?* Do we want the legal system to be enforcing the most sexually closed persons' versions of morality?

• Do we want the long arm of the law to be reaching into our homes? Do we want to be police officers rather than teachers to an even greater degree than we already are?

• Is the abuse we *might* be preventing worse than the "twelve forms of abuse" we are almost guaranteed to be creating? (See preceding section titled **How a Charge of *Possible* Child Abuse Can Create the "Twelve *Guarantees* of Child Abuse"** . . . **Even if the Charge Is True**)

• Are we scaring already cautious female teachers into becoming even more cautious by threatening them with loss of jobs or being arrested if they fail to report any possible sexual abuse?

• Are we understanding that although child-protection agencies self-select for caring people, these people often have backgrounds of being abused themselves, therefore possessing both a "view of the world" and a mission. The agencies usually comprise about an 85 percent-female staff, with most of the men being feminine/sensitive types. Some of the social workers have no heterosexual experience, and many have not raised children, yet their negative judgments about heterosexual sex, 90 percent of which will be directed against men, are legally enforceable. Do we want our children deprived of dads by judgments emanating from such a homogenous perspective?

What Are Therapists and Teachers Doing in the Legal System?

Therapists' and teachers' jobs are to *align* with clients and students; the legal system's job is to *cross-examine*. Therapists' and teachers' mandate is to protect *one* person; the mandate of the legal system is to protect *all* persons equally—the accuser *and* the accused.

The problem is that the legal system is leap-frogging to legal conclusions from therapists' methods. It is treating reports emanating from a system of *alignment with the accuser* with the type of credibility it would give to reports that emanated from multiple interviews of all parties, with both the accuser and the accused interviewed with equal intensity.

The legal system has been blindsided into this by the political atmosphere that pigeonholes men without police records into the same category as men with police records. When this is combined with a prosecutor's fear of being "soft on child molestation," the rights of the accused evaporate. The main *direct* casualty is men—men who spent their lives building reputations in the community only to find that even their best friends are looking at them with an air of suspicion they could never quite undo even if they were proven innocent. The main *indirect* casualty, though, is the families—many of which have become destabilized via these accusations.

The long-term legal result of false accusations becoming public will be libel suits. Suits against therapists, teachers, school systems, and child-protection agencies. Soon, just as the ob/gyns specializing in protecting women found themselves overwhelmed by $60,000-per-year malpractice-insurance premiums, so therapists trying to unquestioningly protect women and children will also be overwhelmed by having to carry therapists' malpractice or libel insurance. And as taxpayers, we will be paying malpractice insurance for school systems and child-protection agencies.

How Can Our Education System Really Protect Children?

By reducing class size to allow teachers to give the child the more individualized attention that is needed in this period of family instability. Children need the payment of adult attention more than the imposition of adult morality; they need teachers helping them to understand their parents more than they need teachers making them fearful of their parents.

What can teachers and therapists do? First, talk informally with *all* parties involved prior to reporting. Second, confront the law that requires teachers and therapists to report regardless of their own judgment—a law that suggests teachers and therapists have little judgment; and a law that undermines students' and clients' ability to "talk things through" in confidence. It is a law which, if teachers and therapists do not organize to change, will ultimately

turn teachers and therapists into arms of the law and make them more concerned with protecting themselves against lawsuits than with the process of
creatively educating and teaching—the best form of child protection.

How Can We Tell When a Sex Abuse Charge Is False?

How do we distinguish accusations that are true (or based on a genuine misunderstanding) versus those that are intentionally false? At Columbia University, Dr. Richard Gardner developed an instrument for making these
distinctions.

When a mother is accusing a father, as Dr. Gardner has found, the accusation is more likely to be *true* the more the following are true:[60]

- The complaint was not made in the context of a dispute over parenting time.

- The woman downplays the abuse, or initially denies it.

- The woman does *not* want to "get back at" or destroy the man.

- She has not sought a "hired gun" attorney or mental health professional.

- She does not exhibit duplicity in aspects of the evaluation *not* directly related to the sex-abuse allegation.

- Her personality is not exhibitionistic or hysterical.

- She appreciates the importance of maintaining the child's relationship with the father.

Drs. Gordon Blush and Karol Ross find that the woman who *falsely* ac-
cuses a man tends to be characterized by a view of herself as a powerless victim whose husband is a physical threat and economically punitive.[61] She
frequently insists that the law punish him before reasonable proof has been
demonstrated. What might seem to an outsider to be vindictive behavior (in
the middle of a parent-time battle) is seen by her as justified due to her view
of herself as powerless.

It is easy to see how this woman's fears could intimidate a helping professional into reporting an alleged incident as an actual incident without considering how a false accusation will hurt the child.

When a child says he or she is sexually abused, Dr. Gardner has found the accusation is more likely to be true the more the following is true:

- The child is very hesitant to divulge the sexual abuse.

- The child feels guilty that the person being accused might get into trouble.

- The child feels guilty about her or his own participation in sexual acts.

- Specific details of the sexual abuse are provided.

- The details do not vary from interview to interview.

- The complaint was not made during a dispute over parent time.

Drs. Blush and Ross find[62] that children whose accusations are false are much more likely to "parrot" or "mirror" the accusing parent's descriptions of the situation; they tend to use descriptions whose meaning they don't really understand and to spontaneously initiate those descriptions while being interviewed by the therapist, even using the same affect as the accusing parent. They look coached; they do not look traumatized. They find the children often act like little dictators as a result of an age-inappropriate awareness of their parent's vulnerabilities deriving from their parent's use of the child to communicate complaints about the other parent.

The president of the American Psychiatric Association found that children initiated the accusations in most of the cases that were ultimately judged to be true. In contrast, in *all* cases of *false* accusation the charges were initiated by the parents.

Adolescents who are actually sexually abused, like children, tend to be tearful, emotionally held back, and embarrassed to speak of the abuse. They look traumatized.

Adolescents whose accusations turn out to be false, Blush and Ross find, are much more public in their criticisms, and typically proclaim they "never, ever" want to see the other parent again. The parent they accuse of abusing them has usually imposed limits on them, or has recently moved in with an adult they dislike. Their hidden agenda is to avoid the limits, the chores, the discipline, the restrictions, or the new adult they either dislike or resent because of the attention it takes away from them.

Men who falsely accuse women very rarely accuse the woman directly— they accuse the woman's boyfriend, or a new stepfather, accusing the mother only indirectly by suggesting that her silence is the equivalent of a passive endorsement. His personality is characterized by intellectual rigidity, a strong need to be "correct," chronic criticism of the mother throughout the marriage, and a tendency to be very nit-picking in his examples of the mother being non-vigilant and unfit.

Men who are actual abusers tend to be passive, dependent, and immature. Unfortunately, men who are falsely accused tend also to be passive, dependent, and immature.[63]

How Can the Law Protect Children and Protect Parents?

What can be done legally to stem the tide of false accusations without providing permission for more abuse? First, since abuse is a crime, follow the law allowed for criminals—innocent until proven guilty. Require the same proof. Second, check whether the accuser has reason to discredit the accused. Third, when *purposely* false reporting is found, exact the same criminal penalty for the accuser as the accused would have received. Fourth, if a parent is found guilty, have a therapist, the child, and the abusing parent *work through* the entire dynamic under close supervision, removing the parent only if necessary. "Working through" creates resolution for the child and also diminishes the motivation to accuse a spouse of sexual abuse to win sole parent time.[64]

The deeper solution comes from an underlying attitude. Just as we understand that a mother might unwittingly have charged a father with abuse after her daughter came home and said, "Daddy touched me down here . . . ," we need to train police and social workers to also ask for the father's perspective before they remove the father or even come to the home. For example, the dad who "touched me down there . . ." might have been bathing his two-year-old daughter and believed that *avoiding* the genitals was a form of abuse because it was a way of giving the daughter the message that her genitals were dirty and that sex was dirty.

We might or might not agree with this perspective, but there is almost a 100 percent guarantee that a child will be traumatized by being removed from its father or mother by police or social workers, and almost no chance that an infant or young child will feel traumatized by a father or mother bathing it fully in a non-exploitive manner. Children do not feel exploited by being cared for. They do feel exploited by the confusion they feel when one parent tells them that the caring they thought they were feeling was really exploitation.

During the early twenty-first century, I believe the misuse of abuse will become increasingly apparent, especially when the "abuse" card is played to eliminate dads from children's lives.

11

The Political Consequences
of Ignoring Fathers

Why, When We Don't Support Fathers' Rights, We Are Really Supporting the "Right-to-Life" Movement

Part of what fuels the "Right-to-Life" Movement is the frequency of abortion and the lack of effort made to avoid abortions. The "Right-to-Life" movement is strengthened in the United States in part because 51 percent of the pregnancies in the United States are unplanned (versus 17 percent in countries like the Netherlands),[1] and about 60 percent of these unplanned pregnancies end in abortion.

The number of fetuses killed by abortion *each year* is more than twice the number of Americans killed in battle during *all* U.S. wars *combined.*[2] We know the type of emotion created by deaths in war. And when those deaths are perceived as unnecessary, a country develops a collective guilt and deep divisions, as in the Vietnam war. Of course, pro-choice women feel there is not a child being killed, and that abortion is necessary. Thus the deep divisions.

When the right-to-life woman sees that the pro-choice woman is not open to a fetus becoming a wanted child if the person wanting to love the child is a dad, it makes her feel that those deaths are unnecessary. It gives credibility to the right-to-life woman's belief that the real agenda of the pro-choice woman is pro-selfishness—her desires over another's life.

The degree to which fetuses find their fathers is the degree to which the "Right-to-Life" movement is less able to tap into the country's collective guilt and ambivalence.

What the Pro-Choice Woman and the Right-to-Life Woman Have in Common

In reality, the right-to-life woman has just as much self-interest at stake as the pro-choice woman. More often than not, for the right-to-life woman, raising children is her job. And raising children is her sense of identity ("I am a mother"). Her "right" to this job is reinforced by the belief of her husband and community that she—the mother—has natural protective instincts. **Other women advocating abortion undermine a woman being seen as a natural protector of children.** It undermines her "natural right" to this territory, and her sense of being naturally superior in this arena. Often her unspoken motto is, "*Our* Children, *my* Turf."

The right-to-life woman can experience abortion as an emotional rejection of her sense of purpose and as jeopardizing her job security—or her economics. Remember the formula for a major movement: a large number of people experiencing simultaneous economic hurt and emotional rejection? There you have it—the Right-to-Life movement. *And* the Pro-Choice movement. Here's why both . . .

Both the pro-choice and right-to-life women have in common three concerns: job rights; job as identity; territoriality:

	Pro-Choice	Right-to-Life
1. Job Rights	Right to Choose Job Over Child	Child Is Job
2. Job as Identity	"I Am a Lawyer"	"I Am a Mother"
3. Territoriality	My Body, My Business	Our Children, My Turf

The Fathers' Rights movement's desire for fathers to have an equal right to child involvement challenges both the Pro-Choice and the Right-to-Life women's job rights, sense of identity, and territoriality. Think about which sex is usually associated with job rights, sense of identity, and territoriality. Correct. In fact, both sexes have these concerns.

These three concerns are one more set of reasons why the journey of

fathers' *rights* to children involves navigation through the minefield of female insecurities to at least the same degree that women's entrance into the
workplace involves navigation through the minefield of male insecurities.

It is difficult for the leaders of either movement to see the other's position. But now there's no choice. Between 1991 and 2000, support for *Roe v.
Wade* fell from 56 percent to 43 percent. And women are more likely to be
its *opponents*.[3] People who want choice will need to expand their political
base so choice is no longer just a woman's right—but a balancing of
women's right to abort, men's right to love, and the fetus's right to become
a child.

There's "Father-Style" and "Mother-Style": Until Courts Understand What "Father-Style" Means, a Father's Contributions Will Be Mistaken for Child Abuse

When women entered the workplace, many men were mentors to them
and, in turn, also learned to respect women's unique contributions (for example, their listening and facilitative skills). Now, as we give men responsibilities to care for children, women must be among the mentors, *and* we
must also learn to respect *men's* unique contributions. Our lack of understanding of men's contributions results in men's legal losses. Not just custody suits, but even child abuse suits. For example . . .

Mark and his daughter, Rosalie, loved to wrestle and roughhouse. Even
when Rosalie fell and hurt herself, he continued doing it some more as soon
as she felt better. Sarah, Rosalie's mother, used that in court to prove him an
irresponsible father. But Mark believed that if he protected Rosalie from
avoiding life's falls, he would prevent her from learning how to protect herself; he believed that **to protect a child from failure was to prevent a
child from achieving success** . . . and *that* was irresponsible because it
would make her dependent on a man. But Mark couldn't articulate why he
was doing this, so he lost primary parent time of his daughter—a daughter
he deeply loved.

Why, if Mark was doing this, was he unable to articulate it? He knew
only intuitively how much he learned from life's falls—he only sensed it was
the best part of what he got from riding his skateboard down a steep hill,
from having his ass kicked in the army, from roughhousing with his dad,
from playing sandlot football, from striking out in baseball, from climbing

tall trees, from riding his bike on one wheel, from skiing downhill too quickly, from learning how to get "tubed" on a surfboard without wiping out. He sensed that girls saw the outcome and feared that boys were just "better at these things." He knew that if his daughter was to succeed, she had to know that temporary failure—striking out or wiping out—*was a part of the process that led to success.* Then, he felt, he would be preparing her to control her own life. For him, that was helping create a truly liberated woman.

Mark also felt differently from his wife about openly discussing sex with Rosalie. He felt—as many men do—that flaunting one's body and hiding one's body were flip sides of the same problem: teaching a child that her or his body is unnatural. But in the courtroom, naturalness became nakedness and, when the only thing that was discussed in court was Rosalie's questions about Mark's penis, the penis became the focus—exactly the opposite of what Mark had accomplished by making bodies natural. As Mark listened, he could see that it was the beginning of the end of his chance for shared parent time. He realized that if he were to ever have a chance of achieving shared parent time in the future, he would have to publicly apologize for these perspectives and openly adopt his wife's perspectives. He would have to feminize. Ironically, to be a father, he had to erase the father in the father.

If neither the mother nor the court is educated to the male contribution and the father is unable to articulate it, fatherhood evolves into imitation motherhood. And that would be as sad as female executives becoming imitation male executives rather than both sexes learning from each other. In each case, society is deprived of the uniqueness of that sex's contribution.

And this is but the iceberg's tip: If we *both* ignore the unique contribution of "male-style" parenting *and* jail a man who responsibly contributes it, fatherhood becomes another hazardous occupation. More precisely, it becomes the *largest 100 percent–male hazardous occupation.* And in the process, our children lose one of the greatest potential gifts of Stage II—genuine fatherhood. That's the bad news. The good news is that there are ways of creating a father and child reunion. . . .

12

Conclusion: Toward a Father and Child Reunion

Dad's role has been the one that has varied most. Sometimes we want him to hold back Hitler and suffer a bullet in his head; other times we want him to hold a baby and put a bottle in its mouth. If someone applauds, men will run in circles and call it a home run. Men goeth to that place from which appreciation cometh.

The challenge is shifting our appreciation: being willing to give up some of Dad's money for more of Dad's love. And, in the process, altering the psyche that makes him lovable.

The fact that we *can* direct men by appreciation does not mean we are willing to *redirect* men: to make the tradeoff of less male money for more male love. How so? Kids often confuse what money buys with love. Women rarely marry future dads whose future income has little future. And the process it takes to support a family is often so inversely related to the time and introspection it takes to love a family, that dads themselves are often afraid to ask what they're being loved for, and whether they are doing what they love. All of these forces make us want to keep appreciating Dad for being a wage slave—denying what we know inside: that appreciation keeps the slave a slave.

Fortunately, children, moms and dads also have feelings that can just as easily turn them into countervailing forces. Kids like who they become when Dad's caring is close and constant. When Mom is getting more attention from Dad she finds herself not having to shop for more attention. And the more Dad invests in his family's love, the less he feels he has to invest in the market to receive his family's love. Love grows love.

Technology is cooperating. Technology is Dad-at-home friendly. It has satisfied some of the hunger for material goods that industrialization magnified but, unlike industrialization, provides options for both dads and moms being at home. It allows people to work from suburbs and rural communities. For dozens of reasons, it allows the family to be more creative and role-flexible than it ever has in the past without being poor in the process.

And in the process, many men are discovering children. (Some are becoming child-aholics.) Many women are discovering that the motherhood instinct implies a responsibility to be certain children have dads—every day, not far away; and some are aware that economic independence requires not holding on to her child as if it were her job.

A mother will hold on to her child as if it were her job until we stop using money that fathers make to pay for children that mothers raise.

How do we make that transition without hurting mothers or children? By resocializing our daughters to know when temporary financial security (child-as-job) creates long-term financial insecurity (no career after child). It is a process that must run parallel to resocializing our sons to know when temporary emotional security (*e.g.,* avoiding counseling) creates long-term emotional insecurity (divorce).

Exactly how do we do that resocialization? By, for example, helping our daughter invest in stocks and to compare her long-term rate of return to that in a bank; or encouraging her to start a small business at a young age (*e.g.,* designing Web sites at twelve or thirteen) without expecting her to "succeed" in order to see it as a success; *encouraging* her to ask boys out that she likes even though the rejection rate will be higher, and having her compare her long-term results to selecting only from among the boys who come to her. Our daughters will let go of child-as-career only when they are at ease with creating their own careers. And in the process they will be even better mothers—mothers who don't protect their children from success by protecting them from failure.

Shifting our attitudes about the future of fathers requires shifting our attitudes about the way our fathers loved. Recognizing that the rigid roles of the past were not designed by men to serve only men is not unrelated to shifting our attitudes about Dad.

We cannot think of dads as being nurturing if we think of men as being self-serving. In the past, rigid roles created survival. Rigid roles were not designed to serve men. "No sex before marriage" is not a male fantasy. Working on front lines served the country, not the self; working in coal mines nourished his family, but collapsed his lungs. Dying on front lines or in coal mines is hardly self-serving. Both sexes socialized their children with rigid roles because both sexes loved their children enough to want them to survive, to want them to have a life better than their own.*

Finally that has been achieved. Rigid roles provided the foundation not only for survival, but also for flexible roles. (And without that survival, of course, flexible roles would be a tad irrelevant.)

So how do we create this father and child reunion? Well, if it's about people, and it isn't political, it doesn't happen. In the U.S., Canada, Great Britain, Australia, and New Zealand, there are hundreds—perhaps a thousand—organizations of fathers and women (mostly second wives) whose agenda is a father and child reunion.[1] Yet the vast majority of these organizations, especially in the United States, have virtually no funding. They are staffed by volunteers, usually men who are fighting shared-parenting battles and holding full-time or multiple jobs, often paying for their apartments, the mortgage on their children's mother's home, mother-subsidy payments, alimony, trips to see the children, legal fees . . . free time is a rare commodity. Money is less rare—it just goes to everyone else. As a political force, all but a handful of these organizations are impotent.

A paucity of funding from private and government sources would be much less a problem if billions of dollars each year were not funding feminist perspectives on men. This funding leads to Women's Studies without Men's Studies; to studies about deadbeat dads, but not dead-broke or dead-ended dads—or moms who deny dads access to children, or make false accusations to obtain children. This creates an atmosphere of political correctness so powerful that even the Census Bureau asks moms about deadbeat dads, but not dads about denial of dad time.

The feminist-only funding leads to studies that misinform the nation that a divorced mother is economically more hurt than a divorced man, so judges feel a mandate to make his future income hers, and legislatures feel

---

* See my *The Myth of Male Power,* Chapter 2, on Stages I and II.

fine about refusing to make his mother-subsidy payments tax-deductible even as she pays no taxes on the money received. And all this perpetuates the belief that he earns more money. . . .

Meanwhile there is virtually no funding to study the validity of the more muted complaints of men: to study when a false accusation is being used as a weapon to keep the children from Dad; or when the child is being badmouthed by the other parent; or when access to the child is being prevented; or when statistics about deadbeat dads are including men who are dead, unemployed, or denied their children; or when men are victims of domestic violence.[2]

The one-sided funding creates one-sided images that reinforce the press defining as progress an examination of only women's issues. Thus, a quarter-century's-worth of studies showing domestic violence against men to be more than equal to domestic violence against women receive so little publicity as to barely make a dent on the public's consciousness.

The problem is that the funding has been motivated by anger felt toward men who have rejected women and disappointed women, but the image impacts the woman's sons, and the father of her sons—affecting the way the son feels about the 50 percent of his genes that are his dad's. It might defeat the man she hates, but it poisons the son she loves and handicaps her daughter's ability to love.

From these biased studies come biased social policy. Hundreds of millions of dollars to enforce sanctions against fathers who don't pay mothers; almost nothing to enforce sanctions against mothers who don't allow fathers to see children. Similarly, funding to prevent domestic violence against only women makes the fear of hurting only a woman so potent that few judges can afford to ask whether the violence was initiated by the woman, or the accusation motivated by a desire to defeat his battle for shared parent time.

In brief, *part* of the need for funding comes from the need to create balance to a third of a century of funding an "attitude" toward men. And part comes from the need to study how both sexes can make a transition from those rigid roles to more flexible roads with a road map clear enough not to go over too many cliffs along the way . . . the cliffs of homicides and suicides because the Boys of Columbine couldn't express their feelings and we didn't know what to ask; or because a man felt he had no way to counter a false accusation of sexual harassment, date rape, domestic violence, or child molestation. There is little life where no one will listen. These are fathers, sons, and families who are needlessly lost.

It is in our genes to sacrifice men each generation in war to protect women, children, and the rest of us. Ignoring these men's needs is just our latest way of acting out our genetic heritage. But today there is less need to prepare men for war, so the appreciation and medals that, in the past, we gave men to die so we could live have become dysfunctional for the communication we will require of men in the future. The process it took to create killer-protectors is inversely related to the process it will take to create nurturer-connectors. This has happened in an evolutionary instant. Part of our evolutionary heritage is the ability to adapt—species that survive, adapt. Humans adapt by altering their priorities to match evolving values.

What we spend is our clearest statement as to what we value. After private spending, the clearest statement as to what a country values is its government's budget. What changes could private and government sources redirect if the country valued the quickest and soundest path to a father and child reunion?

We need to fund research on a men's birth-control pill so teenage boys and men have as much right, responsibility and flexibility as teenage girls and women do. Equal responsibility for childcare begins with equal choice in child creation.

We need to fund research on false accusations, violations of due process and the fourteenth amendment, denial of dad time, and cuckoldry.

The research that discovered that 10 percent of children are being raised by dads who are unaware they are not the child's biological father is more than a half-century old—done at a time when blood tests could not detect but a fraction of what DNA tests can ascertain today. If this does, in fact, mean that 15 to 20 percent of dads are unknowingly raising one or more children who are not their own, this will have volumes worth of ripple effects.

When a dad discovers he has devoted his life to supporting a child he believes is his, but in fact came from his wife's affair with another man, he experiences more than feelings of involuntary servitude. He often feels the deepest level of emotional betrayal. For a man there is no experience that is more likely to generate the feeling of being emotionally raped. If the sexes' reproductive roles were reversed, and a DNA test were needed to assure a woman she was not spending her life raising money for a child her husband had conceived during an affair, DNA tests at the earliest possible moment would be the most fundamental of women's reproductive rights. DNA tests to ascertain paternity must become the most fundamental of men's reproductive rights.

On a more upbeat note, we need to fund relationship language in our schools so that future parents will know how to communicate about whether they want children, to communicate with the children they have, and teach their children how to communicate with the world. Technical progress without social skills is a Tower of Babel.

A first test of that communication is whether we can replace our right-to-life versus pro-choice abortion monologues with dialogues about the overlapping rights of the mother, the father, and the fetus. Abortion rights and wrongs are a perfect metaphor for one of the key differences in a Stage I society's decision-making, in which we needed men and women to follow rigid rules to survive (because, for example, sex before marriage could lead to children no one could afford to care for), to a Stage II society, which allows for much more gray-area thinking (since, for example, technology such as birth control allows sex before marriage without destroying anyone's ability to survive).

To permit abortion in a Stage I world was to begin the trek down the long road of sanctioning sex without a lifetime of responsibility. In a Stage II world, we are happy for that option; we are just divided as to where the option stops—with RU-486 (the French abortion pill), or with a woman who is raped. The question of a Stage II society, then, is much more how to negotiate gray-area issues. When we jump to quick judgments of our opponents being right or wrong, we are engaged in the thinking of a Stage I world. In a Stage II world, we are more likely to find ourselves weighing tradeoffs than making rigid judgments; to be seeing that every solution contains ethical and moral dilemmas, not absolute rights or wrongs.

Both the pro-life and pro-choice sides agree on one thing: it's the woman's issue. Pro-choice people make that very clear—it's a woman's choice; but pro-life people also feel it's a woman's issue—it's her obligation to bear and raise the child. **Neither pro-life nor pro-choice advocates involve Dad in the discussion.**

To focus on only a woman's rights—or only a man's—is not a charac-

teristic of freedom. Politically, it is a characteristic of absolute power—and absolute power corrupts absolutely. Psychologically, it is a characteristic of a spoiled child who says, "Absolute power—what else is there?"

The solution to the abortion question, then, will ultimately involve gray areas—a certain amount of freedom to abort (for example, in the first few months) and a certain amount of restriction to that freedom. It might require no obligation to consider the adoption option in the first few months; an obligation in the second couple of months to prove that the parents had at least considered the option (for example, two adoption agencies certifying that they saw the couple), and in the next couple of months, an obligation to pursue adoption over abortion; in the last few months, abortion might be made increasingly illegal until it is finally considered a special and separate category of killing (in the same way that vehicular manslaughter is a special category).

The solution to the abortion question will also involve understanding that once a woman and a man have created a fetus, they have equal responsibilities and equal rights to determine its destiny.

Perhaps no legal change creates more of a win-win situation (for mother, father, and child) than a legal requirement for a woman to make "every reasonable attempt"[4] to notify the man as soon as she discovers she is pregnant. That one change allows them both to share in the entire emotional process of deciding whether they will have a child together, support each other through an abortion, or put the child up for adoption. For either sex to have more time than the other to process the joy, pain, or decisions is to give that sex unfair rights and unfair responsibilities, and to shortchange the possibility of the fetus having as much chance as possible to live and become a loved child.

Social policy that reunites father and child must always confront itself with the question, "Are we paying dads to stay, or to go away?" If a single mother receives more money when the father isn't around than when he is around, there will be fewer fathers around. The government will become her substitute husband.

Laws that give women incentives to be with children unwittingly discriminate against women's being at work. For women to have genuine equal opportunity in the workplace requires a woman not being pressured to be more of a mother than a man feels to be more of a dad. This doesn't mean more women won't choose to be mothers, only that it will be their and their partner's choice, not their and their partner's response to carrots or sticks.

Until now, the government has stacked the deck against women in the workplace by focusing on women's financial and reproductive rights, and on men's financial and reproductive responsibilities.

To create the framework within which freedom of choice is genuinely exercised requires laws to balance eight considerations: let's call them The Octant of Equal Opportunity Parenting. They look like this:

The Octant of Equal Opportunity Parenting

- Women's reproductive rights

- Men's reproductive rights

- Women's reproductive responsibilities

- Men's reproductive responsibilities

- Women's financial rights

- Men's financial rights

- Women's financial responsibilities

- Men's financial responsibilities

Social policy must not just fund, but inspire. Not just inspire, but create community to sustain and nurture the inspiration—something churches do so well. As churches, schools, and industry partner with governments to create the Fathers' Corps, the Man-in-the-Family Plan, the Man-in-the-School Plan, the Male Teacher Corps, and the Female Work Corps Exchange (each of which I discuss in Chapter 5), we will begin to develop the multiple communities necessary to create permission for men to be everything that it was previously dysfunctional for them to be.

No force is more powerful—or more multiple—than the family. This means that if we want fathers and children to be differently united, we need to ask whether our sons and daughters are being differently appreciated. Are we appreciating our daughter for saving money to ask a boy out so she doesn't begin thinking of a boy as a wallet who pays for love? Are we appreciating our son as much for his ability to listen to a girl as his ability to kick a goal? (Or are we teaching him to catch a girl by catching a pass?) The litmus tests in Chapter 5 on what every dad and mom can do gives us a sense of whether we are using our family as a force to have a father and child reunion.

Perhaps the biggest appreciation adjustment we need is toward the millions of men and women we call stepparents. We have taken for granted especially the stepparents who are raising no children of their own, and receiving no income from a significant other, but who have nevertheless chosen to invest love, time and money in children. May I recommend that we begin this appreciation of stepparents by calling them "social parents," honoring the social role they have chosen to play.

Fathering, as Margaret Mead pointed out, is more of a social role than is mothering. Thus it is not surprising that the great majority of stepparents who are raising no children of their own, and receiving no income from a significant other, are social dads. This is in marked contrast to our image of men as having to impregnate as many women as possible to pass on their genes. Social dads love and protect the genes of other men.

If we are to inspire men to father it also helps to stop reflexively condemning men as afraid of commitment and address what they are afraid of. A study of divorced men's fear of remarrying found that more than two-thirds of divorced men believed "the courts are stacked against men," and that women's interests rule the divorce courts. The study found that men were not afraid of commitment, but of legal marriage, stemming from their "fear of 'getting taken to the cleaners' in court . . . simply because society says 'she gets the kids and men get the shaft.'"[5]

We have, then, our work cut out for us. But just as it takes a lot of computer programming to generate options, it will take a lot of social reprogramming to create social options. Options—and options' tradeoffs—will be the core characteristic of the twenty-first century. There will be less and less of either-or: *either* father *or* mother. Shared parent time introduces the child to a century of options and the plurality of life; and to the understanding that while divorce produces change and instability, it also produces *the ability to make changes* and develop inner resources in times of instability; that the twenty-first century is marked by flexibility, not decisions made as a child that are written in stone for life; that parents can divorce and both parents can be good and loving. . . .

Ultimately, then, the quietest revolution is not the dad's revolution, but the revolution of all of us to reconfigure Dad into the family and society. It is not only the father and child reunion, it is the discovery of a new way for our sons and daughters to be—within themselves, and with each other. A way that leaves their parents with the emotions mixed of envy and pride.

Appendix:
What a Man Needs to Do if
Divorce Cannot Be Avoided

I think of attorneys' fees as the karmic price paid by people who fail to communicate.

*"If it's all right with your mother and her attorney,
then it's all right with me and my attorney."*

Attorneys' fees can be thought of as a special tax paid by those who need to be right. In return for a swimming pool in her or his backyard, the attorney gives us the opportunity to be a gladiator in our home court. So you won't be surprised to hear me rant that neither a divorce nor attorneys should precede a year of competent counseling and attempts to mediate.

But if divorce and attorneys are inevitable, then men especially will need to protect themselves against a system built on the assumption that the children need their mother and their mother needs the courts (to provide the money the husband "should" have provided).

What a Man Needs to Do if Divorce Cannot Be Avoided. . . .[2]

Protect the Kids and Avoid a Battle over Parent Time if at All Possible

- Put more focus on the children and less on work.

- Be sure the children understand you are not divorcing *them*.

- Give your wife books, articles, and audiotapes on the value of the dad in a child's life. Appeal to her mothering instinct to provide good fathering.

- Contract with her on never badmouthing each other to the kids.

- Close joint accounts and credit cards that can be jointly used.

- Make sure you and your wife both have your own business and personal financial records. Keep your copy in a more secure location than your home.

- Try for a reasonable, out-of-court settlement if possible.

- Contact various men's-rights/divorce-reform groups and consider joining them. Ask their advice on choosing an attorney.

- Attempt to determine what the lawyer's fees will be.

- Learn about the judges who might sit on your case. Ask for a different judge if you are assigned one who seems prejudiced.

- Keep a written record of all incidents pertinent to the divorce: names, dates, etc.

- Rent a post-office box to receive correspondence that you do not wish to risk having your wife open or see.

- Don't entertain lavishly or travel extensively; cut down on purchases of clothing and household goods. Judges usually award maintenance payments based on a couple's standard of living before the divorce, so the sooner you lower the standard, the less you might have to pay.

- Develop your friendship network of men you can talk with and men you can play with.

- Stay in the home of your wife and children until a settlement is finalized.

- Form a men's group—especially with men who have been divorced with children and had *minimal* conflict.

- Consider having your lawyer present if a court-appointed social worker interviews your children.

Before Trial, DON'T—

- Don't use your wife's lawyer.

- Don't work with a lawyer who is defeatist about your chances for some success.

- Don't be afraid to ask a potential lawyer for your case any and all questions you want to ask.

- Don't discuss any proposed settlement with your wife and/or her lawyer unless *your* lawyer is present.

- Don't avoid your children if you move out of the house, even though you will probably be tested by them much of the time.

- Don't take your children with you if you leave home unless you are absolutely sure you know what you are doing and what effect it will have on them.

- Don't rely on psychiatrists, psychologists, or social workers to support you once the case is scheduled for court. They are reluctant witnesses in such situations.

During Trial, DO—

- Attend all depositions, court sessions, etc., even if your attorney tells you he or she has no need for you.

- Obtain and keep copies of transcripts of all proceedings.

- Get specific visitation rights if you don't get primary dad time.

- Claim tax exemptions for the children you are supporting.

- Keep a tab on your attorney's fees. Also estimate your wife's fees.

- Take a reasonable settlement any time you can get it. Just because you have begun a court case does not mean you have to end it.

- Fight with everything you have to keep the kids from appearing in court.

- Understand that you are undergoing a test that drives some men to suicide. The anxiety you might feel is not abnormal or a sign of weakness; the male is almost inevitably the underdog in divorce court, and what you are feeling matches the facts.

During Trial, DON'T—

- Don't sign any decree or settlement until you understand every word.

- Don't be afraid to change lawyers if your interests are not being defended as you think they should be.

- Don't panic when, as is likely, the court assigns your ex-wife the children. Remember how high the odds were against you and realize that no institution, state, or malicious person can dictate your children's feelings about you. That is a matter between you and your kids.

- Don't agree to alimony beyond what it takes to get your wife financially capable of supporting herself while you are involved with the children to the degree you can be.

- Don't agree to mother subsidies based strictly on your income.

- Don't agree to pay all medical expenses for the children, as you could find incredible bills for not much illness. Medical insurance is another matter.

- Don't be sloppy about wills, trusts, and insurance. Make sure the beneficiaries are who you want them to be.

After Trial, DO—

- See your children regularly.

- Obey the divorce agreement, even if your ex-wife violates it; continue to pay mother subsidies even if she denies you dad time. You want a solid case should you have to go back to court.

- Keep a complete record of all the financial support you give your children. Keep all correspondence relating to the divorce.

- Confront your children as a man who has self-respect and who has made the best of a bad situation.

After Trial, DON'T—

- Don't review the details of the divorce with your children.

- Don't be overly possessive of your children. They, too, need time to adjust to the new situation.

Resources

Selected Organizations

Alliance for Non-Custodial Parents Rights (ANCPR)
Lowell Jaks, Director
www.ancpr.org

American Coalition for Fathers and Children (ACFC)
David A. Roberts, president
www.acfc.org

Bay Area Male Involvement Project (BAMIN)
Stan Seiderman
www.bamin.org

Center on Fathering
www.geocities.com/Heartland/
Meadows/5042/cof.htm

Center on Fathers, Families and Public Policy
David Pate, executive director
www.cffpp.org

Children's Rights Council (CRC)
David L. Levy, president
www.childrensrightscouncil.org

Coalition of Parent Support (COPS)
Robert Bennett, president
www.copss.org

Dads Against Discrimination (DADS)
Victor Smith, president
www.dadsusa.com

Domestic Rights Coalition
George T. Gilliland Sr., executive director
home.earthlink.net/~proadvocate

False Allegations of Child Sexual Abuse
Edward Nichols, author
www.falseabuse.com

Families and Work Institute
Ellen Galinsky, president
www.familiesandwork.org

The Fatherhood Project/Families and Work Institute
James A. Levine, director
www.fatherhoodproject.org

Fathers Raising Children (FRC)
John R. Sims, executive director
www.frcpgh.org

Fathers' Resource Center, Inc
David Bruer, executive director
www.fathersresourcecenter.org

Fathers' Rights and Equality Exchange (F.R.E.E.)
Anne Mitchell, founder
dadsrights.org/anne.html

Institute for Responsible Fatherhood and Family Revitalization
Charles Ballard, president
www.responsiblefatherhood.org

Joint Custody Association
James Cook
www.jointcustody.org

Men's Defense Association
Rich Doyle
www.mensdefense.org

Men's Health Network
Ron Henry, co-founder
www.menshealthnetwork.org

Men's Rights, Inc.
Fred Hayward
www.mens-rights.org

National Center for Fathering
Ken Canfield
www.fathers.com

National Center for Strategic Non-Profit Development and Community Leadership
Jeffery M. Johnson, president
www.npcl.org

National Center on Fathers and Families
Vivian Gadsden, director
www.ncoff.gse.upenn.edu

National Coalition of Free Men (NCFM)
Tom Williamson
www.ncfm.org

National Congress for Fathers and Children (NCFC)
Larry Hellmann, president
www.ncfc.net

National Fatherhood Initiative
Wade Horn, president
www.fatherhood.org

National Fathers' Resource Center (NFRF)
Steve Finstein, director
www.fathers4kids.org

National Organization of Circumcision Information Resource Centers (NOCIRC)
www.nocirc.org

National Parental Alienation Foundation
www.fact.on.ca/facthomepage/npaf.htm

National Partnership for Women and Families
Ellen R. Malcolm, chair
www.nationalpartnership.org

Parental Responsibility Project
Susan Damron Krug, director
www.state.ok.us/~oja/parental.htm

Second Wives Crusade
Dianna Thompson
www.secondwives.org

United Fathers of America (Washington State)
David MacDonald, director
www.ufa.org

Victims of Child Abuse Laws (VOCAL)
www.vocalny.org

Women's Freedom Network
Rita J. Simon, president
www.womensfreedom.org

Australia

Fathers for Family Equity
Malcolm Mathias, president
www.familyequity.asn.au

MENDS
Daryl Sturgess
www.peerleadership.com.au/mends

Men's Rights Agency
www.mensrights.com.au

Canada

Equal Parents of Canada (EPOC)
Contact: Eric Tarkington.
www.interlog.com/~parental/epocnews/home.htm

Equitable Child Maintenance and Access Society (ECMAS)
Bob Bouvier, president (Edmonton Chapter)
www.ecmas.net

Family of Men Support Society
Contact: Earl Silverman
www.familyofmen.com

Fathers Are Capable Too (F.A.C.T.)
www.fact.on.ca

**Groupe d'entraide aux pères et de
soutien à l'enfant inc. (GEPSE)**
Yves Ménard
www.cam.org/~gepse

**Men's Educational Support Association
(MESA)**
Gus Sleiman
www.mesacanada.com

Vancouver MEN Support Association
www.vcn.bc.ca/vmsa

Victoria Men's Center (VMC)
Keith Harris, president
victoria.tc.ca/Community/
MensCentre

Windsor Men's Forum
Daniel Cahill
winforum@mnsi.net

Ireland

Parental Equality
Liam O'Gogain, chairman
parentalequality.ie

New Zealand

Men's Centre North Shore
Jim Bailey, chairman
www.menz.org.nz

United Kingdom

Families Need Fathers
Jim Parton, chairman
www.fnf.org.uk

Mankind
Robert Whiston, chairman
www.mankind.org.uk

United Kingdom Men's Movement
George McAulay, chairman
www.ukmm.org.uk

Bibliography

Abraham, Jed H. *From Courtship to Courtroom.* New York: Bloch Publishing Company, Inc., 1999.

Amneus, Daniel. *The Case for Father Custody.* Alhambra, CA: Primrose Press, 1999.

Baber, Asa. *Naked at Gender Gap.* New York: Birch Lane Press, 1992.

Biller, Henry B. *Fathers and Families.* Westport, CT: Auburn House, 1993.

Blankenhorn, David. *Fatherless America.* New York: Basic Books, 1995.

Braver, Sanford L. & Diane O'Connell. *Divorced Dads.* New York: Jeremy P. Tarcher/Putnam, 1998.

Brennan, Carleen and Michael Brennan. *Custody for Fathers.* Costa Mesa, CA: Brennan Publishing, 1996.

Brott, Armin A. *The Single Father.* New York: Abbeville Press, 1999.

Farrell, Warren. *The Liberated Man.* New York: Random House, 1975; Bantam, 1975; Putnam/Berkley, 1993.

Farrell, Warren. *The Myth of Male Power.* New York: Simon & Schuster, 1993; Putnam/Berkley, 1994; revised intro, 2001.

Farrell, Warren. *Why Men Are the Way They Are.* New York: McGraw-Hill, 1986; Putnam/Berkley, 1988.

Farrell, Warren. *Women Can't Hear What Men Don't Say.* New York: Jeremy P. Tarcher/Putnam, 1999.

Gilder, George. *Men and Marriage.* Gretna, LA: Pelican Publishing Company, 1987.

Greenberg, Martin. *The Birth of a Father.* New York: Continuum, 1985.

Gurian, Michael. *The Wonder of Boys.* New York: Jeremy P. Tarcher/Putnam, 1996.

Halpern, Howard. *Cutting Loose.* New York: Simon & Schuster, 1976.

Heinowitz, Jack. *Pregnant Fathers.* San Diego, CA: Parents As Partners Press, 1995.

Horn, Wade F. *Father Facts 3.* Lancaster, PA: National Fatherhood Initiative, 1998.

Horn, Wade F. and Jeffrey Rosenberg. *The New Father Book.* Des Moines, IA: Better Homes and Gardens Books, 1998.

Jeffers, Susan. *I'm Okay; You're a Brat.* Los Angeles: Renaissance Books, 1999.

Kimball, Gayle. *50/50 Parenting.* Lexington, MA: Lexington Books, 1988.

Kipnis, Aaron R. *Angry Young Men.* San Francisco: Jossey-Bass Publishers, 1999.

LaFramboise, Donna. *The Princess at the Window.* Toronto: Penguin Books, 1996.

Levine, James A. and Todd L. Pittinsky. *Working Fathers.* New York: A Harvest Book, 1998.

Leving, Jeffery M. & Kenneth A. Dachman. *Fathers' Rights.* New York: Basic Books, 1997.

Levy, David L., ed. *The Best Parent is Both Parents.* Norfolk, VA: Hampton Roads Publishing Company, 1993.

Masson, Jeffrey Moussaieff. *The Emperor's Embrace.* New York: Pocket Books, 1999.

Novak, James. *Wisconsin Father's Guide to Divorce and Custody.* Madison, WI: Prairie Oak Press, 1996.

Osherson, Samuel. *Finding Our Fathers.* New York: The Free Press, 1986.

Popenoe, David. *Life Without Father.* Cambridge, MA: Harvard University Press, 1999

Prengel, Serge. *Still a Dad.* New York: Mission Creative Energy, 1999.

Pruett, Kyle D. *Fatherneed.* New York: The Free Press, 2000.

Seidenberg, Robert. *The Father's Emergency Guide to Divorce-Custody Battle.* Takoma Park, MD: JES Books, 1997.

Sommers, Christina Hoff. *The War Against Boys.* New York: Simon & Schuster, 2000

Tiger, Lionel. *The Decline of Males.* New York: Golden Books, 1999

Walker, Glynnis. *Solomon's Children.* New York: Arbor House, 1986.

Wallerstein, Judith S. & Sandra Blakeslee. *Second Chances.* New York: Ticknor & Fields, 1989.

Warshak, Richard A. *The Custody Revolution.* New York: Poseidon Press, 1992.

Whitehead, Barbara Dafoe. *The Divorce Culture.* New York: Alfred A. Knopf, 1997.

Wilber, Ken. *The Eye of Spirit.* Boston: Shambhala, 1997.

Audio/Video Tapes:

Cooper, Kat. *Family Ties and Knots* series. www.familytiesandknots.com

Farrell, Warren. *The Myth of Male Power.* www.warrenfarrell.com.

Farrell, Warren. *Understanding Each Other I/II.* www.warrenfarrell.com.

Farrell, Warren. *Why Men Are the Way They Are.* Abridged. www.warrenfarrell .com

Farrell, Warren. *Why Men Are the Way They Are.* Unabridged. Costa Mesa, CA: Books-on-Tape, 1988.

Farrell, Warren. *Women Can't Hear What Men Don't Say.* New York: Audio Renaissance, 1999.

Periodicals:

At-Home Dad
Peter Baylies, editor
www.parentsplace.com/family/dads/gen/0,3375,10234,00.html

Everyman: A Men's Journal.
David Shackleton, editor
www.everyman.org

Fathers' Rights Newsline
www.microserve.net/~steflink/index.htm

Full Time Dads
James McLoughlin, editor
www.fathersworld.com/fulltimedad/

The Liberator
Rich Doyle, editor
www.mensdefense.org

Mensight
www.themenscenter.com/mensight/

The Networker
Larry Hellmann, editor
www.ncfc.net

Speak Out for Children
David L. Levy, editor
www.childrensrightscouncil.org

Transitions
Jerry Bissett, editor
www.ncfm.org

Notes

Introduction (pages 1–25)

1 *Der Spiegel,* No. 47/1997, November 17, 1997, p. 101. Sent by Hans-Günther Tappe.

2 Radcliffe Public Policy Center,"Life's Work: Generational Attitudes Toward Work and Life Integration, " (Cambridge, MA.: Radcliffe Public Policy Center, July, 2000). The Harris Interactive Poll was commissioned by the Radcliffe Public Policy Center. The Poll also found that 80% of men 21–39 put a flexible work schedule at the top of their list of desired job characteristics. See also Joyce Madelon Winslow, "Dads Can Learn from Moms," *USA Today,* July 12, 2000, p.15A.

3 Richard Serrano and Mike Clary, *Los Angeles Times,* "Elián's Father Arrives, Says He Feared for Son," April 7, 2000, p. A1 and A18.

4 Peter T. Kilborn, "A Bumpy Path for Miami Kin of Cuban Boy," *The New York Times,* February 9, 2000, pp. A1 and A13.

5 The father's name is Juan Miguel González.

6 Steve Kelley, *San Diego Union-Tribune/*Copley News Service, June 29, 2000.

7 Ralph Vigoda, "Stepfather Wins Battle For Custody," *The Philadelphia Inquirer,* January 22, 2000, p. A1.

8 U.S. Department of Commerce, Bureau of the Census, *Statistical Abstract of the United States, 1999* [hereinafter *Statistical Abstract, 1999,* Table 81] (Washington, D.C.: G.P.O.), p. 66, Table 81, "Family Households with own Children under 18, by Type of Family 1980–1998." For 1980 single fathers vs. single mothers: 10.2% vs. 89.8%; for 1998 single fathers vs. single mothers: 18.9% vs. 81.1%

9 Promise Keepers does not keep any hard ethnic numbers, but Roger Chapman, Manager of Media Relations for the Promise Keepers, estimated informally that the organization was about 11 to 15% minority (African-American, Asian-American, or Hispanic), with the rest being white. Interview on June 19, 2000.

10 See, for example, Second Wives'Crusade, in Resources.

11 *Parade,* April 23, 2000, p. 9.

12 Augustine J. Kposowa, "Marital status and suicide in the National Longitudinal Mortality Study," *Journal of Epidemiology and Community Health,* Vol. 54, April 2000, p. 256. It is now 4.8 times higher in men than in women.

13 Ibid., *Epidemiology.* The figure is 9.94 higher in divorced men than in divorced women. The 9.94 figure was obtained from Dr. Kposowa using information from Table 1 on p. 256. Personal correspondence June 29, 2000.

14 Separated and divorced men commit suicide at 13.4 times the rate of separated and divorced women. Augustine J. Kposowa, Department of Sociology, University of California, Riverside, derived this number from information taken from C. H. Cantor and P. J. Slater, "Marital Breakdown, Parenthood, and Suicide," *Journal of Family Studies*, Vol. 2, No. 2, October, 1995, p. 99. Personal correspondence April 18, 2000.

15 Kposowa, *Epidemiology*, op. cit., pp. 254–261.

16 D. A. Luepnitz, *Child Custody* (Lexington: D. C. Heath & Company, 1982), cited in Richard A. Warshak, "Father Custody and Child Development: A Review and Analysis of Psychological Research," *Behavioral Sciences & the Law*, Vol. 4, No. 2, 1986, p. 194. Half of custodial mothers reported spending less time with the children than before the divorce.

17 Frank Cotham ©The New Yorker Collection 1997.

Part One. What's Missing When Dad's Missing

1 U.S. Department of Health and Human Services, "HHS Launches 'Be Their Dad' Parental Responsibility Campaign," Press Release, March 26, 1999. <http://www.hhs.gov/news/press/1999pres/990326.html>

Chapter 1. Why Dad Is Crucial (pages 29–54)

1 *Statistical Abstract, 1999*, Table 81, op. cit.

2 Rachel Levy-Shiff, Michael A. Hoffman, Salli Mogilner, Susan Levinger, and Mario B. Mogilner, "Fathers' Hospital Visits to their Preterm Infants as a Predictor of Father-Infant Relationship and Infant Development," *Pediatrics*, Vol. 86, 1990, pp. 291–292. The authors are from Bar-Ilan University and Kaplan Hospital in Israel.

3 Ibid.

4 Frank A. Pedersen, Judith L. Rubenstein, and Leon J. Yarrow, "Infant Development in Father-Absent Families," *Journal of Genetic Psychology*, Vol. 135, 1979, pp. 55–57.

5 The Binet IQ measurement was used. See L. J. Yarrow, R. P. Klein, S. Lomonaco, and G. A. Morgan, "Cognitive and Motivational Development in Early Childhood," in B. Z. Friedlander, *et al.*, *Exceptional Infant 3* (NY: Brunner/Mazel, 1974), as cited in ibid., p. 57.

6 Ibid., see especially pp. 55–57.

7 Richard Koestner, C. Franz, and J. Weinberger, "The Family Origins of Empathic Concern—A Twenty-Six-Year Longitudinal Study," *Journal of Personality and Social Psychology*, Vol. 58, No. 4, April, 1990, pp. 709–717.

8 Bryce J. Christensen, "America's Academic Dilemma: The Family and the Schools," *The Family in America*, Vol. 2, No. 6, June, 1988. Cited in Nicholas Davidson, "Life Without Father: America's Greatest Social Catastrophe," *Policy Review*, Winter 1990, p. 41.

9 Martin Deutsch and Bert Brown, "Social Influences in Negro-White Intelligence Differences," *Journal of Social Issues*, Vol. 20, No. 2, 1964, p. 29.

10 Sara McLanahan and Gary Sandefur, *Growing Up with a Single Parent* (Cambridge, MA: Harvard University Press, 1994), p. 41. The four national surveys are: the National Longitudinal Survey of Youth, the Panel Study of Income Dynamics, the High School and Beyond Study, and the National Survey of Families and Households. The socioeconomic variables that were controlled included race, mother's education, father's education, income, number of siblings, place of residence, and other background differences. See page 12 and Appendix B.

11 Henry Biller, *Paternal Deprivation: Family, School, Sexuality, and Society* (Lexington, MA: Lexington Books, 1974).

12 John Guidubaldi, Joseph D. Perry, and Bonnie K. Nastasi, "Growing Up in a Divorced Family: Initial and Long Term Perspectives on Children's Adjustment," in Stuart Oscamp, ed., *Applied Social Psychology Annual, Vol. 7: Family Processes and Problems* (Beverly Hills, CA: Sage Publications, 1987), p. 212.

13 U.S. Department of Health and Human Services, National Center for Health Statistics, "Family Structure and Children's Health: United States, 1988," *Vital and Health Statistics,* [hereinafter *Vital and Health Statistics/*"Family Structure . . ."] Series 10, No. 178 (Hyattsville, MD: Public Health Service, 1991), p. 24, Table 10, "Number of Children 5–17 Years of Age and Percent Who Ever Repeated a Grade of School, by Family Type and Selected Demographic and Social Characteristics: United States, 1988." Specifically, 11.6% (about 1 in 9) of children living with their biological mother and father repeated a grade of school; 24.1% (about 1 in 4) of children living with either a formerly married mother and no father, *or* a never-married mother and no father, repeated a grade of school.

14 The greater absentee rate, as well as suspensions, expulsions, dropouts, and truancy of children from one-parent families was found by the National Association of Elementary School Principals after surveying the records of more than 8,000 students from elementary and high schools around the country. Reported in "Woe Is One," *Time,* September 8, 1980.

15 Sheila Fitzgerald Krein and A. Beller, "Educational Attainment of Children from Single-Parent Families: Differences by Exposure, Gender, and Race," *Demography,* Vol. 25, May 1988, pp. 403–426.

16 Ibid., pp. 403–426.

17 Lyn Carlsmith, "Effect of Early Father Absence on Scholastic Aptitude," *Harvard Educational Review,* Vol. 34, 1964, pp. 3–20.

18 Ibid.

19 Christensen, "America's Academic Dilemma" op. cit., in Davidson, op. cit.

20 Guidubaldi, op. cit., in Oscamp, op. cit., *Applied Social Psychology Annual,* pp. 214–217.

21 B. Sutton-Smith, *et al.,* "Father-Absence Effects in Families of Different Sibling Compositions," *Child Development,* Vol. 39, 1968, pp. 1213–1221.

22 McLanahan, op. cit., pp. 48-49; 49-50. The four national surveys are: the National Longitudinal Survey of Youth; the Panel Study of Income Dynamics; the High School and Beyond Study; and the National Survey of Families and Households. The socioeconomic variables that were controlled for included race, mother's education, father's education, number of siblings, place of residence, and other background differences. See page 12 and Appendix B.

23 Christine Nord, DeeAnn Brimhall, and Jerry West, "Fathers' Involvement in their Children's Schools." *U.S. Department of Education, National Center for Education Statistics,* Washington, D.C., 1997, pp. viii–ix.

24 Linda W. Warren and C. Tomlinson-Keasey, "The Context of Suicide," *American Journal of Orthopsychiatry,* Vol. 57, No. 1, January 1987, p. 42.

25 Carmen Noevi Velez and Patricia Cohen, "Suicidal Behavior and Ideation in a Community Sample of Children: Maternal and Youth Reports," *Journal of the American Academy of Child and Adolescent Psychiatry,* Vol. 273, 1988, pp. 349–356.

26 U.S. Department of Health and Human Services, National Center for Health Statistics, *Vital Statistics of the United States* (Washington, D.C.: G.P.O., 1991), Vol. II, Part A,

"Mortality" p. 51, Table 1–9 "Death Rates for 72 Selected Causes by 5-Year Age Groups, Race, and Sex: U.S., 1988." The exact rates are:

Suicide Rates by Age and Sex Per 100,000 Population

Age	Male	Female
5–9	0.1	0.0
10–14	2.1	0.8
15–19	18.0	4.4
20–24	25.8	4.1

27 John S. Wodarski and Pamela Harris, "Adolescent Suicide: A Review of Influences and the Means for Prevention," *Social Work*, Vol. 32, No. 6, November/December, 1987, pp. 477–484.

28 M. Main and D. R. Weston, "The Quality of the Toddler's Relationship to Mother and to Father: Related to Conflict Behavior and the Readiness to Establish New Relationships," *Child Development*, Vol. 52, 1981, pp. 932–940.

29 R. Dalton, *et al.*, "Psychiatric Hospitalization of Pre-School Children: Admission Factors and Discharge Implications," *Journal of the American Academy of Child and Adolescent Psychiatry*, Vol. 26, No. 3, May, 1987, pp. 308–312.

30 H. S. Merskey and G. T. Swart, "Family Background and Physical Health of Adolescents Admitted to an In-Patient Psychiatric Unit, I: Principle Caregivers," *Canadian Journal of Psychiatry*, Vol. 34, 1989, pp. 79–83.

31 Davidson, op. cit., p. 42.

32 U.S. Department of Justice, Bureau of Justice Statistics, *Special Report: Survey of Youth in Custody, 1987* (Washington, D.C.: U.S. Department of Justice, Bureau of Justice Statistics, Sept. 1988), p. 3, Table 2, "Family Structure and Peer Group Involvement of Youth in Long-Term, State-Operated Juvenile Institutions, Year End 1987."

33 *Vital and Health Statistics/*"Family Structure . . ." op. cit., p. 27, Table 13, "Number of Children 3-17 Years of Age and Percent Treated for Emotional or Behavioral Problems in the Past 12 Months, by Family Type and Selected Demographic and Social Characteristics: United States, 1988." In the previous 12-month period, 2.7% of children living with their biological mother and father, and 8.8% of children living with a formerly married mother and no father, were treated for emotional and behavioral problems.

34 *Vital and Health Statistics/*"Family Structure . . . ," op. cit., p. 19, Table 5, "Number of Children 17 Years of Age and Under and Percent Who Had Frequent Headaches in the Past 12 Months, by Family Type and Selected Demographic and Social Characteristics: United States. 1988." In the previous 12-month period, 2.5% of children living with their biological mother and father, and 4.1% of children living with a formerly married mother and no father, had frequent headaches.

35 Ibid., p. 21, Table 7, "Number of Children 17 Years of Age and Under and Percent Who Had Chronic Enuresis in the Past 12 Months, by Family Type and Selected Demographic and Social Characteristics: United States, 1988." In the previous 12-month period, 2.3% of children living with their biological mother and father, and 2.9% of children living with a formerly married mother and no father, had chronic enuresis (bed-wetting).

36 Ibid., p. 20, Table 6, "Number of Children 17 Years of Age and Under and Percent Who Had a Stammer or Other Speech Defect in the Past 12 Months, by Family Type and Selected Demographic And Social Characteristics: United States, 1988." In the previous 12-month period, 2.3% of children living with their biological mother and father, and 3.2% of children living with a formerly married mother and no father, had a stammer or other speech defect.

37 Ibid., p. 10. In the previous 12-month period, 39% of children living with their biolog-
    ical mother and father, and 55.3% of children living with a formerly married mother
    and no father, had one or more indicators of anxiety or depression.
38 Ibid., p. 10. In the previous 12-month period, 34.9% of children living with their bio-
    logical mother and father, and 51.1% of children living with a formerly married
    mother and no father, had one or more indicators of hyperactivity.
39 Guidubaldi, op. cit., in Oscamp, op. cit., *Applied Social Psychology Annual,* p. 230.
40 Frank Mott, "When Is a Father Really Gone? Paternal-Child Contact in Father-Absent
    Homes," *Demography,* Vol. 27, No. 4, November 1990, pp. 499–518.
41 P. Frankel, C. F. Behling, and T. Dix, "The Parents of Drug Users," *Journal of College Stu-
    dent Personnel,* Vol. 16, No. 3, 1975, pp. 244–247.
42 The only factor more important than father involvement was the child's age. Robert H.
    Coombs and John Landsverk, "Parenting Styles and Substance Use During Childhood
    and Adolescence," *Journal of Marriage and the Family,* Vol. 50, May 1988, p. 479, Table 4.
    The factors considered were age, sex, ethnicity, social class, closeness to parent, parent
    trust, parental rules, parent strictness, etc. Age accounted for about 17% (.17 out of a
    max of 1) of the variation in drug use among the youth in their sample; positive father
    sentiment (closeness) accounted for another 10%, and no other factor accounted for
    more than 2%.
43 U.S. Bureau of the Census,
44 Francis Ianni, *The Search for Structure* (NY: Free Press, 1989).
45 Duke Hefland, "L. A. Skinhead Forms Unlikely Alliance," *Los Angeles Times,* August 12,
    1996.
46 *Vital and Health Statistics/* "Family Structure . . . ," op. cit., p. 18, Table 4, "Number of
    Children 17 Years of Age and Under and Percent Who Had Chronic Asthma in the Past
    12 Months, by Family Type and Selected Demographic and Social Characteristics:
    United States, 1988." In the previous 12-month period, 3.9% of children living with
    their biological mother and father, and 5.9% of children living with a formerly married
    mother and no father, had chronic asthma.
47 Daniel Patrick Moynihan, "Half the Nation's Children: Born Without a Fair Chance,"
    The New York Times, September 25, 1988, p. E25. And these figures are just for whites.
    It's even worse among blacks. See also Edward Teyber and Charles D. Hoffman, "Miss-
    ing Fathers," *Psychology Today,* April, 1987, pp. 36–38.
48 Frank F. Furstenberg, Jr. and Kathleen Mullan Harris, "When and Why Fathers Matter:
    Impacts of Father Involvement on the Children of Adolescent Mothers." Cited in
    Robert I. Lerman and Theodora J. Ooms, eds., *Young Unwed Fathers: Changing Roles and
    Emerging Policies* (Philadelphia: Temple University Press, 1993), pp. 127 and 130. The
    sample size of all children in this portion of the study was 253. Among the sons of
    inner-city teenaged mothers, 15% had had a baby by age 19; none who had a close re-
    lationship with their biological father did.
49 Survey conducted by Mark Clements Research, of 720 teenage girls, 6% of whom had
    been pregnant. Sample representative of U.S. Census data geographically, and accord-
    ing to household income and size. Research commissioned by, and reported in, *Parade,*
    February 2, 1997, pp. 4–5.
50 Ibid. Eighty-five percent of the girls saw female friends as significant influences; 83%
    saw pressure from boys as being significant.
51 McLanahan, op. cit., p. 53, Figure 4: "The risk of teen births for women." The four na-
    tional surveys are: the National Longitudinal Survey of Youth, the Panel Study of In-
    come Dynamics, the High School and Beyond Study, and the National Survey of

Families and Households. The socioeconomic variables that were controlled included race, mother's education, father's education, number of siblings, place of residence, and other background differences. See page 12 and Appendix B.

52 E. M. Hetherington, "Effects of Father Absence on Personality Development in Adolescent Daughters," *Developmental Psychology*, Vol. 7, 1972, pp. 313–326; and Teyber, op. cit., pp. 36–38.

53 E. M. Hetherington, "My Heart Belongs to Daddy: A Study of the Marriages of Daughters of Divorcees and Widows," unpublished manuscript, University of Virginia, 1977.

54 Dewey G. Cornell (University of Virginia), in "Juvenile Homicide: Personality and Developmental Factors," final report to the Harry Frank Guggenheim Foundation, New York, NY, 1989.

55 Raymond A. Knight and Robert A. Prentky, "The Developmental Antecedents of Adult Adaptions of Rapist Sub-Types," *Criminal Justice and Behavior*, Vol. 14, December, 1987, pp. 413–414. Knight and Prentky labeled this type of rapist as one with "displaced anger."

56 Wray Herbert, "Dousing the Kindlers," *Psychology Today*, January, 1985, p. 28.

57 *Special Report: Survey of Youth in Custody, 1987*, op. cit.

58 Douglas A. Smith and G. Roger Jarjoura, "Social Structure and Criminal Victimization," *Journal of Research in Crime and Delinquency*, Vol. 25, No. 1, February, 1988, pp. 27–52.

59 John Johnson and Ronald L. Soble, "The Brothers Menendez," *Los Angeles Times*, July 22, 1990, cover.

60 Ibid., p. 6.

61 Warshak, op. cit., pp. 199–200.

62 E. M. Hetherington, M. Cox, and R. Cox, "Effects of Divorce on Parents and Children," in M. Lamb, ed., *Non-Traditional Families* (New Jersey: Lawrence Erlbaum, 1982), pp. 233–288; Judith Wallerstein and Joan B. Kelly, *Surviving the Breakup* (NY: Basic Books, 1980); and John W. Santrock and Richard A. Warshak, "The Impact of Divorce in Father-Custody and Mother-Custody Homes: The Child's Perspective," in L. A. Kurdek, ed., *Children and Divorce* (San Francisco, CA: Jossey-Bass, 1983).

63 Ibid.

64 Ibid.

65 E. B. Karp, "Children's Adjustment in Joint and Single Custody: An Empirical Study," doctoral dissertation, California School of Professional Psychology, Berkeley, CA, 1982.

66 L. P. Noonan, "Effects of Long-Term Conflict on Personality Functioning of Children of Divorce," doctoral dissertation, The Wright Institute Graduate School of Psychology, Berkeley, CA, 1985.

67 E. G. Pojman, "Emotional Adjustment of Boys in Sole Custody and Joint Custody Compared with Adjustment of Boys in Happy and Unhappy Marriages," unpublished doctoral dissertation, California Graduate Institute, Los Angeles, 1982.

68 Paula M. Raines, "Joint Custody and the Right to Travel: Legal and Psychological Implications," *Journal of Family Law*, Vol. 24, June 1986, pp. 625–656.

69 D. A. Luepnitz, "Maternal, Paternal, and Joint Custody: A Study of Families After Divorce," doctoral dissertation, State University of New York at Buffalo, 1980.

70 Karp, doctoral dissertation, op. cit.

71 D. B. Cowan, "Mother Custody Versus Joint Custody: Children's Parental Relationship and Adjustment," doctoral dissertation, University of Washington, 1982.

72   Isabel A. Lehrman, "Adjustment of Latency Age Children in Joint and Single Custody Arrangements," summarized in *Dissertation Abstracts International,* Vol. 50, No. 8, February 1990. (order #DA8925682)

73   B. H. Granite, "An Investigation of the Relationship Among Self-Concept, Parental Behaviors, and the Adjustment of Children in Different Custodial Living Arrangements Following a Marital Separation and/or a Divorce," doctoral dissertation, University of Pennsylvania, Philadelphia, 1985.

74   Margaret Crosbie-Burnett, "Impact of Joint vs. Sole Custody and Quality of Co-Parental Relationship on Adjustment of Adolescents in Remarried Families," *Behavioral Sciences & the Law,* 1991, Fall, Vol. 9, No. 4, pp. 439–449.

75   Luepnitz, doctoral dissertation, op. cit.

76   Shirley M. H. Hanson, "Healthy Single Parent Families," *Family Relations,* Vol. 35, 1986, p. 131.

77   *Statistical Abstract, 1999,* Table 81, op. cit. By 1998, the total number of fathers was 1,798,000, and increasing each year.

78   U.S. Bureau of the Census, Public Use Microdata Samples (PUMS), 1990, a 5% sample of the U.S. population, as cited in David J. Eggebeen, Anastasia R. Snyder, and Wendy D. Manning, "Children in Single-Father Families in Demographic Perspective," *Journal of Family Issues,* Vol. 17, No. 4, July 1996, p. 450, Table 2, "Characteristics of Single-Father Families." Fifty-two percent of fathers are in the top two family income quintiles. Conversely, only 12% are in the lower fifth.

79   Carmen Noevi Velez, J. Johnson, and P. Cohen, "A Longitudinal Analysis of Selected Risk Factors for Childhood Psychopathology," *Journal of the American Academy of Child and Adolescent Psychiatry,* 1989, Vol. 28, pp. 861–864, as cited in ibid., Eggebeen, p. 453.

80   F. C. Verhalst, G. W. Akkerhuis, and M. Althaus, "Mental Health in Dutch Children: I. A Cross-Cultural Comparison," *Acta Psychiatrica Scandinavica,* 1985, Vol. 72 (Suppl.), pp. 1–108; and E. E. Werner, "Stress and Protective Factors in Children's Lives," in A. R. Nichoe, ed., *Longitudinal Studies in Child Psychology and Psychiatry* (NY: John Wiley & Sons, 1985), pp. 335–355, as cited in ibid., Eggebeen, p. 453.

81   J. T. Gibbs, "Assessment of Depression in Urban Adolescent Females: Implications for Early Intervention Strategies," *American Journal of Social Psychiatry,* 1986, Vol. 6, pp. 50–56, as cited in ibid., Eggebeen.

82   G. J. Duncan and W. L. Rodgers, "Longitudinal Aspects of Child Poverty," *Journal of Marriage and the Family,* 1988, Vol. 50, pp. 1007–1021; and M. S. Hill and G. J. Duncan, "Parental Family Income and the Socioeconomic Attainment of Children," *Social Science Research,* 1987, Vol. 16, pp. 39–73, as cited in ibid., Eggebeen.

83   K. Alison Clarke-Stewart and Craig Hayward, "Advantages of Father Custody and Contact for the Psychological Well-Being of School-Age Children," *Journal of Applied Developmental Psychology,* Vol. 17, No. 2, April–June 1996, pp. 239–270.

84   Warshak, op. cit., p. 190.

85   Mary Jo Coiro, Nicholas Zill, and Barbara Bloom, "Health of Our Nation's Children," U.S. Department of Health and Human Services, National Center for Health Statistics, Centers For Disease Control and Prevention, *Vital and Health Statistics,* Series 10, No. 191, December 1994. The National Health Interview Survey is based on a Census Bureau sample of over 122,000 individuals, including over 17,000 children.

86   John W. Santrock and Richard A. Warshak, "Father Custody and Social Development in Boys and Girls," *Journal of Social Issues,* Vol. 35, No. 4, Fall 1979.

87   Ibid., pp. 112–125.

88   E. M. Hetherington, "Divorce: A Child's Perspective," *American Psychologist*, Vol. 34, 1979, pp. 831–858.

89   Kyle D. Pruett, "The Nurturing Male: A Longitudinal Study of Primary Nurturing Fathers," in *Fathers and Their Families*, ed. Stanley H. Cath, Alan Gurwitt, and Linda Gunsberg (Hillsdale, NJ: The Analytic Press, 1989), p. 390.

90   Three percent of children with their fathers felt victimized, vs. 10% of children with their mothers. Mogens Nygaard Christoffersen, "An Investigation of Fathers with 3- 5-Year-Old Children." Paper presented at the Social Research-Institute Ministerratskonferenz, Stockholm, Sweden, 27–28 April 1995, Chart 3, "Psychosomatic Symptoms of the Parents and Development of the Children." Translated by David Bedard. E-mail, March 12, 1997. Dr. Christoffersen is with the Social Research Institute in Denmark. The study is especially significant because it examined more than one-quarter of all the 3- to 5-year-old children in Denmark who lived with their biological fathers (600 out of 2,040). The study compared these children to a group of about 600 (out of 33,708) living with their biological mothers.

91   Armin A. Brott, *The Single Father* (NY: Abbeville Press, 1999), p. 80.

92   Ibid. Thirty percent of the children living with moms and 15% of those living with dads had concentration problems.

93   Ibid.

94   Ibid., Chart 2, "Parents Living Alone With 3- To 5-Year-Old Children."

95   Pruett, op. cit., in *Fathers and Their Families*, op. cit., p. 390.

96   See H. S. Goldstein, "Fathers' Absence and Cognitive Development of 12- to 17-Year-Olds," *Psychological Reports*, 1982, Vol. 51, pp. 843–848. See also N. Radin, "The Role of the Father in Cognitive, Academic, and Intellectual Development," in M. E. Lamb, ed., *The Role of the Father in Child Development* (NY: John Wiley & Sons, 1981), pp. 379–427; and N. Radin, "The Influence of Fathers on Their Sons and Daughters," *Social Work in Education*, 1986, Vol. 8, pp. 77–91.

97   Ibid., Radin, "Role of the Father"; ibid., Radin, "Influence of Fathers," and N. Radin and G. Russell, "Increased Paternal Participation and Childhood Outcomes," in M. E. Lamb and A. Sagi, eds., *Fatherhood and Family Policy* (Hillsdale, NJ: Lawrence Erlbaum, 1983), pp. 191–218.

98   E. Bing, "The Effect of Child-Rearing Practices on the Development of Differential Cognitive Abilities," *Child Development*, Vol. 34, 1963, pp. 631–648, as cited in David Popenoe, *Life Without Father* (NY: The Free Press, 1996), p. 148.

99   Nord, op. cit., pp. viii–ix.

100 Douglas B. Downey, "The School Performance of Children from Single-Mother and Single-Father Families: Economic or Interpersonal Deprivation?" *Journal of Family Issues*, 1994, Vol 15, No. 1. The children were 13- and 14 year-olds, thus limiting its generalizability.

101 U.S. Bureau of the Census, *Current Population Reports: Population Characteristics*, Series P 20, No. 488, "Household and Family Characteristics: March, 1995," October, 1996, pp. 59–60, Table 6, "Families, by Type, Age of Own Children, and Educational Attainment, Race, and Hispanic Origin of Householder: March 1995." This data compares single mothers and fathers who are heads of households, and thereby does not include most teenage mothers, who are unlikely to be heads of households and more likely to live with their parents. The education gap is likely to be even greater between teenage mothers and the fathers, since the teenage mothers, by virtue of their age, will be limited to a high school education or less, while the teenage fathers, who are usually about

eight years older than the mothers, have a greater likelihood of more years to educate themselves.

102 D. C. Scheck and R. Emerick, "The Young Male Adolescent's Perception of Early Childrearing Behavior: The Differential Effects of Socioeconomic Status and Family Size," *Sociometry,* 1976, Vol. 39, pp. 39–52; and J. D. Wright and S. R. Wright, "Social Class and Parental Values for Children: A Partial Replication and Extension of Kohn's Thesis," *American Sociological Review,* 1976, Vol. 41, pp. 141–161, as cited in Eggebeen, op. cit., p. 452.

103 P. Blau and O. D. Duncan, *The American Occupational Structure* (NY: John Wiley & Sons, 1967); D. L. Featherman and R. M. Hauser, *Opportunity and Change* (NY: Academic Press, 1978); W. H. Sewell and R. M. Hauser, *Education, Occupation, and Earnings* (NY: Academic Press, 1975), as cited in ibid., Eggebeen.

104 Douglas B. Downey, James W. Ainsworth-Darnell, and Mikaela J. Dufur, "Sex of Parent and Children's Well-Being in Single-Parent Households," *Journal of Marriage and the Family,* Vol. 60, November 1998, pp. 878–893.

105 Luepnitz, *Child Custody,* op. cit., cited in Warshak, op. cit., p. 192.

106 On the "children with moms get along better" side is Downey, "Sex of Parent . . . ," op. cit., pp. 886 and 887. On the "children with dads get along better" side is Christoffersen, op. cit., Chart 2.

107 Ibid., Christoffersen, Chart 2.

108 U.S. Department of Health and Human Services, National Center on Child Abuse and Neglect, *Third National Incidence Study of Child Abuse and Neglect: Final Report Appendices* (Washington, D.C.: U.S. Department of Health and Human Services, National Center on Child Abuse and Neglect, 1997), pp. A-63–A-64. Table A-11B, "Parent Structure by Categories of Maltreatment and Severity for Children Countable Under the Harm Standard." The estimated total for Mother Only Household is 264.1 children killed. For Father Only Household the estimated total is 10.8.

109 Christoffersen, op. cit., Chart 3.

110 Coiro, op. cit., Table 13, p. 43.

111 Ibid., Table 16, p. 49. Nine percent of children with only biological fathers have late or irregular bedtimes; 33% of children with only biological mothers had late or irregular bedtimes.

112 Christoffersen, op. cit., Chart 4, "Psychosomatic Symptoms and Select Background Situations of the Parents."

113 Clarke-Stewart, op. cit.

114 Christoffersen, op. cit.

115 Glynnis Walker, *Solomon's Children* (NY: Arbor House, 1986), pp. 27, 84–85.

116 Clarke-Stewart, op. cit., p. 257.

117 Ibid., pp. 257–258 (including Table 4).

118 Douglas B. Downey and Brian Powell, "Do Children in Single-Parent Households Fare Better Living with Same-Sex Parent?" *Journal of Marriage and the Family,* Vol. 15, February, 1993, p. 55–71.

119 Credit to Chandler Arnold for gathering most of the research in this section. Chandler Arnold, "Children of Stepfamilies: A Snap Shot," publication from the Center for Law and Public Policy, November, 1998. <http://www.clasp.org/pubs/familyformation/stepfamiliesfinal.BK!.htm> The undocumented portions are my perspectives, and can be discounted accordingly.

120 Paul Glick, "Remarried Families, Stepfamilies, and Stepchildren: A Brief Demographic Analysis," *Family Relations,* Vol. 38, 1989, pp. 24–27.

121 E. Mavis Hetherington and Kathleen M. Jodl, "Stepfamilies as Settings for Child Development," in Alan Booth and Judy Dunn, eds., *Stepfamilies: Who Benefits? Who Does Not?* (Hillsdale, N.J.: L Erlbaum, 1994).

122 Paul Glick, "Remarriage: Some Recent Changes and Variations," *Journal of Family Issues,* Vol. I, pp. 455–478.

123 McLanahan, op. cit.

124 Furstenberg, "Fathers Matter . . . ," op. cit. Cited in Lerman & Ooms, op. cit., pp. 127 & 130.

125 Hetherington, "Stepfamilies . . . ," op. cit., in Booth, op. cit.

126 N. Zill, D. Morrison, and M. Coiro, "Long-Term Effects of Parental Divorce on Parent-Child Relationships, adjustment, and Achievement in Young Adulthood," *Journal of Family Psychology,* Vol. 7, No. 6, 1993, pp. 1–13, as quoted in Hetherington, "Stepfamilies," ibid.

127 McLanahan, op. cit., p. 53.

128 Nan Marie Astone and Sara S. McLanahan, "Family Structure, Residential Mobility, and School Dropout: A Research Note," *Demography,* Vol. 31, No. 4, November 1994, pp. 575–583.

129 W. Glenn Clingempeel, at al., "Stepparent-Stepchild relationships in Stepmother and Stepfather Families: A Multimethod Study," *Family Relations,* Vol. 33, 1984, pp. 465–473.

130 Hetherington, "Stepfamilies . . . ," op. cit., E. Mavis Hetherington and Kathleen M. Jodl, "Stepfamilies as Settings for Child Development," in Booth, op. cit.

131 D. R. Morrison, K. A. Moore, C. Blumenthal, M. J. Coiro, and S. Middleton, *Parent-Child Relations and Investments of Parental Time in Children* (Washington, D.C.: Child Trends, Inc., 1994).

132 Nan Astone, op. cit., pp. 575–583.

133 McLanahan, op. cit.

134 William R. Beer, *American Stepfamilies* (New Brunswick, NJ: Transaction Publishers, 1992), p. 217. The biological mom and dad led to 11% of the males saying they were "not too happy." The father and stepmother combination led to 14% "not too happy." And the mother-stepfather combination to 1.3%. The average of the stepparent combinations is less than that of the mother-father combination.

135 Ibid.

136 See Maura Dolan, Legal Affairs Writer, "Justices Ease Relocation of Children in Divorce Cases," *Los Angeles Times,* April 16, 1996, p. 1.

137 McLanahan, op. cit.

138 Clarke-Stewart, op. cit., p. 239.

139 The California Supreme Court decreed this major shift in family law in the *Marriage of Burgess* (1996) 13 Cal. 4th 25. See also Dolan, op. cit.

140 Christoffersen, op. cit., Chart 3. Three percent of children with their fathers felt victimized versus 10% of children with their mothers. Seizures of fear were experienced by 1% of children with their fathers and 4% of children with their mothers. Nightmares were experienced by 6% of children with their fathers and 13% of children with their mothers.

Chapter 2. Is There a Mothering Instinct?/Fathering Instinct? (pages 55–74)

1 Popenoe, op. cit., p. 144. The first sentence of the swing example is also from this source, same page.

2 Brott, op. cit., p. 130.

3 John Nicholson, *Men and Women: How Different Are They?* (Oxford: Oxford University Press, 1984), p. 131; and Kyle Pruett, *The Nurturing Father* (NY: Warner Books, 1987), pp. 34–35. As cited in Gayle Kimball, *50/50 Parenting* (Lexington, MA: D. C. Heath and Company, 1988), p. 134.

4 Colette Jones, "Father-Infant Relationships in the First Year of Life," in Shirley Bozett and Frederick Bozett, eds., *Dimensions of Fatherhood* (Beverly Hills: Sage, 1985), p. 103. As cited in Kimball, ibid.

5 Brott, op. cit., p. 131.

6 Popenoe, op. cit., p. 144.

7 Ibid. See also John Snarey, *How Fathers Care for the Next Generation* (Cambridge, MA: Harvard University Press, 1993), pp. 163–164.

8 Lina Tarkhova, "Men: What's the Matter with Them?" *Soviet Life*, March, 1987, p. 31. (Reprinted from the youth daily newspaper *Komsomolskaya pravda*.)

9 David Brandon Lynn, *Daughters and Parents: Past, Present, and Future* (Monterey, CA: Brooks Cole Publishing Company, 1979), p. 89.

10 Interview on September 4, 1998, with Cynthia Epstein, author of *Women's Place: Options and Limits in Professional Careers* (Berkeley, CA: University of California Press, 1970) and of continuing studies of mentorship through the Graduate Center in New York City.

11 Jeffrey Moussaieff Masson, *The Emperor's Embrace* (NY: Pocket Books/Simon and Schuster,1999), p. 44.

12 Ibid.

13 Ibid., p. 38.

14 Ibid.

15 Ibid., p. 43.

16 Ibid., p. 45.

17 Lydia Scoon-Rogers and Gordon H. Lester "Child Support Custodial Mothers and Fathers: 1991," *Current Population Reports*, P60-187, U.S. Department of Commerce, Bureau of Census, August 1995, p. 6.

18 Masson, op. cit., p. 38.

19 For the suicide after spousal *death* figure, see: Jack C. Smith, James A. Mercy, and Judith M. Conn, "Marital Status and the Risk of Suicide," *American Journal of Public Health*, Vol. 78, No. 1, January 1988, p. 79, Figure 3. For the suicide after spousal *divorce* figure, see Kposowa, *Epidemiology*, op. cit.. The figure is 9.94 higher in divorced men than in divorced women. The 9.94 figure was obtained from Dr. Kposowa using information from Table 1 on p. 256. Personal correspondence June 29, 2000.

20 Ann Landers survey. Results ran in her syndicated column in 1,200 papers on January 23, 1976.

21 Walker, op. cit., p. 87.

22 H. R. Schaffer and P. E. Emerson, "The Development of Social Attachments in Infancy," *Monographs of the Society for Research in Child Development*, Vol. 29, 1964 in Lamb, op. cit., *The Role of the Father...*, in his chapter called "The Role of the Father: An Overview" p. 5.

23 Ibid., Lamb, *The Role of the Father*, p. 5. Here is the list of studies mentioned by Lamb that found no preference for either parent concerning infant separation protest:

- L. J. Cohen and J. J. Campos, "Father, Mother and Stranger as Elicitors of Attachment Behaviors in Infancy," *Developmental Psychology,* Vol. 10, 1974, pp. 146–154.
- M. Kotelchuck, "The Nature of the Child's Tie to His Father," Unpublished doctoral dissertation, Harvard University, 1972.
- M. Kotelchuck, P. Zelazo, J. Kagan, and E. Spelke, "Infant Reaction to Parental Separations When Left with Familiar and Unfamiliar Adults," *Journal of Genetic Psychology,* Vol. 126, 1975, pp. 255–262.
- M. E. Lamb, "Separation and Reunion Behaviors as Criteria of Attachment to Mothers and Fathers," Unpublished manuscript, Yale University, 1975.
- M. E. Lamb, "Interactions Between Two-Year-Olds and Their Mothers and Fathers," *Psychological Reports,* Vol. 38, 1976, pp. 447–450.
- G. Ross, J. Kagan, P. Zelazo, and M. Kotelchuck, "Separation Protest in Infants in Home and Laboratory," *Developmental Psychology,* Vol. 11, 1975, pp. 256–257.
- E. Spelke, P. Zelazo, J. Kagan, and M. Kotelchuck, "Father Interaction and Separation Protest," *Developmental Psychology,* Vol. 9, 1973, pp. 83–90.

24 Main, "Toddler's Relationship to Mother and to Father," op. cit., pp. 932–940.

25 Spelke, op. cit.

26 Bob Harvey, "First Breath," *Men's Health,* Summer 1988, p. 53.

27 David Rothstein, among others, in his analysis of 27 inmates of the Medical Center for Federal Prisoners in Springfield, Missouri, found that most had domineering mothers and had joined the military at an early age. See David A. Rothstein, "Presidential Assassination Syndrome," *Archives of General Psychiatry,* Vol. 11, September 1964, pp. 245–254.

28 See Michael Janofsky, "Capriati's Dad Joins Others in Watching a Star's Ascent," *The New York Times,* August 31, 1990, p. B11; and Pat Jordan, "Daddy's Big Test," *The New York Times Magazine,* March 16, 1997, pp. 28–31.

29 Rothstein, op. cit.

30 George Bernard, Kenneth Fuller, Lynn Robbins, and Theodore Shaw, *The Child Molester: An Integrated Approach to Evaluation and Treatment* (NY: Brunner/Mazel Clinical Psychiatry Series, No. 1, 1988).

31 Rothstein, op. cit. David Rothstein conducted the study of 27 inmates at the Medical Center for Federal Prisoners in Springfield, Missouri. See James F. Kirkham, Sheldon G. Levy, and William J. Crotty, *Assassination and Political Violence: A Report to the National Commission on the Causes and Prevention of Violence* (NY: Bantam Books, 1970), p. 65f. See also Patricia Cayo Sexton's *The Feminized Male* (NY: Random House, 1969).

32 Ibid., Sexton, p. 4.

33 Ibid.

34 Hans Sebald, *Momism: The Silent Disease of America* (Chicago: Nelson Hall, 1976), p. 180ff.

35 Walker, op. cit., p. 87.

36 Ibid.

37 "The Facts of Life . . . Happiness is a Family," *Psychology Today* March, 1989, p. 10.

38 "Survey, How Fathers Feel . . . ," *Parents Magazine,* December, 1993, p. 234.

39 Between 1980 and 1998, single-mother families increased by 41.3%; single-father families increased by 192%. *Statistical Abstract, 1999,* Table 81, op. cit. These changes are very similar in many other industrialized nations such as Germany, England, Denmark, and Sweden.

40 Lynne M. Casper, "My Daddy Takes Care of Me! Fathers as Care Providers," *Current Popluation Reports,* P70-59, U.S. Department of Commerce, Bureau of the Census, September 1997, p. 7.

41   Robert A. Frank, Ph.D., "Research on At-Home Dads" in *At-Home Handbook,* 1997. Data is from his 1996 study of 371 Primary Caregiving Fathers and 490 Primary Caregiving Mothers. See <http://slowlane.com/research/laymen_research.html>

42   Ibid.

43   U.S. Department of Commerce, Bureau of the Census, Survey of Income and Program Participation, *Current Population Reports,* Household Economic Studies, Series P-70, No. 20, "Who's Minding the Kids? Childcare Arrangements: Winter 1986–87," p. 14, Table 1. "Primary Child Care Arrangements Used by Employed Mothers for Children Under 15, by Marital and Employment Status of Mothers—Part B. Fall 1987," by Martin O'Connell and Amara Bachu.

44   Joseph Pleck, "Family-Supportive Employer Policies: Are They Relevant to Men?" unpublished paper, p. 5, presented at the 98th Annual Convention of The American Psychological Association at Boston, August, 1990.

45   Ibid.

46   Walker, op. cit., p. 83. This data is based on a nationwide study of 368 children of divorce from 32 states, responding to questionnaires an average of 7 years after the divorce.

47   Ibid., p. 77.

48   Stephen Coz, "Kenny Rogers Turns Down $10 Million a Year—So He Can Spend More Time with 6-Year-Old Son," *National Enquirer,* July 12, 1988, p. 7.

49   Rick Kirkman and Jerry Scott, "Baby Blues," *Los Angeles Times,* November 12, 1990.

Chapter 3. Are Dads More Likely to Abuse? (pages 75–86)

1   Fredric Hayward, "I.Q. Test Questions/Answers," submitted for 1989 Farrell Fellowship awards.

2   Selwyn M. Smith, Ruth Hanson, and Sheila Noble, "Social Aspects of the Battered Baby Syndrome," in Joanne Valiant Cook and Roy Tyler Bowles, eds., *Child Abuse: Commission and Omission* (Toronto: Butterworths, 1980), p. 214, Table VIII, "Characteristics of Identified Perpetrators Compared with Total Sample." At the .01 level of significance, mother as head of household is responsible for twice the proportion of abuse in cases where parents are identified as perpetrators vs. other cases.

3   U.S. Department of Health and Human Services, Administration on Children, Youth, and Families, *Child Maltreatment 1997: Reports From the States to the National Child Abuse and Neglect Data System* (Washington, D.C.: G.P.O., 1999).

4   Ibid., Table 7-3, p. 7-3. In chapter one I mention a 24 to 1 ratio; that was comparing single moms to single dads, not to be confused with this 2 to 1 ratio, of all moms to all dads.

5   Ibid., Table 6-1, p. 6-2.

6   *Third National Incidence Study of Child Abuse and Neglect,* 1996, op. cit., p. 6-11, Table 6-4: "Distribution of Perpetrator's Sex by Severity of Outcome and Perpetrator's Relationship to Child." This report states that 81% of children seriously injured from child abuse or neglect by the natural parents are injured by the mother; 43% by the father. The percentages exceed 100% because some children were injured by both parents.

7   Ibid., p. 6-9, Table 6-3: "Distribution of Perpetrator's Sex by Type of Maltreatment and Perpetrator's Relationship to Child." Eighty-seven percent of children who are victims of neglect were victimized by their natural mother; 40% by their natural father.

8   Ibid., p. 4-3, Table 4-1: "Sex Differences in Incidence Rates per 1,000 Children for Maltreatment under the Harm Standard in the NIS-3 (1993)." The serious injury rate for boys is 9.3 per 1,000; for girls, it is 7.5 per 1,000.

9   National Center on Child Abuse and Neglect, *National Study of the Incidence and Severity of Child Abuse and Neglect* (Washington, D.C.: NCCAN, 1981).

10   Christoffersen, op. cit., Chart 2.

11   *Third National Incidence Study of Child Abuse and Neglect/Appendices*, 1997, op. cit., pp. A-63–A-64. Table A-11B, "Parent Structure by Categories of Maltreatment and Severity for Children Countable Under the Harm Standard; The estimated total for Mother Only Household is 264.1 children killed. For Father Only Household the estimated total is 10.8.

12   The National Longitudinal Study of Youth (see Appendix C). Murray A. Straus, *Beating the Devil Out of Them* (NY: Lexington Books, 1994), p. 25.

13   Ibid.

14   The show was "The Dr. Fad Show." See "If One Dad Is Not Enough . . . ," *Sunday Camera* (Colorado), September 24, 1989. No author given.

15   Henry B. Biller and Richard Solomon, *Child Maltreatment and Paternal Deprivation* (Lexington, MA: Lexington Books, 1986), pp. 68–69.

16   David Finkelhor, *Child Sexual Abuse* (NY: Free Press, 1984); M. E. Fromuth, "The Long-Term Psychological Impact of Childhood Sexual Abuse," unpublished doctoral dissertation, Auburn University, 1983; S. D. Peters, "The Relationship Between Childhood Sexual Victimization and Adult Depression Among Afro-American and White Women," unpublished doctoral dissertation, University of California at Los Angeles, 1984.

17   Ibid., Finkelhor. Cited by David Finkelhor and Larry Baron, "High Risk Children," in David Finkelhor and Associates, *Sourcebook on Child Sexual Abuse* (Beverly Hills: Sage Publications, 1986), p. 74.

18   D. E. H. Russell, *The Secret Trauma* (NY: Basic Books, 1986). Cited by Finkelhor, ibid., "High Risk Children," in ibid., Finkelhor, *Sourcebook,* p. 78.

19   Ibid.

20   Ibid.

21   Martin Daly and Margo Wilson, "Child Abuse and Other Risks of Not Living with Both Parents," *Ethnology and Sociobiology,* Vol. 6, 1985, pp. 197–209. Cited by Bryce J. Christensen, "The Child Abuse 'Crisis': Forgotten Facts and Hidden Agendas," *The Family in America,* Vol. 3, No. 2, February 1989.

22   Michael Petrovich and Donald I. Templer, "Heterosexual Molestation of Children Who Later Became Rapists," *Psychological Reports,* Vol. 54, 1984, p. 810.

23   Douglas J. Besharov and Lisa A. Laumann, "Child Abuse Reporting," *Social Science and Modern Society,* Vol. 33, May/June, 1996, p. 42. The actual number of substantiated reports fell 41%, from 14,000 to 8,000, even though 12,000 additional families had been investigated.

24   Hollida Wakefield and Ralph Underwager, "Personality Characteristics of Parents Making False Accusations of Sexual Abuse in Custody Disputes," *Issues in Child Abuse Accusations,* Vol. 2, 1990, pp. 121–136. False accusations were made by 72 parents: 68 mothers; 4 fathers—or 94% mothers. There were 103 falsely-accused parents: 4 mothers, 99 fathers—or 96% fathers.

25   Ibid.

26   Hollida Wakefield and Ralph Underwager, "Sexual Abuse Allegations in Divorce and Custody Disputes," *Behavioral Science and the Law,* Vol. 9, 1991, pp. 451–468.

27   The research was conducted by Dr. Jane Rawls, a child and clinical psychologist from Hamilton, New Zealand. She is also a specialist report writer for the Family Court in New Zealand and a consulting expert witness for the high court. Cited in Alan Samson,

"Research on Children's Sexual Abuse Fibs Goes to NATO Forum: Children Often Fabricate Stories of Sexual Abuse," *New Zealand Herald,* May 29, 1996, p. 24.

28   Ibid.

29   Mark Clements Research, op. cit., in *Parade,* February 2, 1997, pp. 4–5.

30   Furstenberg, "Fathers Matter . . . ," op. cit., as cited in Lerman & Ooms, op. cit., pp. 127 and 130. The sample size of all children in this portion of the study was 253. Among the sons of inner-city teenaged mothers, 15% had had a baby by age 19; none who had a close relationship with their biological father had.

31   Alfred A. Messer, M.D., "Boy's Father Hunger: The Missing Father Syndrome," *Medical Aspects of Human Sexuality,* Vol. 23, No. 1, January 1989, pp. 44–50.

32   Carol Murley, "Male Sex Offenders Speak Out About Female Perpetrators in Their Sex Histories," unpublished manuscript, pp. 1–18. Study conducted 1990-1991. Murley was previously with Tarrant County (TX) Department of Mental Health and Mental Retardation.

33   Diana Korte and Roberta Scaer, *A Good Birth, A Safe Birth* (NY: Bantam, 1984) in "Sexual Pleasures of Childbirth," *Glamour,* March, 1984.

34   See both U.S. Department of Commerce, Bureau of the Census, *Statistical Abstract of the United States, 1996,* p. 65, Table 81, "Children Under 18 Years Old by Presence of Parents, 1970-1995" and *Statistical Abstract, 1999,* Table 81, op. cit.

35   See my *Why Men Are the Way They Are* (NY: Berkley Books, paper, 1988), Chapter 8, pp. 237–267.

36   Korte, in *Glamour,* op. cit.

37   Credit for the phrase to Mark Podolner, as quoted in Jon Nordheimer, "Caring for Children, Men Find New Assumptions and Rules," *The New York Times,* August 5, 1990, p. 1.

Chapter 4. What Prevents Dads from Being Involved? (pages 87–110)

1   Wylie, Washington Post Writers Group, August 13, 1995.

2   Birgitta Silen, "The Truth About Sexual Equality," *Inside Sweden,* April, 1987, p. 13 (available free of charge: S-105 53, Stockholm, Sweden); and Staffan Herrstrom, "Swedish Family Policy," *Current Sweden* (Swedish Institute, Stockholm), September 1986, p. 5.

3   Ibid.

4   Maggie Jackson, Associated Press, "Dads Reluctant to Take Leave," *The Press Democrat,* February 5, 1999, p. E-1.

5   U.S. Department of Commerce, Bureau of the Census, *Current Population Reports* (Washington, DC: G.P.O., 1987), "Male-Female Differences in Work Experience, Occupation, and Earnings: 1984," Series P-70, No. 10, p. 13, Table 1: "Workers with One or More Work Interruptions Lasting Six Months or Longer, by Reason for Interruption." This is the latest data available as of 1997.

6   *Der Spiegel,* op. cit.

7   Research on the films from 1994 to 2000 is by Jerry A. Boggs of Westland, MI. Private correspondence on November 27, 1996 and March 10, 2000.

8   Credit to Jerry Boggs, whose sources were Martin Connors and Jim Craddock, *Video-Hound's Golden Movie Retriever 2000* (Farmington Hills, MI: Visible Ink Press,1999) for movies between 1950 and 2000, and his own notes on movies he personally watched between 1980 and 2000.

9   *Parents* magazine subscription insert, approximately 1990.

10   Nordheimer, op. cit.

11 Interview with Darrell Watkins, Assistant Scout Executive of the Desert Pacific Council, Boy Scouts of America, June 22, 2000.

12 Christoffersen, op. cit., Chart 3.

13 Bill Watterson, "Calvin and Hobbes," *Los Angeles Times,* June 1, 1990.

14 Walker, op. cit., p. 89.

15 Julie A. Fulton, "Parental Reports of Children's Post-Divorce Adjustment, *Journal of Social Issues,* Vol. 35, 1979, p. 133. Fulton reported that 53% of the non-custodial fathers claimed their ex-wives had refused to let them see their children.

16 Wallerstein, *Surviving the Breakup,* op. cit., p. 125. This 50% figure is particularly surprising because it is from the suburban San Francisco area, generally considered more conscious of the importance of fathers.

17 Ibid., p. 125.

18 Ibid.

19 Ibid., p. 126.

20 Rick Kirkman and Jerry Scott, "Baby Blues," *Los Angeles Times,* April 24, 1990.

21 Carolyn Pape Cowan and Philip A. Cowan, "Men's Involvement in Parenthood: Identifying the Antecedents and Understanding the Barriers," *Men's Transition to Parenthood: Longitudinal Studies of Early Family Experience,* ed. Phyllis W. Berman and Frank A. Pedersen (Hillsdale, NJ: Lawrence Erlbaum Associate, 1987).

22 Interview with Dr. Frances K. Grossman on April 2, 1997, based on her research in Frances K. Grossman, William S. Pollack, and Ellen Golding, "Fathers and Children: Predicting the Quality and Quantity of Fathering," *Developmental Psychology,* Vol. 24, No. 1, February 1988, pp. 82–91.

23 S. Philip Morgan, *American Journal of Sociology,* Vol. 94, No. 1, as cited in Mia Adessa, "Divorce Insurance: Have a Son," *Psychology Today,* May 1988, p. 14.

24 John W. Santrock and Richard A. Warshak, "Children of Divorce: Impact of Custody Disposition on Social Development," in E. J. Callahan and K. A. McClusky, eds., *Life-Span Developmental Psychology* (NY: Academic, 1983), as cited in Warshak, op. cit., p. 191.

25 Walker, op. cit., pp. 84–85. Walker reports that 24% of the children said both parents spoke badly of each other; 10% said neither parent said anything derogatory about the other.

26 From a letter from Sam Downing, May 28, 1989.

27 Walker, op. cit., p. 84.

28 John Robertson and Louise Fitzgerald "The (M.I.S.) Treatment of Men: Effects of Client Gender Role on Diagnosis and Attribution of Pathology," *Journal of Counseling Psychology,* Vol. 37, No. 1, January 1990, pp. 3–9.

29 *Los Angeles Times,* December 3, 1989. Medical Center of North Hollywood ad about fathers having beepers: "Where Dad is only a heartbeep away."

30 Michael Segell, "Of Human Bonding," *Parenting,* May 1989, p. 60.

31 James A. Levine and Edward W. Pitt, *New Expectations* (NY: Families and Work Institute, 1995).

Chapter 5. Toward the Best Interests of Everyone . . . (pages 111–122)

1 Credit to Hans-Günther Tappe.

2 Robert Bly, *Iron John* (NY: Addison-Wesley, 1990).

3   Paul Lewis, *The Five Key Habits of Smart Dads* (Grand Rapids, MI: Zondervan, 1994), quoted in Sheryl Stolberg, "No Longer Missing in Action," *Los Angeles Times,* June 16, 1996, p. A16.

Part Two: Introduction. The Politics of Bringing Dad Home Again

1   Interview with Gordon Clark by Donna Foote, "You Have to Take Care of the Kids," *Newsweek,* April 17, 1995.

2   From *The New York Times,* as cited in Hugh Rawson and Margaret Miner, eds., *The American Heritage Dictionary of American Quotations* (NY: Viking Penguin, 1997), p. 368.

Chapter 6. Men's ABC Rights (pages 127–159)

1   "Males . . . Babies and Ohio Law," 1987 brochure distributed by Planned Parenthood of Northwest Ohio, 1301 Jefferson Avenue, Toledo, Ohio 43624, (419) 255-1115.

2   Marriage of Dennis 117 Wisc. 2d 249, 344 N.W. 2d 128.

3   Matter of Audrey G. [Robert T.]; New York Family Court, Kings County, *New York Law Journal,* August 17, 1989.

4   Milne v. Milne, 556 A2d 854.

5   Bedford v. Bedford; Pennsylvania Superior Court, No. 02705, Philadelphia, 1988.

6   Paul Dean, "Two Men and a Baby," *Los Angeles Times,* October 29, 1989, p. E1. The court's decision was in June 1989.

7   *Good Housekeeping,* April 1989. Good Housekeeping Institute Poll.

8   Associated Press, "Poll: Ohio Residents Support Fathers' Rights in Abortions," *Dayton Daily News,* July 10, 1989, p. 14-A.

9   Sam Downing, February 25, 1991.

10   "Our Bodies; Our Business"—Top border from *Ms.;* July/August, 1989, pp. 42–43.

11   Ann Landers, "Pay the Piper If You're Going to Tango," *Los Angeles Times,* January 17, 1989.

12   Letter from Steve DeLuca, Mendocino, CA.

13   Credit to Christine Eberl, a Canadian biologist.

14   See the following: John Elson, "The Rights of Frozen Embryos," *Time,* July 24, 1989, p. 63; "A Trial of An Embryonic Issue," Currents section, *US News & World Report,* August 21, 1989, p. 13; Ronald Smothers, "Woman Given Custody in Embryo Case," *The New York Times,* September 22, 1989; and "Whose Lives Are These?" "Nation" section, *Time,* October 2, 1989, p. 19.

15   Mike Luckovich, "Frozen Embryo Case," *Atlanta Constitution.*

16   Fredric Hayward, "How the System Represses Men: Our Lady of Maternity, Church of the Woman I Serve," as reprinted in Francis Baumli, Ph.D., *Men Freeing Men* (NJ: New Atlantis Press, 1985), pp. 173–174.

17   The National Center for Lesbian Rights is a San Francisco public-interest law firm. See Kathleen Hendrix, "A Case of Two 'Moms' Test Definition of Parenthood," *Los Angeles Times,* August 15, 1990.

18   David Margolick, "Lesbians' Custody Fights Test Family Law Frontier," *The New York Times,* July 4, 1990.

19   Catherine Gewertz, "Genetic Parents Given Sole Custody of Child," *Los Angeles Times,* October 23, 1990, front page.

20   Carol Lawson, "Couples' Own Embryos Used in Birth Surrogacy," *The New York Times,* August 12, 1990, front page and p. 16.

21 Gewertz, op. cit.

22 *Ms.,* June, 1987, p. 28.

23 Lori B. Andrews, *Between Strangers* (NY: Harper & Row, 1989).

24 Once a man has an *ongoing* relationship with a woman, the woman is likely to trust the man. Only 2% of women do not trust their ongoing male partners to use the male pill. See A. F. Glasier, *et al.,* "Would Women Trust Their Partners to Use a Male Pill?" *Human Reproduction,* Vol. 15, No. 3, 2000, pp. 648–649.

25 Ann Landers, "'Planned' Pregnancy," syndicated article, October 13, 1989.

26 Robert L. Cox, "Law in Brief," U.S. Department of Health and Human Services, Federal Office of Child Support Enforcement, January 1983, <http://www.acf.dhhs.gov/programs/cse/new/csr8301.htm> The Court of Appeals, New York's highest court, sustained the decision of the Appellate Division, in L. Pamela P. v. Frank S., 462 N.Y.S.2d 819 (Ct.App. 1983), which overturned the initial decision ruling that Serpico's common-law constitutional right of "procreative freedom" was abridged by his girlfriend's fraud.

27 Michelle Green and Linda Kramer, "Baby Doesn't Make Three," *People,* November 14, 1988, pp. 60–65.

28 Ibid.

29 "Fathers by Force," *The New York Times,* October 31, 1987. Cited in Transitions, Vol. 7, No. 6, November/December 1987.

30 Ibid.

31 Jim Unger, "Herman," *Los Angeles Times,* April 1, 1990.

32 Glasier, *et al.,* op. cit.

33 John K. Amory and William J. Bremner, "Newer Agents for Hormonal Contraception in the Male," *Trends in Endocrinology and Metabolism,* Vol. 11, No. 2, March 2000, p. 61.

34 Jared Diamond, "Everything Else You Always Wanted to Know About Sex: But That We Were Afraid You'd Never Ask." *Discover,* Vol. 6, No. 4, April 1985, pp. 76–77. Diamond points out that this research was done in the 1940s and that the true incidence is doubtless much higher because "many blood-group substances now used in paternity tests were not known in the 1940s. . . ." As I discuss in *Women Can't Hear What Men Don't Say,* research that shows the shadow side of women, or of men as victims, is rarely re-funded. I am unaware of this research having been repeated since the 1940s.

35 Amory, op. cit.

36 Nifedipine was introduced in 1982. Nifedipine is the generic name for a variety of brand-name drugs such as Adalat, sold by Bayer. It is being worked on by Dr. Susan Benoff of the New York University School of Medicine. See Marlene Habib, "Research Into Male Birth-Control Pill Hits Snag," *The Canadian Press,* September 28, 1999. <http://www.canoe.ca/Health9909/28_men.html>

37 Ibid.

38 David G. Savage, "Justices to Rule on Unwed Fathers," *Los Angeles Times,* April 19, 1988.

39 Real name. Based on the true story behind the U.S. Supreme Court case, McNamara v. County of San Diego, 87–5840.

40 U.S. Supreme Court case, McNamara v. County of San Diego, 87–5840.

41 The story of Mary Lou is a composite story, drawn from the experiences of a few people I have interviewed.

42 Bruce Kovacs, Bejan Shahbahrami, Arnold Medearis, and David Comings, "Pre-Natal Determinations of Paternity by Molecular Genetic 'Fingerprinting,'" *Journal of Obstetrics and Gynecology,* Vol. 75, No. 3, Part 2, March 1990, pp. 474–479. As cited in the *Los Angeles Times,* March 5, 1990, p. B3.

43 By "every reasonable attempt," I mean mailing him a letter by express mail, leaving messages to "please call, it's important" on his answering machine, etc. While the burden of proof that she has done these things is on her, she cannot be held responsible if he is not available or doesn't respond.

44 Former Chief Judge Richard Huttner, Kings County (Brooklyn) Family Court and Member of the New York State Commission on Child Support, quoted in Jane Young, "The Fathers Also Rise," *New York Magazine,* November 18, 1985, p. 75.

45 *Sentinel-Tribune* (Bowling Green, OH), April 25, 1989.

46 Drake University School of Law, "Physical Custody Awards in Cases That Proceeded to Trial, Polk County District Court, Polk County, Iowa, 1988." Research directed by Judy Nusbaum. Referred by Dick Woods.

47 Michael J. Geanoulis, Sr., "New Hampshire Men and Divorce," New Hampshire Department of Health and Human Services, Bureau of Vital Records/Health Statistics, May 1991.

48 Patrick Kurp, "Dad Wins 6-Year Area School Fight," *The Knickerbocker News,* Friday, August 9, 1985.

49 Wakefield, "Personality Characteristics," op. cit., pp. 121–136. Seventy-two parents made false accusations: 68 mothers; 4 fathers, or 94% mothers. One hundred three parents were falsely accused: 4 mothers, 99 fathers—or 96% fathers.

50 Apologies to Star Trek and Star War fans! But who knows, in the future, there may be a "Star Wars: The Next Generation." Besides, "Bar Trek: The Next Generation" makes no sense!

Chapter 7. Does Divorce Make Women Poorer and Men Richer? (pages 160–168)

1 Ann Landers' syndicated column, *Herald-Star* (Steubenville, OH), April 13, 1990.

2 Lenore J. Weitzman, *The Divorce Revolution* (NY: The Free Press, 1985).

3 The latest figures available are from the U.S. Department of Commerce, Bureau of the Census, *Statistical Abstact of the United States* in 1991 in a table titled "Household Net Worth-Percent Distribution, by Selected Characteristic: 1988." The figure for this year is 104%. This statistic was last published in 1991.

4 U.S. Department of Commerce, Bureau of the Census, *Statistical Abstracts of the U.S.* (Washington, D.C.: G.P.O., 1989), 109th Edition, p. 459, Table 747—"Household Net Worth—Median Value of Holdings: 1984." Lenore J. Weitzman's *The Divorce Revolution,* op. cit., was published in 1985.

5 Greg J. Duncan and Saul D. Hoffman, "The Economic Consequences of Marital Instability," Figure 14.3 and Table 14.A.8, in Martin David and Timothy Smeeding, eds., *Horizontal Equity, Uncertainty & Economic Well-Being* (Chicago: University of Chicago Press, 1985)

6 When we look at six income studies, the average fathers' gross income was only $18,000 (in 1984 dollars). All six studies are listed in "Estimates of National Child Support Collections Potential and the Income Security of Female-Headed Families—Final Report," April 1, 1985, p. xi. Bush Institute for Child and Family Policy, Frank Porter Graham Child Development Center, University of North Carolina at Chapel Hill.

7 See Chapter 8, "Is Child Support Helping or Hurting the Family?"

8 Greg J. Duncan and Saul D. Hoffman, "The Economic Consequences of Marital Instability," Table 14.A.2., cited in David and Smeeding, op. cit.

9   See generally Duncan, "Marital Instability," ibid.; and Greg J. Duncan and Saul D. Hoff-
     man, "A Reconsideration of the Economic Consequences of Marital Dissolution,"
     Demography, Vol. 22, No. 4, 1985, pp. 485–497.

10   Ibid.

11   Freya L. Sonenstein and Charles Calhoun, "The Survey of Absent Parents/Pilot Re-
     sults," U.S. Department of Health & Human Services, Office of the Secretary for Plan-
     ning & Evaluation, July, 1988, p. iv.

12   Greg J. Duncan, "Do Women 'Deserve' to Earn Less Than Men?" *Years of Poverty, Years of
     Plenty*, Vol. 164, 1984, p. 162.

13   See, for example, R. Haskins, A. Dobelstein, J. Akin, and J. Schwartz, University of
     North Carolina, Bush Institute for Child and Family Policy, "Estimates of National
     Child Support Collections Potential and the Income Security of Female-Headed Fami-
     lies," Vol. 38, No. 54, 1985.

14   Credit to Bernard R. Goldberg, "Love and the Deadbeat Dad," *The New York Times*, Au-
     gust 20, 1986, for the phrase "masculinization of loneliness."

15   Walker, op. cit., pp. 84–85. Please see Chapter 4, the section on the bad-mouthing bar-
     rier, for more details.

16   Lenore J. Weitzman, "Legal Regulation of Marriage: Tradition and Change," *California
     Law Review*, Vol. 62, 1974, pp. 1169 and 1194.

17   Weitzman, *Divorce Revolution*, op. cit.; Phyllis Chesler, *Mothers on Trial* (NY: McGraw
     Hill, 1986).

18   Lenore J. Weitzman, "A New Look at Career Assets," *Ms.*, February, 1986, pp. 67–68,
     and Phyllis Chesler, "Phyllis Chesler on Custody," *Ms.*, February, 1986, pp. 69–70.
     Weitzman, the author of *The Divorce Revolution*, ibid., espouses both the "career asset"
     and "primary parent" theories, as does Chesler in *Mothers on Trial*, ibid.

Chapter 8. Is Child Support Helping or Hurting the Family? (pages 169–185)

1   Sixty-one percent of all divorce cases (legally); the remainder are initiated either by the
     husband (33%), or jointly (6%). Men file 33%, and 6% are filed jointly. See "Monthly
     Vital Statistics Report: Advance Report of Final Divorce Statistics, 1987," National
     Center for Health Statistics, Vol. 38, No. 12, Supplement 2, May 15, 1990, p. 5. This is
     the latest data available as of 2000. As is apparent throughout the book, the data sug-
     gesting that women are not the victims tend not to be updated. When the couple has
     children, women are more than twice as likely to initiate (65% vs. 29%). See National
     Center of Health Statistics, 1989.

2   Margaret F. Brinig and Douglas W. Allen, "These Boots Are Made for Walking: Why
     Most Divorce Filers Are Women," *American Law and Economics Review*, Vol. 20, No. 1,
     Spring 2000, pp. 126–169. See also Richard Kuhn and John Guidubaldi, "Child Cus-
     tody Policies and Divorce Rates in the U.S." Paper presented at the 11th Annual Con-
     ference of the Children's Rights Council, October 23-26, Washington, D.C., 1997.
     <http://www/vix.com/crc/sp/spcrc97.htm>

3   John Rink, "Two Generations of Tradition—Divorce in Amerika," *Liberator*, Vol. 16,
     No. 5, May, 1990, p. 1. Some quotes are modified slightly to condense.

4   Fitzgerald v. Fitzgerald, No. 87-1259 (DC Cir.) in Ronald K. Henry, "Litigating the Va-
     lidity of Support Guidelines," *The Matrimonial Strategist*, Vol. VII, No. 12, January 1990.

5   Section 423 of the Tax Reform Act of 1984, which was signed into law on July 18,
     1984, amended the Internal Revenue Service code section 152 such that after January
     1, 1985, the custodial parent claims exemption unless both parents sign forms to

change this. Verified by Fred Tubbs (802) 223-0873, an expert on child support and the law who works with the National Council for Children's Rights.

6   Chris Cobb, "Father's Suicide Fuels Battle Over Divorce Act: Man Ordered to Pay Ex-Wife Amount Twice His Monthly Income," *The Ottawa Citizen,* March 27, 2000. <http://www.ottawacitizen.com/national/000327/3825383.html>

7   Photo accompanying Cobb, ibid.

8   Ibid.

9   Kposowa, op. cit., Table 1, p. 256. The figure is 9.94 higher in divorced men than in divorced women. The 9.94 figure was obtained from Dr. Kposowa using information from Table 1 on p. 256. Personal correspondence June 29, 2000. Dr. Kposowa teaches at the Department of Sociology, University of California, Riverside.

10   Mothers with sole custody were awarded mother subsidies 61% of the time; fathers with sole custody were awarded father subsidies 40% of the time. Lydia Scoon-Rogers, "Child Support for Custodial Mothers and Fathers: 1995," in U.S. Department of Commerce, Bureau of the Census, *Current Population Report* (Washington, D.C.: G.P.O., 1999).

11   Ibid.

12   Patricia G. Tjaden, Nancy Thoennes, and Jessica Pearson, "Will These Children Be Supported Adequately?" *The Judges' Journal,* Fall, 1989, p. 40. Findings based on a random sample of 4,721 cases.

13   Personal letter, March 16, 2000, from a San Francisco Bay area dad who requested anonymity.

14   John Siegmund, "Preliminary Analysis of the Database of the D.C. Office of Paternity and Child Support Enforcement," compiled for National Council for Children's Rights, November 9, 1990. The Freedom of Information Act request was made by the National Council for Children's Rights. The computer printout is dated August 3, 1990, and contains 6,103 names, addresses, amounts owed, and amounts paid, from which a random sampling of 610 names was taken.

15   Ibid. In that 10% sample, there were 81 records of overpayment totaling $37,106.27, showing that 13% of men had overpaid.

16   Bennett Stark, Ph.D., "Child Support Delinquency: Are Men and Women Treated Differently?" *Today's Dads,* March 1990, p. 3.

17   Associated Press, "Ex-Hostage Jailed in Child Support Case," *Greensboro News and Record,* December 16, 1990.

18   Stephanie Finucane, staff writer, "Failure to Pay Child Support," *Santa Barbara News-Press,* March 1, 1989.

19   Interview by Fred Hayward with Max Cline, California bankruptcy attorney with offices statewide, January 7, 1991.

20   Poster from Family Support Division; Santa Barbara and Santa Maria Counties (California), May, 1988.

21   Michael deCourcy Hinds, "Better Traps Being Built for Delinquent Parents," *The New York Times,* December 9, 1989, p. 107. Procedures mentioned are taken by Pennsylvania's Delaware County Domestic Relations Court.

22   Television reporter Janet Tamaro on the topic of child support, *Inside Edition,* January, 1990. Prosecutor Angela Martinez was interviewed, as was David Levy of the National Council for Children's Rights.

23   Interview November 7, 1990, with John Conine at (206) 586-4775. Conine, former director of the state of Washington's Child Support Recovery Office, is the author of *Fathers' Rights: The Sourcebook for Dealing with the Child Support System* (NY: Walker & Company, 1989).

24 Richard Woods, former executive director of the National Congress for Fathers and Children in "Fathers Rights: The Human Rights Issue of the 1990s," a lecture delivered at Coe College, Iowa, June 24, 1989, and published in *Fathers for Equal Rights* (now called *Networker*), July, 1989, Vol. VII, No. XII, p. 1.

25 As of 1991, the latest Census Bureau data on child support is available in Gordon H. Lester, "Child Support and Alimony: 1987," *Current Population Reports,* Series P-23, No. 167, U.S. Department of Commerce, Bureau of the Census, June 1990.

26 The women in this survey reported receiving between 55% and 83% of their awards, similar to the Census Bureau reports. Sonenstein, op. cit., p. 26.

27 Ibid., p. iv, and other citations.

28 This is documented in a memorandum from Robert Helms (Assistant Secretary, Department of Health & Human Services) to Wayne Stanton (Administrator, the Family Support Administration), October 1, 1988. The complete letter can be obtained from the National Council for Children's Rights, (202) 547-6227.

29 Lester, "Child Support and Alimony: 1987," op. cit., p. 40.

30 One study is by Carol Jones, Nancy Gordon, and Isabel Sawhill ("Child Support Payments in the United States," 1976, Working Paper 992-03, Washington, DC: The Urban Institute); a second is by Martha Hill in "PSID Analysis of Matched Pairs of Ex-Spouses: The Relation of Economic Resources and New Family Obligations to Child Support Payments," University of Michigan, Institute for Social Research, 1984. Hill used the Panel Survey of Income Dynamics (PSID), one of the few containing longitudinal information about a national sample of couples. The third study is by Sonenstein, op. cit., p. 5.

31 Ibid., p. 45.

32 Ibid., pp. vi and viii. See also David L. Chambers, *Making Fathers Pay* (Chicago: University of Chicago Press, 1979) and Judith S. Wallerstein and Dorothy S. Huntington, "Bread and Roses: Non-Financial Issues Related to Fathers' Economic Support of Their Children Following Divorce," in *The Parental Child Support Obligation: Research, Practice, and Social Policy,* Judith Cassetty, ed. (Lexington, MA: Lexington Books, 1983).

33 Ibid., Sonenstein.

34 Ibid.

35 Hill, "PSID Analysis," op. cit., as cited in ibid., Sonenstein.

36 Ibid.

37 Ibid.

38 Ibid., Sonenstein, pp. vi and viii.

39 "Child Support and Alimony: 1983 (Supplemental Report)," 1986, *Current Population Reports,* Series P-23, No. 148, U.S. Bureau of the Census as cited in ibid., Sonenstein, p. 5.

40 Hill, "PSID Analysis," op. cit., as cited in ibid., Sonenstein.

41 Goldberg, op. cit. Study conducted at the University of Toronto by Dr. Howard Irving. See also F. Furstenberg and N. Zill, "Supporting Children After Divorce: The Influence [of] Custody on Support Levels and Payments," *Family Law Quarterly,* Vol. XXII, No. 3, Fall, 1988.

42 R. Mnookin, "Child Custody Adjudication: Judicial Functions In the Face of Indeterminacy," *Law and Contemporary Problems,* Vol. 39, pp. 226–93, 1975. Also see Chambers, op. cit., as cited in *Liberator,* Vol. 16, No. 5, May 1990, p. 3.

43 Julie A. Fulton, "Children's Post-Divorce Adjustment," *Journal of Social Issues,* 35:4, 1979, p. 133. Study sponsored by the National Institute of Mental Health.

44 Judith Greif, "Why Fathers Don't Visit," *American Journal of Orthopsychiatry,* April, 1979. See also John Jacobs, "The Effect of Divorce on Fathers," *American Journal of Psychiatry,* Vol. 139:10, October 1982.

45 For the $3.4 billion figure, see Elain Sorensen and Ariel Halpern, "Child Support Enforcement Is Working Better Than We Think," The Urban Institute, Series A. No. A-31, March 1999, p. 4. For the $10 million figure, see the Department of Health and Human Services, "93.597 Grants to States for Access and Visitation Programs." <http://www.cfda.gov/static/93597.asp>

46 Hugh Nations, "Analysis of Access and Visitation Enforcement Grants in Texas, FY 1999." Private correspondence, July 21, 2000. Nations found ten out of twelve access and visitation enforcement grants were given to agencies without access and visitation enforcement programs, but only with visitation limitation programs (e.g., visitation under supervision).

47 Fairrow v. Fairrow, Indiana Court of Appeals, Second District, September 13, 1989, as cited in *Liberator,* Vol. 15, No. 12, December 1989.

48 Cassady, *Liberator,* Vol. 15, No. 10, November 1989.

49 Tibbett v. Tibbett, California Court of Appeals, First District, No. A046030, February 28, 1990, released in March 20, 1990, *Speak Out for Children* (newsletter published by the National Council for Children's Rights), Summer, 1990, Vol. 5, No. 3, p. 13. Cited in "In The Courts: Child Support Due for Concealed Child," *Liberator,* October, 1990.

50 Goldberg, op. cit.

Chapter 9. "Visitation" Is for Criminals (pages 186–199)

1 Stayskal, *Tampa Tribune,* 1996 as reprinted in the *San Diego Union-Tribune,* April 25, 1996.

2 Credit to Asa Baber.

3 Walker, op. cit., p. 83.

4 Credit for "dollar bill" sentence to Kevin Roy, "Low-Income Single Fathers in an African-American Community and the Requirements of Welfare Reform," *Journal of Family Issues,* Vol. 20, No. 4, July 1999, p. 432.

5 Louis Genevie and Eva Margolies, in their survey of 1,100 women, ages 18–80 (see *The Motherhood Report* (NY: Macmillan Publishing Company, Inc., 1987), found that, for women, finances were the biggest source of stress after divorce.

6 Larry Hugick, the Gallup Organization, "The Family Still Is Thriving, Poll Says," *Seattle Times,* July 3, 1989, Section F, pp. 1 and 7. Copyright 1989, the Gallup Organization. Distributed by the *Los Angeles Times* Syndicate.

7 Dr. Maurice M. Small, "Freedom—From Jail," *Today's Dads,* October 1989, p. 3.

8 See Goldberg, op. cit.

9 Kposowa, op. cit. The figure is 9.94 higher in divorced men than in divorced women. The 9.94 figure was obtained from Dr. Kposowa using information from Table 1 on p. 256. Personal correspondence, June 29, 2000.

10 William Congreve, *The Mourning Bride* (1697): "Heaven has no rage like love to hatred turned, Nor hell a fury like a woman scorned."

11 The Supreme Court ruled (in Griswold v. Connecticut, 85 S. Ct. 1678) that the Federal Courts can protect, under the "life, liberty, and pursuit of happiness" phrase of the Declaration of Independence, the right of a father to enjoy the mutual care, company, love, and affection of his children, and that this cannot be taken from him without due

process of law. Cited in "In The Courts: Fundamental Rights of Fathers," *Liberator,* Vol. 16, No. 3, March 1990.

12   Mabra v. Schmidt, D.C. Wisconsin 1973, 356 f. Sup. 620. Cited in ibid., "In The Courts" *Liberator.*

13   Peter McCabe, "Disposable Fathers," *Penthouse,* November, 1982, reporting on *The Disposable Parent* by William Haddad and Mel Roman.

14   Jane Jaffe Young (of New York), Letters to the Editor, *The New York Times,* June 28, 1990.

15   Edward Nichols and J. Annette Vanini, "Divorced Fathers' Estrangement From Children As a Result of 'Visitational Interference' and Its Correlation to Child Support Default Rates: An Empirical Analysis Utilizing a Large Data Base," 1978, p. 11, published by FAIR—The National Father's Organization, 1 NE Tenth Street, Milford, DE 19963, (302) 422-8460. The study is of 2,228 men randomly selected from 6,720 persons who called a national, toll-free hotline in 1986 in response to 1,350 radio announcements in 48 states.

16   Ibid.

17   Jack Kammer, "The Gender Bias in the Maryland Report on Gender Bias in the Courts," *The Matrimonial Strategist,* October 1988, p. 12.

Chapter 10. Playing the "Abuse" Card (pages 200–233)

1   Associated Press, "Official Takes Life, Unaware Accuser Recanted Her Story," *The New York Times,* July 7, 1988. Tarrant was employed by the Pinellas (Florida) County Schools.

2   Dr. Robert Emans, "Abuse in the Name of Protecting Children," *Phi Delta Kappan,* June, 1987, p. 740.

3   *The Orlando Sentinel,* February 7, 1989, and *The Bradenton Herald,* February 15, 1989.

4   Emans, op. cit.

5   Diane Schetky, forensic psychiatrist, as quoted in David Gelman, "The Sex-Abuse Puzzle," *Newsweek,* November 12, 1989, pp. 99–100. The latest estimates (as of 1986) were 325,000 allegations per year.

6   Martha Brannigan, "The Accused: Child-Abuse Charges Ensnare Some Parents in Baseless Proceedings," *The Wall Street Journal,* August 23, 1989.

7   Associated Press, "Norway Man Frees Last of 35 Hostages After He's Granted TV Time," *San Diego Union Tribune,* May 16, 2000, p. A-7. Notice I did not give the man's name. In Norway, Australia, and many other countries, unlike in the U.S., the names of the unconvicted are not released in the press. Since the great majority of people accused—and falsely accused—of crimes are men, this is an important men's issue.

8   Ibid.

9   U.S. Department of Health & Human Services, National Study of the Incidence and Severity of Child Abuse and Neglect, *Study Findings* (Washington, D.C.: G.P.O., 1981), Publication 81-03-325, p. 11. Cited in LeRoy Schultz, "One Hundred Cases of Unfounded Child Sexual Abuse: A Survey and Recommendations," *Issues in Child Abuse Accusations,* Vol. 1, No.1, 1989, p. 29. Schultz was a Professor in the School of Social Work at West Virginia University.

10   U.S. Department of Health and Human Services, Andrea J. Sedlak and Diane D. Broadhurst, "Third National Incidence Study of Child Abuse and Neglect: Final Report," Ad-

ministration for Children and Families, Washington, D.C., September, 1996. The 1-in-4 figure was supplied by Andrea J. Sedlak, Ph.D., from tabulations of the original NIS-3 findings report. Dr. Sedlak is Associate Area Director of Westat. Personal correspondence, April 4, 2000.

11 The percentage of fathers is, in reality, still overstated, since the measure used by DHHS includes only adults over 18, so it excludes babysitters, some friends, etc., making the percentage of investigations in which the natural father ends up being a sexual abuser in reality closer to 1 in 1,000. (The measure used was the Harm Standard; only the Endangerment Standard includes adults and those under 18.)

12 "Child Abuse and Neglect in Missouri: Report for Calendar Year 1998." Missouri Department of Social Services, September 1999.

13 U.S. Department of Commerce, Bureau of the Census, Population Estimates Program, Population Division, Washington, D.C., December 8, 1999.

14 *The Orlando Sentinel,* op. cit., and *The Bradenton Herald,* op. cit.

15 Interview, October 23, 1990, with Tom Young, attorney for the Florida Education Association—United.

16 John Caher, "Child Protection, Parental Rights on Collision Course," [Albany, NY] *Sunday Times Union,* April 30, 1989, p. A-1.

17 Interview, April 11, 1990, with Frank Brennan, Australian psychologist, author, and university professor. Brennan can be reached for comment at 95 Clydesdale Street, Como, Perth, WA (Western Australia), 6152.

18 Susan Ager, "'Daddy Hurt Me'," *Detroit Free Press,* February 22, 1987.

19 Daniel Goleman, "Perils Seen in Warnings About Abuse," *The New York Times,* November 21, 1989, p. B5.

20 Ibid.

21 Ibid. Found in a study by Dr. Neal Gilbert, School of Social Welfare, University of California at Berkeley.

22 Ibid. Survey by the National Committee for the Prevention of Child Abuse, 1989. See also review conducted by N. Dickon Repucci, a University of Virginia psychologist, for *The American Psychologist,* November 1989.

23 Caher, op. cit.

24 Ibid.

25 Journal News Service, "Almost Over: Court Will Clear Man on Molest Charge," *Livingston County Press,* November 9, 1989.

26 Ibid.

27 This account is an integration of reports from Pat Plarski, "'The System,' Not Dad, Abused Tot," *Palm Beach Post,* July 30, 1989; and interviews with Peter Gianino (Janet's attorney), Richard Kibbey (Cecil's attorney), and Cecil Smith, October 23, 1990.

28 Janet Singer's attorney was Peter Gianino of Stuart, Florida.

29 Fran Hovey, "Five Life Sentences for Nothing," *Transitions,* November/December 1989, pp. 1–2.

30 *St. Paul Pioneer Press/Dispatch,* October 13, 1989.

31 Fred Hayward, *Westworld,* September 5, 1989, and interview, January 7, 1991. The names of the boys and fathers are kept confidential for legal reasons.

32 Kimberly Hart, national office, Victims of Child Abuse Legislation (VOCAL); interview on August 16, 1990.

33 Credit for the "nuclear weapons" phrase to Phoenix attorney Robert Hirschfeld.

34 Emans, op. cit.

35 Study by the University of Michigan's Psychiatry Department, which has evaluated more than 1,000 contested-custody cases. See "Sexuality Update" section, *Medical Aspects of Human Sexuality,* April 1987, p. 8.

36 Dr. Benedek is with the Statewide Center for Forensic Psychiatry in Ann Arbor, Michigan, and is a former president of the American Psychiatric Association.

37 Donna L. Wong discusses both studies in "False Allegations of Child Abuse: The Other Side of the Tragedy," *Pediatric Nursing,* Vol. 13, September/October 1987, pp. 329–332. Cited in Bryce J. Christensen, "The Child Abuse 'Crisis': Forgotten Facts and Hidden Agendas," *The Family in America,* February, 1989, Vol. 3, No. 2.

38 Robert Fay, M.D., F.A.A.P., "Scenario of an 'Incorrect Allegation of Child Sexual Abuse' {Documented}," *AVID* (A Voice In Defense), Vol. II, April 1988, p. 1. A publication of RIP-TITAN, Inc., 4100 US 19 North T-207, Palm Harbor, FL, 34684, (813) 934-6908.

39 Maureen Dowd, "Bush Signs Bill to Release a Mother," *The New York Times,* September 24, 1989.

40 Caryl Murphy, staff writer, *Washington Post,* February 18, 1987.

41 "A Mother's Right: The Elizabeth Morgan Story" aired on ABC as *Shattered Silence* in 1992.

42 Dowd, op. cit.

43 Felicity Barringer, "Prison in Washington Releases a Defiant Mother," *The New York Times,* September, 26, 1989.

44 Paul Clancy, "Morgan Has Media Edge in Battle," *USA Today,* September 29, 1989, p. 1A. Clancy reported that 55% of men also believed Elizabeth's side of the story.

45 See my *Women Can't Hear What Men Don't Say,* Chapter 8, for definition and broader examples.

46 *Time,* July 10, 1989. Photo title for "Doing Time for No Crime."

47 Ibid.

48 "Morgan & Foretich," *Liberator,* Vol. 15, No. 9, September, 1989.

49 Jonathan Groner, *Hilary's Trial* (NY: Simon & Schuster, 1991), especially p. 119.

50 Ibid., pp. 179–180.

51 Ibid., p. 177

52 Op. cit., "Morgan & Foretich."

53 Groner, op. cit., pp. 178–179.

54 Dowd, op. cit.

55 Credit to John Macchietto for this analogy.

56 See section below: **How Can We Tell When a Sex Abuse Charge Is False?**

57 Howard Rosenberg, "Trail of Abuse in the 'Hilary' Custody Case," *Los Angeles Times,* April 24, 1990, p. F1.

58 Ibid.

59 Ibid.

60 Richard A. Gardner, M.D., *The Parental Alienation Syndrome and the Differentiation Between Fabricated and Genuine Child Sex Abuse* (Cresskill, NJ: Creative Therapeutics, 1987). These are only a few of the differentiating criteria from the updated 1990 "Sex Abuse Legitimacy Scale" (SAL Scale). The complete scale can be obtained by writing the publisher at Creative Therapeutics, PO Box R, Cresskill, NJ, 07626.

61 Gordon J. Blush and Karol L. Ross, "Sexual Allegations in Divorce: The SAID Syndrome," March 1986. <http://primenet.com/~azclua/said.txt>

62 Ibid.

63   Ibid.

64   See also Victims of Child Abuse Legislation (VOCAL) "Solutions in Divorce/Custody Disputes," as cited in *Liberator,* Volume. 15, No. 9, September 1989.

Chapter 11. The Political Consequences of Ignoring Fathers (pages 234–237)

1   Study is by the Alan Guttmacher Institute, New York, of use of contraceptives in 20 developed countries between 1982 and 1986. Please see *The New York Times,* June 2, 1988, and *Newsweek,* June 13, 1988.

2   There were 650,604 battle deaths in all U.S. Wars combined; but in 1996 alone, there were 1,365,730 abortions. Abortion source is the Alan Guttmacher Institute, "Facts in Brief," Februrary 2000; <http://www.agiusa.org/pubs/fb_induced_abortion.html> Battle death source is from "Casualties in Principal Wars of the U.S." *The World Almanac and Book of Facts, 1998.* (Mahwah, NJ: World Almanac Books, 1998), p. 161.

3   Alissa J. Rubin, "Americans Narrowing Support for Abortion," *Los Angeles Times,* June 18, 2000, pp. A1 and A14. The question is "Do you favor or oppose *Roe v. Wade,* the Supreme Court decision that permits a woman to get an abortion at any time?" The answer in 2000 is:

	All	Men	Women
Favor	43%	42%	44%
Oppose	42	39	44
Indifferent	15	19	12

Chapter 12. Conclusion: Toward a Father and Child Reunion (pages 238–247)

1   See the **RESOURCES** section for a list of some of these groups.

2   See Chapter 6 of my *Women Can't Hear What Men Don't Say* (NY: Tarcher/Putnam, 1999).

3   Joe Heller, "What is Fusion?" *Green Bay Press Gazette,* 1989.

4   By "every reasonable attempt," I mean mailing him a letter by express mail, leaving messages to "please call, it's important" on his answering machine, etc. While the burden of proof that she has done these things is on her, she cannot be held responsible if he is not available or doesn't respond.

5   Bryan D. Brook, Ph.D., *Design Your Love Life* (NY: Walker and Company, 1989), pp. 28–29. Sadly, Bryan, a friend and colleague, passed away in July, 2000, at the too-young age of 57.

Appendix (pages 248–252)

1   Brott, op. cit., p. 65.

2   Inspired by, and in places adapted from, Asa Baber, "A Divorce Manual For Men," *Playboy,* December 1978.

Index

Page numbers in *italics* refer to illustrations.

Permissions

• Drawing (mommy and daddy frog). By permission of Alex Blanchard. • Drawing (child and mother at dinner table; the child daydreams about father being there, too). By permission of Ms. Marie Marcks, Heidelberg, Germany. • Steve Kelley, June 29, 2000 (Elian/"A father's parental rights"). By permission of Steve Kelley, Editorial Cartoonist, *San Diego Union-Tribune*/Copley News Service. • *Parade,* April 23, 2000 ("I'd never marry a man just because he had a million dollars. Not in today's market.") By permission of William Hoest Enterprises, Inc. • Frank Cotham, 1997 ("Your father was a jackass."). ©The New Yorker Collection 1997, Frank Cotham from cartoonbank.com. All rights reserved. • Lee Lorenz, 1991 ("During the next stage of my development, Dad, I'll be drawing closer to my mother—I'll get back to you in my teens."). ©The New Yorker Collection 1991, Lee Lorenz from cartoonbank.com. All rights reserved. • Chuck Asay (". . . One good dad carries a lot of weight.") By permission of Chuck Asay, Editorial Cartoonist, *The Gazette* (Colorado Springs). • Robert Mankoff, 1989 ("Pass 'em, Pop!"). ©The New Yorker Collection 1989, Robert Mankoff from cartoonbank.com. All rights reserved. • Rick Kirkman and Jerry Scott, *Baby Blues,* 11/12/90 ("I just had the worst day of my life . . ."). Reprinted with special permission of King Features Syndicate. • Wiley Miller, *Non Sequitur,* 1995 (Early man's development of data gathering and decision-making: "The focus group says to go out and kill something.") Non Sequitur ©1995 Wiley. Reprinted by permission of Universal Press Syndicate. All rights reserved. • Bill Waterston, *Calvin & Hobbes,* 6/1/90 ("Hey, Mom, want to hear something great?"). Calvin & Hobbes ©1990 Waterston. Reprinted by permission of Universal Press Syndicate. All rights reserved. • Rick Kirkman and Jerry Scott, *Baby Blues,* 4/24/90 ("Here, let me try."). Reprinted with special permission of King Features Syndicate. • Mike Luckovich (Frozen Embryo Custody Case). By permission of Mike Luckovich and Creators Syndicate, Inc. • Jim Unger, *Herman,* 4/1/90 (". . . we were only married three days."). Herman® is reprinted with permission from LaughingStock Licensing Inc., Ottawa, Canada. All rights reserved. • Photo, Darrin White, 3/27/00 (http://www.ottawacitizen.com/national/000327/3825383.html). By permission of Dave Paulson, City Editor, *Prince George Citizen.* • J. R. "Jack" Cassady ("The judge gave her everything—the kids, the car, even the house.") By permission of J. R. "Jack" Cassady. • Wayne Stayskal, 4/25/96 ("You call this a stress test? . . ."). By permission of Wayne Stayskal, Editorial Cartoonist, *Tampa Tribune.* • Joe Heller, 1989 ("What is fusion?") By permission Joe Heller, Editorial Cartoonist, *Green Bay Press-Gazette.* • Michael Maslin, 1994 ("If it's all right with your mother and her attorney, then it's all right with me and my attorney.") ©The New Yorker Collection 1994, Michael Maslin from cartoonbank.com. All rights reserved.

About the Author

Dr. Warren Farrell is the author of two award-winning bestsellers, *Why Men Are the Way They Are* and *The Myth of Male Power,* as well as *The Liberated Man* and *Women Can't Hear What Men Don't Say,* a Book-of-the-Month Club selection. His books are in more than fifty countries, in ten languages.

Dr. Farrell is the only man ever elected three times to the Board of NOW in New York City. He taught in the School of Medicine at the University of California in San Diego, and has taught psychology, sociology, and political science at Georgetown University, Rutgers University, and Brooklyn College. *The Financial Times* of London has chosen Dr. Farrell as one of one hundred "Thought Leaders" worldwide to consult with top corporate executives.

Warren appears regularly on CNN, and has appeared eight times on *Donahue* and repeatedly on *The Oprah Winfrey Show.* He has been interviewed by Peter Jennings, Barbara Walters, and Larry King, and been the subject of features on *20/20* as well as in *People, Parade, The New York Times, The Times* of London, *Japan Times, Australian Times, The Wall Street Journal,* and *Forbes.*

Dr. Farrell lives in Encinitas, a seaside community in north San Diego County. He can be reached virtually at www.warrenfarrell.com, or at:

Warren Farrell, Ph.D.
PMB 222
315 South Coast Highway 101, Suite U
Encinitas, California 92024-3555